40

RAMBUSCH

The First 100 Years, 1898–1998

ORO Editions
Publishers of Architecture, Art, and Design
Gordon Goff: Publisher

www.oroeditions.com
info@oroeditions.com

Published by ORO Editions

Author: Catha Jackson Grace
Editor: Barbara S. Christen
Indexer: David A. Luljak
Project Manager: Jake Anderson
Book Design: Pablo Mandel, layouts by Micaela Carraro / CircularStudio
Typeset in Lyon Text and Tenez

10 9 8 7 6 5 4 3 2 1 First Edition

ISBN: 978-1-961856-05-9

Prepress and Print work by ORO Editions Inc
Printed in China

ORO Editions makes a continuous effort to minimize the overall carbon footprint of its publications. As part of this goal, ORO, in association with Global ReLeaf, arranges to plant trees to replace those used in the manufacturing of the paper produced for its books. Global ReLeaf is an international campaign run by American Forests, one of the world's oldest nonprofit conservation organizations. Global ReLeaf is American Forests' education and action program that helps individuals, organizations, agencies, and corporations improve the local and global environment by planting and caring for trees.

Facing page and p. 256: *Garland with flowers and Marian symbols* and *detail, Gate of Heaven*, respectively, mosaic and golden Sienna marble, Italian Chapel, Basilica of the National Shrine of the Immaculate Conception, Washington, DC, 2008. The Rambusch Decorating Company has maintained a working relationship with the Shrine from 1930 to the present.

RAMBUSCH

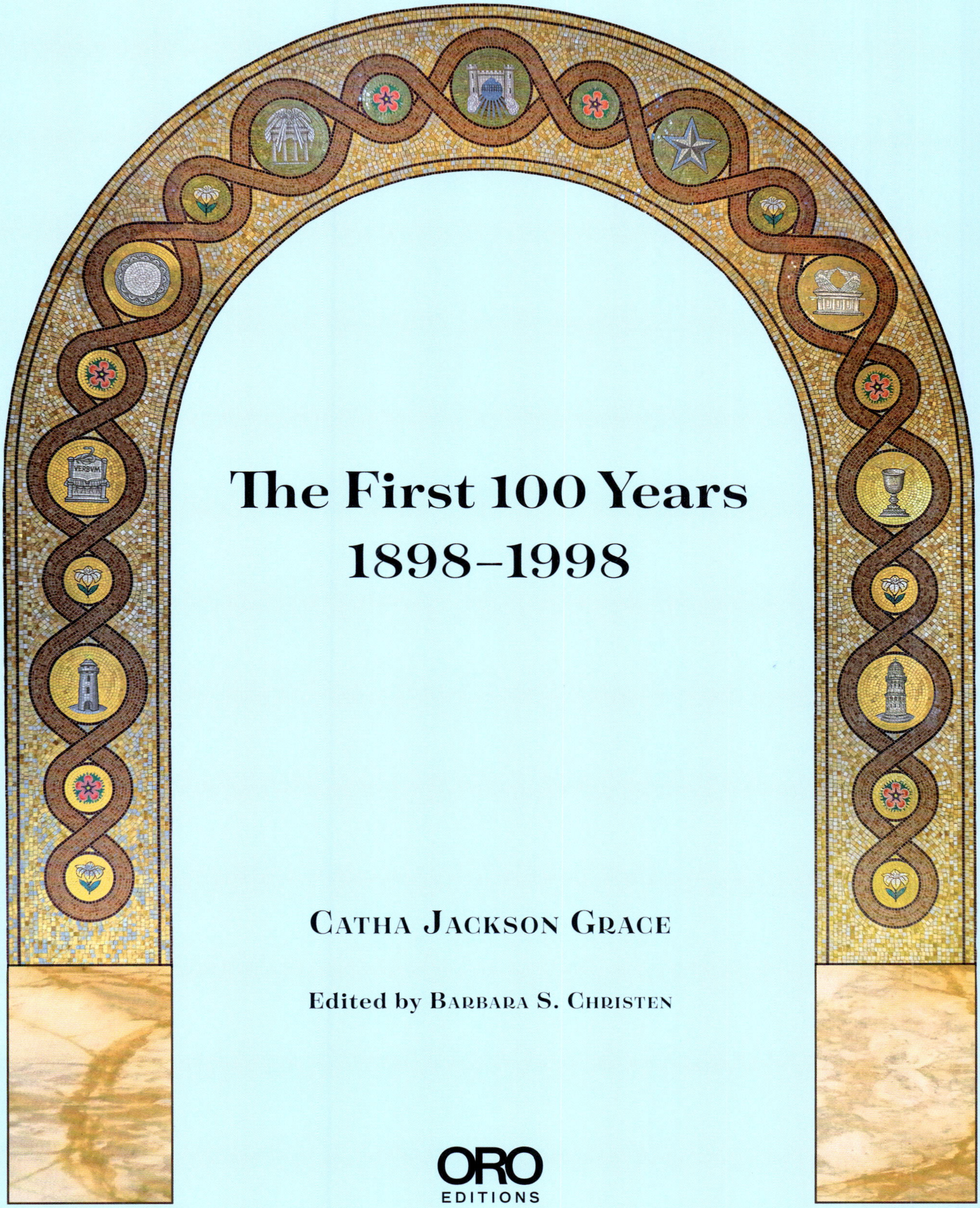

The First 100 Years
1898–1998

CATHA JACKSON GRACE

Edited by BARBARA S. CHRISTEN

ORO EDITIONS

TABLE OF CONTENTS

PROLOGUE 7

INTRODUCTION 9

NOTE ABOUT ILLUSTRATIONS 15

CHAPTER

I	History of the Rambusch Decorating Company	17
II	Church Interior Design and Decoration	31
III	Art Metal: Techniques, Trends, and Styles	45
IV	Lighting Fixtures: Innovation, Technology, and Design	65
V	Stained Glass: Techniques and Styles	85
VI	Hotels, Restaurants, and Shops	101
VII	Theaters and Movie Houses	115
VIII	New York World's Fair, 1939	131
IX	War Effort	145
X	State Capitols and Other Public Spaces	157
XI	Restoration	175
XII	International Commissions	195

EPILOGUE 207

ACKNOWLEDGMENTS 219

APPENDIXES

A	Interior Decoration firms, Manhattan: 1880s–1890s and Previous Rambusch Affiliations	221
B	Letter of Incorporation	222
C	Impressions of an Early Employee	227
D	List of Jobs (selected), 1926–1932	230
E	New York World's Fair, 1939: Partial List of Commissions	233
F	Rambusch Decorating Company: Design Studios and Workshops	237
G	Staff of the Rambusch Decorating Company, 1976	239

ABOUT THE AUTHOR AND EDITOR 241

CREDITS 243

INDEX 244

PROLOGUE

Some years ago, Classical America president Henry Hope Reed reviewed two books that were both titled *McKim, Mead & White, Architects*—one by Leland M. Roth and the other by Richard Guy Wilson. In his review, Reed incisively wrote:

> "What is wholly lacking from both books—and this is true of most surveys of our architecture—is mention of the vast backing enjoyed by the great architects of those days. The art historian likes to concentrate on the *primi tenori* of the architectural opera. No notice is given [to] the equivalent of musicians, costume and set designers, members of the chorus and others—the crowd of talented workers who gave the designer such wonderful support. There were, for example, the trained draftsmen who were as bookish as the senior partners. Beyond the drafting room was the army of skilled craftsmen who were at home in the classical style. In our time the architects disdain the craftsmen, just as landscape architects, bent on basic planting with no maintenance, brush aside the gardeners. In so doing, the architects have come close to destroying the crafts, whose survival has been largely due to interior decorators. To fulfill their aim of achieving originality for its own sake . . . the architects have cleared the building site of all but themselves."
>
> *New York Times Book Review*, June 17, 1984, p. 9.

INTRODUCTION

Geraldine M. Rohling, Ph.D., MAEd., D.S.G.
Archivist-Curator Emerita
Basilica of the National Shrine of the Immaculate Conception
Washington, DC

Where does one begin: At the pedigree of the Rambusch Decorating Company, its works of art, inventions and patents, its achievements? How about its departments and workshops, the multitude of craftspeople, its industry and innovation, the company's national and international recognition, its clients? One must pause to take a breath! It is almost beyond listing, even though this book makes every effort to offer a full picture of a century of its work. This story is not just about the past but also about the future and the firm's ability to navigate prevailing worldwide aesthetic, social, and economic trends as it continues to prosper.

The arts are wonderful! They are essential to every culture and society, representing the soul of a nation and people as WWII has acutely shown us. To look back over several generations of achievement is, in itself, something to be valued. How gratifying for a family to realize—and carry on—the dream that was begun by an ancestor many decades ago, and witness its impact on so many lives in communities across the country and abroad. As such, *Rambusch: The First 100 Years, 1898–1998* provides a sweeping narrative of one of the most enduring and successful design companies in the United States today. It recounts the vision of company founder Frode Christian Valdemar Rambusch (1859–1924), the craftsmanship of its pioneers, the resourcefulness of its promoters, and its trademark in both ecclesiastical and civil settings. Their work notably is not to be confused with a "studio style," such as that of other workshops in the same period. Instead, Rambusch was (and still is) distinctive in its design excellence, craftsmanship, and technique—hallmarks from the very beginning. The company has never limited the scope of its inspiration or originality.

Between 1820 and 1920, more than one million Scandinavians immigrated to the United States. Nordic people, however, arrived as early as AD 1000 with the voyage of Leif Erikson, and over the course of centuries, they left their imprint on American history. Danish names populate registries of both the Revolutionary War and Civil War, where they served both in number and with distinction. Among the gifts they brought to the New World was a love of culture: Old Norse sagas, wondrous tales, and the art of imagery. Danish immigrants quickly settled across many states. Their rapid assimilation into local communities, and particularly their adaptation of the English language, stimulated their economic success. Yet, they maintained their Danishness by holding onto various customs and foods. (Think about how we still enjoy Danish butter cookies!)

One of the greatest purveyors of Nordic heritage was Nikolai Frederik Severin Grundtvig (1783–1872), noted historian, poet, educator, religious leader and philosopher, hymn writer, and folklorist of Denmark. He advocated a holistic approach to community and culture with an emphasis on Danishness. Through an exploration of Old Norse mythology and Anglo-Saxon literature, Grundtvig discovered and came under the influence of spirituality in the early church in northern Europe. As a pastor and educator, he promoted a spirit of freedom, of poetry, and of creativity. In 1883, his youngest son Frederik Lange Grundtvig (1854–1903) immigrated to the United States and became a pastor to the Danish community in Clinton, Iowa. The Danish-American Grundtvigians became known as the "Happy Danes" because they enjoyed forms of merriment along with their prayers and devotions. Their relaxed lifestyle thrived within American culture, and they maintained a healthy respect for Danish language and culture, particularly the folk-school concept, an autonomous place of learning. Like his father, Frederik became a polymath of sorts as an author, folklorist, artist, and recognized ornithologist.

This book's opening pages introduce the central character of the firm in its fledgling years: Frode Christian Valdemar Rambusch, founder of the Rambusch Decorating Company and contemporary of Frederik Lange Grundtvig. Frode, like Frederik Sr., was also the son of a Lutheran pastor and this background similarly factored into his development. While Frederik nurtured the virtues of the Danish-American community from the pulpit, Frode Rambusch used the palette of the artist to a comparable end. The gifted and precocious young Frode was the second son of a Grundtvigian Lutheran pastor. At an early age, he was already creating detailed sketches of Scandinavian sagas and more relatively recent Viking and Native American heroes (see fig. 1-1). It is important to note that the author does not simply refer to a Lutheran pastor but a *Gruntvig*-Lutheran pastor.

It is evident from these sketches that Frode was smitten, when he was young, by the combination of Danish and American culture and history. This interest, however, began more along archaeological rather than artistic lines. Indeed, later in life, Frode noted that above all, he wanted to become an archaeologist. Because his father did not believe this field would yield compensation, Frode chose to train as a painter, leaving archaeology as an avocation. He intermingled the two fields effortlessly and skillfully, forming the backbone of the design company that would be characterized by both elegance *and* erudition. From the very beginning and to this very day, the firm maintains an extensive library with periodicals, scrapbooks, folios, and books for its pursuit of design and craftsmanship, suited to integrated interior environments of stained glass, art metal, decorative painting, and other elements that bear the Rambusch name.

By his early twenties, Frode was a journeyman and worked in many major European cultural centers: Vienna, Dresden, Berlin, Paris, Zurich, and Munich. The golden ring, so to speak, increasingly within his reach, had yet to be grasped. To achieve this goal, he had to go to the cultural centers of the day—either Saint Petersburg or New York. It was courage and the serendipitous "toss of a coin" that determined his fate. In February 1889, Frode Rambusch arrived in New York on the SS Fulda. Almost two years later, on December 16, 1890, he was joined by Valborg Olsen, his Norwegian fiancé. They were married two days later in the Danish Seaman's Church in Brooklyn.

By the turn of the century, the United States had gone from being an outpost of the British Empire to an established world power. In part, this was manifested by the enormous tonnage of steel the nation was producing. The steel mills of Pittsburgh, which were the largest built by Andrew Carnegie, were churning out ten million tons a year, making the city the largest supplier of steel in the world. This aided in the rebuilding of cities that were recovering from catastrophic, ground-leveling fires. Urbanization increased not only by using this material in construction but also by advances in electrification and corresponding developments in communication with the telegraph and telephone. Coinciding with these changes in American society was the beginning of the automobile age and experiments in flight, which brought further dimensions to the realm of travel. Moving pictures were a curiosity; radio was in its infancy. World's fairs by the turn of the twentieth century continued traditions begun decades before, serving as stages upon which nations displayed their triumphs, inventions, and achievements. Similarly, architects, artisans, and designers competed for international recognition regarding emerging tastes in elegance and sophistication. It was a golden age and the perfect time for men and women of talent and imagination to pursue their dreams. Having tossed a coin to begin his journey, Frode now tossed his hat into the ring with architects and designers. For Frode, New York was the place, and this was the moment.

In the trades, there existed an unspoken social order in which architects saw themselves at the apex. Granted, they were artists. But they were not, as sometimes thought, an exclusive solo act. The talents of a skilled and inventive designer were critical to their success. Each structure, each space was singular as were the needs of its occupants. It was the task of the designer to ornament the interior of a building, remaining true to the ethos and plan of the architect. The designer was to make the interior functional, stylish, and inviting. It was to be a place where people wanted to come, spend time, and, as social and economic changes occurred, spend money. A healthy competitive spirit also existed among designers. The ability to survive and thrive rested in the ability to adapt.

In the United States inventions and patents were in an upward spiral. Growth was burgeoning without pause. Immigration helped to accelerate the process. Like Frode, many craftsmen came to seek their fortune and practice their craft. European monarchies and the

Roman Catholic Church held a monopoly as patrons of the arts. The United States, free of any such constraints, offered an array of independent patrons in business, finance, academies, churches, government, and individual and organizational philanthropies—particularly those who wished to create a New World version of "old" Europe. In addition, the growth of merriment and diversions, such as those in the restaurant and entertainment industry, exerted new market forces. Entrepreneurs looked for ways to profit. Eateries, theaters, and churches popped up in large and small communities. In each case, the architect or builder invariably constructed the building but it was the designer who breathed life, style, and sophistication into it. The Rambusch Decorating Company found its niche in the fanciful decoration of restaurants, theaters, ballrooms, and private residences as well as church interiors and the design and fabrication of altar furnishings and appointments.

From its beginning, the company adhered to the structure and practices of the medieval European system of the craft guild. It was within this context that Frode, his sons, and his sons' sons, came of age. Individual skills were tested within a shop and master artisans would pass on their skills to younger, less-experienced workers. Such guilds were particularly competitive in certifying the highest level of quality in a product. By definition, the masterwork was required to meet the standard of excellence in style and execution. A useful analogy that might be made is to the baseball "farm" club, or feeder system, which had begun in approximately 1919. It was created to train and season potential players. The workshops within the Rambusch Decorating Company had their own farm clubs, of a sort, for aspiring craftspeople long before Branch Rickey made it fashionable. Such systems rely on the same principle: the reputation of the owner. In the case of Rambusch, the name spoke persuasively as to the promise of the apprentice. Artists and craftspeople came to the United States either independently or by contract. The company initially hired so many Scandinavians that the Danish language was the default in the design shops. The Danishness of the company, in the early years, was also reflected in the payroll sheets that list one Danish name after another. Still, within the Rambusch workshops, there was always room for one more. During the first ten years of its being established, the Rambusch company also employed full-time designers, painters, and cartoonists who were women.

The first Rambusch apprentice was Frederick "Fred" R. Rickeman (1874–1951), the son of a German immigrant whose surname was Rückermann. During a post-WWII visit to the firm, Rickeman was asked by Michael McCarthy, company treasurer, to write a "sketchy description of how I met dear Mr. Frode Rambusch and what happened as well as I can remember during the firm's infancy." The letter provides an excellent first-person account of the life, work ethic, and guild system in America and its application at the Rambusch company (see Appendix C). Rickeman also offers a bit of whimsy with the tale of the "dirty sponge" and the "full Dutch brush full of green, top of my head." That this letter still exists underscores the value and benefit of the company archives. Rickeman eventually moved to California circa 1920 and became a scenic designer for theater and film. Like so many other artists, he maintained a warm relationship with the Rambusch Decorating Company.

Another aspect of the guild system was that of the itinerant artist who traveled from one studio to the next according to his or her temperament and the availability of work. Some itinerant artists employed by Rambusch included Lithuanian-American Albinas Elskus; stained-glass artist and Dominican priest, Father Marcolino ("Marco") Maas (Arnold Johannes Wilhelmus Maas, under his correct baptismal name); Dutch-American artist Joep Nicholas; and the Colombian-born painter Leandro Velasco. Velasco worked on the domes and vaults at the National Shrine of the Immaculate Conception in Washington, DC, particularly the mosaics of the three domes in the Great Upper Church (2001–2017).

While some craftspeople spent their entire career associated with the firm, others launched their own workshops with the support and encouragement of the company. Such was the case with Costante Crovatto, who had been a foreman for Vittorio Foscato (also known as Fascato), a New York–based Italian marble and mosaic company. In 1953, Crovatto launched his own company with the pledge from Rambusch that they would get more work, along with the free use of Rambusch designers. Crovatto and Rambusch are still collaborating today, speaking to the survival of craft.

In their hometown of Sønder Omme, Denmark, by necessity, the life of Frode's family intermingled with ecclesiastical culture. The second chapter about church interior design and decoration offers a Grundtvig-oriented discussion of art in relation to style, imagery, and technique. In a sense, trade secrets are being shared because the techniques used were tailored to specific objects or interiors. A reader and art enthusiast can visit, with book in hand, any cited places of worship and spend an hour or two in personal or professional enrichment.

Subsequent material about the techniques, trends, and styles of art metal continues the ecclesiastical conversation. This section of the book includes an engaging discussion about the development and evolution of the candlestick in its many forms as executed by the company (see fig. 3-13). Changes in shapes and styles, and differences in materials and techniques, illustrate changing trends in American decorative arts. Frequently, production of these appointments was affected by rising costs and creative means by which Rambusch met its clients' budget. For example, a set of four candlesticks and a crucifix designed in 1919 for the Church of Our Lady of Lourdes, Manhattan, are steeped in both old-world design and innovation. The candlesticks are ornamented with an ancient economical technique of applying bands of silverplated, repoussé copper. The bands, worked into a soft, wave-like design, suggest the borders in a Norwegian stave church, the oldest type of wooden Christian churches that resemble both the buildings themselves and smaller ornaments of the Viking era as well as the frame of Viking ships. Although materials for church appointments (such as candlesticks) were inexpensive, the scale and proportion of them provides an almost monumental effect to the entire altar set. As a ritual element, candlesticks in general for Catholic and Protestant worship services lost some of their practicality as the use of electricity grew. The candlestick and candlestand was soon relegated to the realm of a ritual appointment. By 1908, the Rambusch Decorating Company was illuminating interior decorative wall painting with distinguished electrical light fixtures. Consequently, the lighting division of Rambusch has become one of its hallmarks and core areas of production.

Edward Vilhelm August Rambusch (1896–1978), a Danish-born cousin of Frode, joined the firm in 1924. The following year he became the head of the lighting division, a position he held until his retirement in 1966. From the start of his involvement in the company, Edward wrote articles for the journal produced by the Illuminating Engineering Society. In one such piece, he described the principles of good lighting in a church setting. Not surprisingly, his solution to good lighting was a Rambusch fixture. This was not hubris; it was fact because of the integration possible of employing products and techniques within one firm. As a brilliant engineer, Edward secured several US patents for his lighting fixtures, most notably the Downlite (see figs. 4-18 to 4-20). He was a man of discovery who created an in-house laboratory to test new fixtures and offer precision, custom-made products—not shop style. The original test site for the Downlite, this lab was also the place where four revisions were made to this fixture to accommodate ever-increasing lamp wattage over time. In addition to his engineering skills, Edward also excelled as a company promoter and teacher. Under his watch, the company developed an independent national sales force trained in the distinctive qualities of Rambusch fixtures and custom-engineered lighting solutions.

The New York World's Fair of 1939 provided the Rambusch Decorating Company with several special opportunities to strut its stuff—and they did. The size of this fair was second only to that of Saint Louis, Missouri, in 1904. Maintaining old-world ease and gentility, Rambusch dominated the illumination of the New York fair with 500 Downlites being used in dozens of buildings and pavilions. The Soviet Pavilion alone incorporated 250 fixtures made by Rambusch that were later shipped to the USSR, where engineers could study how the lights were made in order to reproduce them. Rambusch was now an acknowledged player on the world stage. The hospitality and friendliness once enjoyed among the tradesfolk of 1939 would soon give way and parity would not return in the face of coming world events. The New York World's Fair of 1939 was the last hurrah of a world on the edge of war.

In the United States, during the first half of the century, much religious art was imported from Europe. By 1930, the Rambusch company had filled this void by creating its own stained-glass studio, staffed with its own designer-artists. For centuries, the embellishment of church interiors was both devotional and catechetical. The sophistication and scholarship of the Rambusch staff contributed to the success of its designs and imagery. Discussions throughout this book concerning imagery are educational, particularly when referring to such arcane symbols and images as that of a pelican vulning (wounding) itself to give life to its chicks (see fig. 2-8). The use of this symbol of sacrifice and charity waned after the war, but today is enjoying somewhat of a resurgence.

The company's experience in scenic design and theater interiors from the twenties into the forties enabled it to contribute to the American WWII effort. Chief designer Leif Neandross had served in a World War I camouflage unit and used this knowledge to create a method using four different colors on surfaces to appear as representations of four different natural elements when dry. The US Army Corps of Engineers provided him and his team scale drawings of areas to be camouflaged. The Rambusch designers and artists then created a gridded template with ropes to realize the design (see figs. 9-1 and 9-2). From Maryland to Nebraska, at military and civilian airfields, ordinance depots, factories, and chemical plants, the landscape was transformed into Potemkin orchards, meadows, and hillsides intended to deceive the enemy.

At the opposite end of this spectrum, Rambusch was hired by the military not to hide from, but to "light up," opposing forces by creating an instrument and a method to train technicians for anti-aircraft searches. The company was also brought on board by the Sperry Gyroscope Company to design an "Echo Box," a top-secret military device (see fig. 9-5). This box was a component of a cutting-edge, experimental radar system. Together with other smaller components created and manufactured by Rambusch, the unit was colloquially known for its "Mickey Mouse ears," or parabolic reflectors. The final product was the prototype of a radar receiver. Handmade composite units were then mass produced. One of the original models with a Rambusch-fabricated Echo Box at its center was installed on the USS *Missouri* battleship, where the Japanese Empire surrendered on September 2, 1945. The radar antenna of this vessel was one of sixteen units that Rambusch produced as a result of their knowledge of optics, which they skillfully adapted to the needs of radar detection.

The names, dates, places herein reflect a rich facet of American history as experienced by a multi-generational artisanal firm. Nothing short of reading this book will provide a reader with an understanding of the company's role in business history amid wider trends and forces. The Rambusch Decorating Company is an art and design company for all seasons, spaces, and people. The seeds of success planted in 1898 by its Danish forebear have blossomed to yield nearly countless stunning lighting, stained-glass, art-metal, painting and decorating, and mosaic projects. While this book offers a history of the firm's first hundred years, it also provides a touchstone for the work that the company has done since then, including the FDNY Memorial Wall that remembers the sacrifices of the firefighters during 9/11 and also the restoration of the original torch of the Statue of Liberty, among many other commissions. By looking to the past, we can see the foundation of the present as well as visions for the future.

NOTE ABOUT ILLUSTRATIONS

Preference has been given to period photographs, wherever possible. Clarity sometimes varies. If there was a choice between a fuzzy, second-generation photo or none at all, I chose the former. My thanks go to Doris Gottscho Schleisner for her help in identifying some images. Her father photographed commissions that were completed by the Rambusch Decorating Company throughout his distinguished career. In fact, some of his first work was at Rambusch. Fay S. Lincoln, another dean of American architectural photographers, also documented Rambusch projects for many years. Jeanette C. Parsons, at the Labor Archives of Pennsylvania State University, willingly identified many photographs from the index of the Fay S. Lincoln Collection in that repository. Thanks are also due to Michael Hauser and Patrick Seymour at the Theatre Historical Society of America because of their assistance in tracking down a period image of Radio City Music Hall. Unless otherwise noted, illustrations are from the archives of the Rambusch Decorating Company.

Regarding captions, because many projects have taken years to complete, from initial design through fabrication and installation, I have tried to include the completion date for consistency and simplicity although sometimes have noted fuller date ranges. All designers and craftspeople indicated in captions were, or are, associated with the Rambusch Decorating Company, unless otherwise noted. For the five boroughs of the city of New York, the state designation "NY" has been omitted.

King Valdemar the Victororious

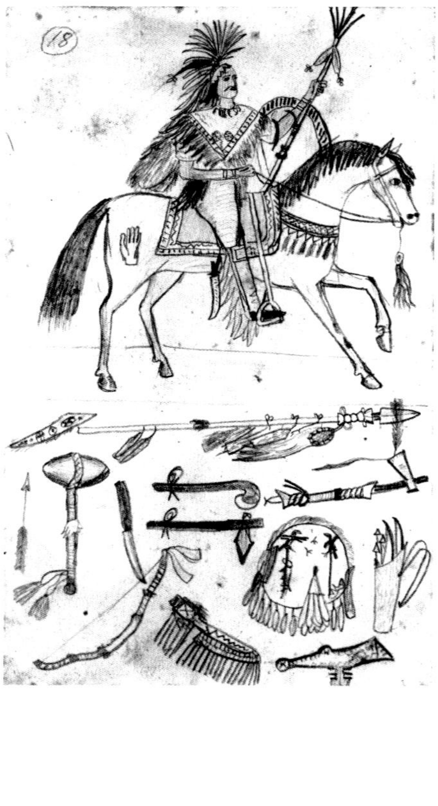

Crest's of danish towns

CHAPTER I

History of the Rambusch Decorating Company

It was the flip of a coin, the family story goes, that determined the destination of Frode Christian Valdemar Rambusch (1859–1924), the second son of a Grundtvig-Lutheran pastor, born on March 23, 1859, in Sønder Omme, Denmark. His childhood sketchbooks show a surprising knowledge of history. Images from Greek mythology, Scandinavian sagas, and Native American and Danish history stride across the pages (fig. 1-1). He depicted historical incidents, along with intricately drawn imaginary scenes and inventions. These drawings portray a remarkable attention to detail and deftness—unusual for a young child. At the age of thirteen, Frode was indentured to the master painter Andersen in Odense, a nearby town. In later years, he wrote: "Until my sixteenth year, I received instruction from our private tutor. I desired, above all, to become an archeologist, a field of study which I always pursued and still pursue for my own enjoyment; but since my father regarded archeology as an unremunerative profession, I abandoned thought of pursuing advanced studies and chose to become a trained painter."

In 1871, Frode's father was moved north to serve another church. A painting from this period shows the young teenager's interest in church interiors, creating a mood with color and light-filled space as a special environment for prayer (fig. 1-2). At the age of seventeen, Frode was accepted to the Danish Design School of the Royal Danish Academy of Art, Copenhagen. He studied drawing and decoration, while simultaneously being apprenticed to the master painter Markussen. After seven years of study, Frode advanced to the level of journeyman. Stamps on his passport of 1884 show his beginning travels (fig. 1-3). Eventually, he worked in Vienna, Dresden, Berlin, Paris, Zurich, and Munich. Returning to

1-1 Frode C. V. Rambusch, *Childhood sketchbook drawings (selected)*, from the top, clockwise: *King Valdemar, the Victorious*; *Crests of Danish towns*; *Thor*; and a *Native American, with tribal tools and clothing*, ca. 1864. **1-2** Frode C. V. Rambusch, *Church interior*, oil on canvas, ca. 1871.

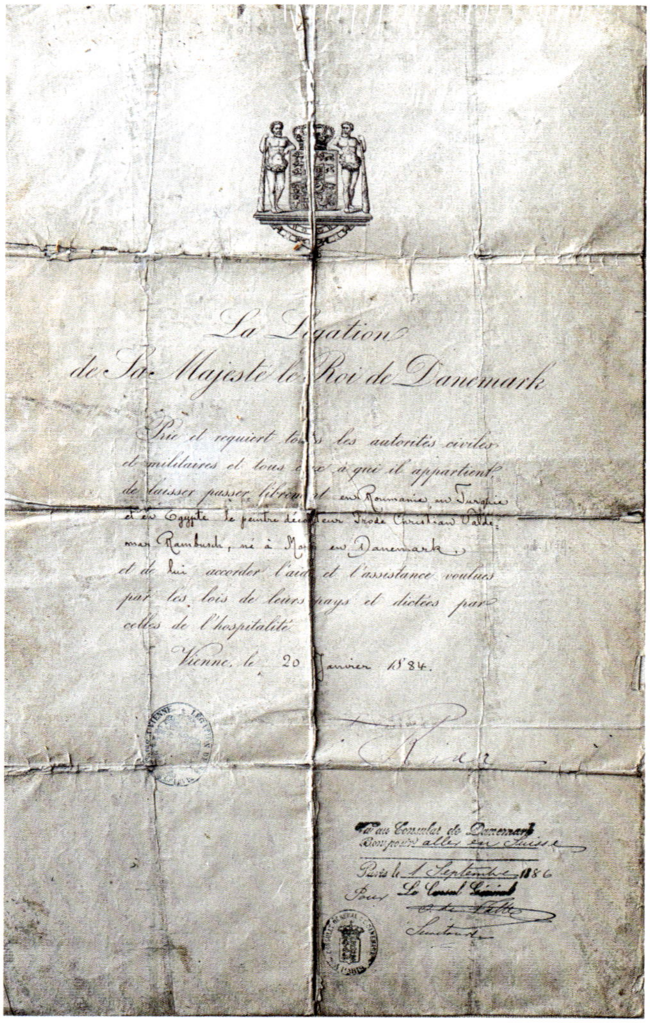

La Légation
de Sa Majesté le Roi de Danemark

Prie et requiert toutes les autorités civiles et militaires et tous ceux à qui il appartient de laisser passer librement en Roumanie, en Turquie et en Egypte le peintre décorateur Frode Christian Valdemar Rambusch, né à ... en Danemark et de lui accorder l'aide et l'assistance voulues par les lois de leurs pays et dictées par celles de l'hospitalité.

Vienne, le 20 Janvier 1884.

Vu au Consulat de Danemark

Paris le 1 Septembre 1886

Pour Le Consul Général

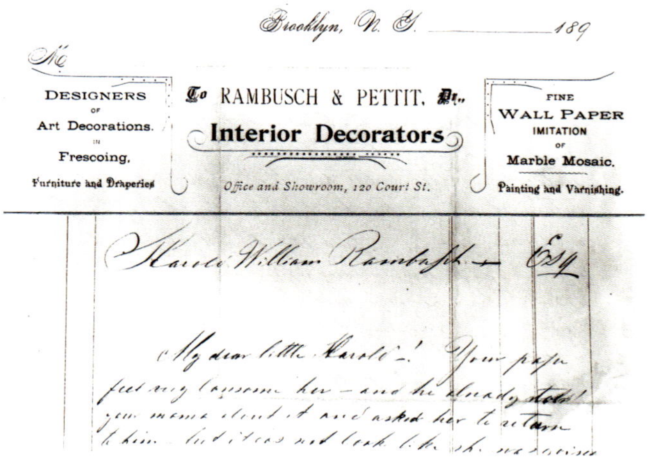

Brooklyn, N. Y. ________ 189

M

DESIGNERS OF Art Decorations. IN Frescoing, Furniture and Draperies

To RAMBUSCH & PETTIT, Dr.

Interior Decorators

Office and Showroom, 120 Court St.

FINE WALL PAPER IMITATION OF Marble Mosaic. Painting and Varnishing.

Harald William Rambusch Esq

1-3 *Passport of Frode C. V. Rambusch*, size: approximately 15" x 25", 1884. **1-4** *Letterhead stationery*, Rambusch & Pettit, Interior Decorators, Brooklyn, ca. 1893.

Denmark in 1888, he saw little opportunity for advancement at home and was determined to emigrate. His options were either St. Petersburg or New York. At the end of the nineteenth century, for a man with his skills and training, both cities were lands of opportunity. The toss of the coin determined his destination: the latter would become his home.

Frode arrived in New York City in February 1889. He found employment immediately. One of his employers was a Brooklyn decorating and painting firm, Arnold & Locke. He quickly rose to become foreman and was known as the "Stencil King," which, at that time, was a highly complimentary epithet. After working for one year, he sent for his Norwegian fiancée, Valborg Olsen, whose father and two brothers were painter-decorators. Valborg and Frode had met when he visited her brothers in Oslo during a holiday. Frode and Valborg were married in the Danish Lutheran Seaman's Church, located in the heart of the Scandinavian community in Bay Ridge, Brooklyn. Their carefully dovetailed wedding chest, with sturdy wrought-iron handles and the bride's name lovingly lettered "Valborg Olsen New York" in fluid gold on the faux-painted, burled surface, is still in the family's possession.

Arnold & Locke decorated churches as far away as Montreal, Canada. Frode's proficiency provided constant employment, unusual in a trade that tended to have seasonal work patterns. He was often away from his wife, buying her silver spoons from the towns where he worked. Even so, he longed to be his own man. In 1892, Frode made the first of two unsuccessful attempts at having his own company.

Evidence of his first short-lived partnership can be found in the ornate stationery of Rambusch & Pettit, Interior Decorators. In 1893 it was located at 120 Court Street, Brooklyn (fig. 1-4). This year, however, was auspicious in other respects. D. C. Laub, an architect in that borough, wrote to C. G. Christensen, president of the Brooklyn Trust Company, and an active member at Saint Anne's Church in Brooklyn. Laub heartily recommended Frode for the interior design work of the church (fig. 1-5). The success of this project resulted in a series of commissions with the Irish clergy across New York and the northeast. But this success took years to take hold: in the immediate term, establishing commercial footing was a challenge.

By 1894, the firm of Rambusch & Pettit, Interior Decorators, was located at 1193 Broadway, near 28th Street, Manhattan (fig. 1-6), where it remained established for at least a few years (fig. 1-7). Their letterhead identifies the firm as "Designers of Art Decorations in Ecclesiastical and Domestic Work, Marble and Mosaic." Notably, after this business venture ceased, Frode remained on good terms with H. McEwen Pettit because records indicate that he later collaborated with his former partner.

At the Gibson Art Glass and Decorating Company, Frode's second early venture, Frode was responsible for a complex job: Saint Michael's Monastery Church, Union City, New Jersey. Five decades later, after a disastrous fire at this church, the Rambusch Decorating Company did extensive work for the new building that would be designed by architect Charles D. Maginnis.

Insufficient funds likely were a factor in these early ventures, along with perhaps a certain naiveté or lack of business acumen. Even as a successful partner in his own firm, by 1900, Frode wrote to his brother, Sigurd:

> I am so busy from early morning 'till late evening that it is an exception when I have a little extra time in the evening. The struggle for existence is hard and I probably have no talent for making money. The business conditions are such that it is almost impossible to be

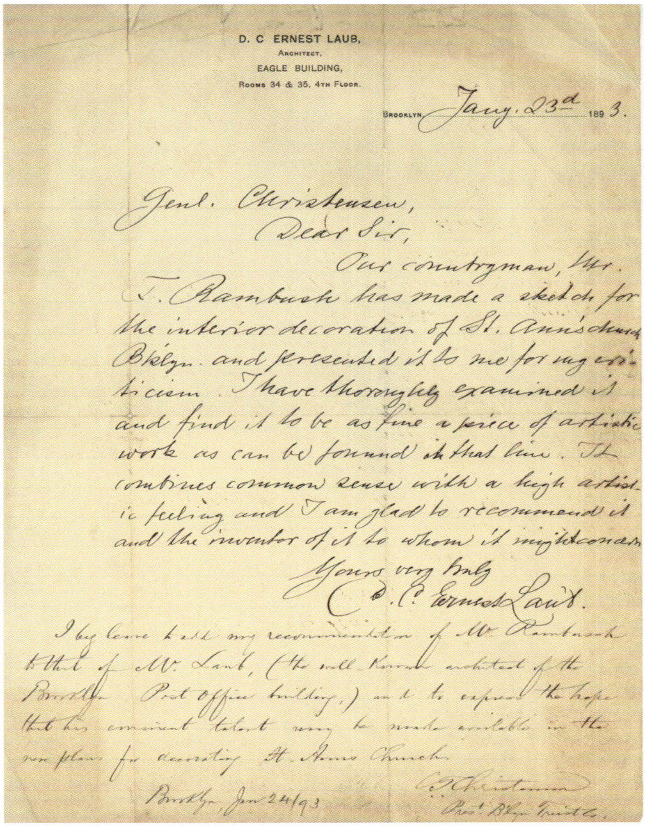

D. C ERNEST LAUB,
ARCHITECT,
EAGLE BUILDING,
ROOMS 34 & 35, 4TH FLOOR.

BROOKLYN, Jany. 23d 1893.

Genl. Christensen,
Dear Sir,

Our countryman, Mr. F. Rambusch has made a sketch for for the interior decoration of St. Ann's church Bklyn. and presented it to me for my criticism. I have thoroughly examined it and find it to be as fine a piece of artistic work as can be found in that line. It combines common sense with a high artistic feeling and I am glad to recommend it and the inventor of it to whom it might concern.

Yours very truly
D. C. Ernest Laub.

I beg leave to add my recommendation of Mr. Rambusch to that of Mr. Laub, (the well known architect of the Brooklyn Post Office building,) and to express the hope that his eminent talent may be made available in the new plans for decorating St. Ann's Church.

Brooklyn, Jan 24/93
C. T. Christensen
Prest. Bklyn Trust Co.

1-5 *Letter of recommendation*, from D. C. Laub to General Christensen, January 23, 1893. **1-6** *Studio Interior, Rambusch & Pettit, Interior Decorators*, left to right: H. McEwen Pettit, Frode C. V. Rambusch, F. Rickeman, 1193 Broadway, near 28th Street, Manhattan, ca. 1895.

> honest and at the same time make money, but my business is continually growing. At the present time I have 40 men working—it is a weekly payroll of more than 2,000 Krone in Danish money. But the business is, as you probably know, a stock company, so even if for a while we are making good money, I still have no greater personal income.

The decades that bracketed the turn of the century were eras of congenial and extraordinarily productive collaboration between architects, artists, decorators, and craftsmen. Associations in Philadelphia, Chicago, Cleveland, Detroit, and other cities promoted collaboration in their club rooms. These spaces provided stimulating atmospheres for mutually beneficial exchanges and club staff organized regular public exhibitions of their members' work. One example was the Architectural League of New York, founded in 1881. Its earliest exhibitions were held in the newly built headquarters of the American Fine Arts Society on West 57th Street. The façade of the building designed by architect Henry J. Hardenbergh clearly proclaimed its purpose. Below the cornice were three tablets: "Architecture" was carved in the center, flanked by "Painting" and "Sculpture."

The firm of Rambusch and Pettit participated in the annual exhibition of the Architectural League of New York for 1893–1894. A connection with the League continued until the eventual demise of these exhibitions in the early 1940s which, at their height, drew large and enthusiastic crowds. Rambusch was invited again and again to exhibit. However, weakened by the Depression, the hiatus caused by World War II, and the increasing dominance of the International Style (with its truculent proponents and their avowed disinterest—and even disdain—for craft and decoration), sealed the fate of these exhibitions. (Despite the cessation of their annual exhibitions, however, the Architectural League of New York is still thriving as an organization).

Finally in 1898, through a family acquaintance, Frode (fig. 1-8) was introduced to William F. Hencken (1872–1953; fig. 1-9). Hencken was fresh out of Princeton University, and his family wanted him to obtain some practical business experience. He and his brother George D. Hencken advanced $2,500 in capital that launched the Rambusch firm. Although George's name appears on stationery as late as 1911, he seems never to have taken an active part in the new company.

On January 1, 1899, the first Board meeting of the Rambusch Glass and Decorating Company was held at 175 Broadway. The Hencken brothers held forty-eight shares, Valborg Olsen Rambusch held twenty-five, and Frode held one, which was immediately transferred to his young son, Harold. William Hencken became treasurer with an annual wage of $780. Frode was elected superintendent with a yearly salary of $1,500. The two purchased a partners' desk made of walnut, with cabriole legs that terminated in ball-and-claw feet. It is still in use at the firm today, symbolizing the ideal partnership, each of the pair bringing an equal, but different, contribution. The old and the new were joined together, as they had been in other business and cultural spheres in the United States. The company's history was to become an archetypal American success story.

Hencken had a sharp eye for numbers, a good head for accounts, and helpful local connections. His parsimonious nature befitted his role as company treasurer. An office boy later reminisced—and lamented—that he had to pay his own nickel for transportation. Then, with receipt in hand, Mr. Hencken would reimburse him from the petty cash box that he kept in his desk drawer.

Frode, reputed to have been a man of great charm and erudition, had the talent and skill necessary to design and execute attractive decorative interiors. He could design, cut, and apply stencils. He could also glaze, pounce, marbleize, create woodgrain, and draw and do free-hand decoration. All these skills were applicable in both domestic and public interiors. The partners did not enter an area devoid of competition. Since the end of the Civil War and the amassing of great fortunes in the United States, the interior decorating profession had developed rapidly. Such firms as William Baumgarten, Herter Brothers, and Pottier & Stymus supplied all the furnishings, drapery, and decorative wall and ceiling treatments required for interior decorating jobs. "The works" were readily available in every imaginable combination and mélange of styles for the client who could pay. Louis Comfort Tiffany at Tiffany Studios, John La Farge, and Francis Lathrop were some of those supplying original designs in stained glass, murals, and mosaics to complete interiors (see Appendix A).

In 1899 the Rambusch Decorating Company took offices at 160 Fifth Avenue, right in the center of an area where competing firms existed. The paint shop, by contrast, was a subterranean space on Sixth Avenue near 13th Street. Until 1917, the firm maintained these two locations. The Rambusch advertisement in *Sweet's Indexed Catalogue of Building Construction* of 1906 shows the interior of Benjamin Henry Latrobe's Baltimore Cathedral (fig. 1-10), which the firm had decorated two years earlier, and would decorate twice more in the

1-7 *Letterhead stationery*, Rambusch & Pettit, Interior Decorators, Manhattan, 1899. **1-8** Harold Slott-Møller, *Frode Christian Valdemar Rambusch*, oil on canvas, 1922; founder, Rambusch Decorating Company; Knight of Dannebrog (1911); founder, at the behest of Cardinal Farley, of Saint Ansgar's Scandinavian League. **1-9** *William F. Hencken*, ca. 1930. **1-10** *Advertisement, showing the interior of the Basilica of the Assumption, Baltimore, Maryland*, from *Sweet's Indexed Catalogue of Building Construction*, 1906.

INTERIOR DECORATIONS 391 RAMBUSCH GLASS AND DECORATING CO.

RAMBUSCH GLASS AND DECORATING CO.

Interior Decorations, Mural Paintings, etc.

160 Fifth Avenue

NEW YORK CITY, N. Y.

TELEPHONE, 3954 GRAMERCY

PRODUCTS. Interior Decorations, Mural Paintings, Wall Hangings, Relief Work, Painting and Wood Finishing, and Cabinet Work.

BALTIMORE (MD.) CATHEDRAL

Decorations by Rambusch Glass & Decorating Co.

EXAMPLES. The following are some of the notable buildings which we have decorated:

BALTIMORE CATHEDRAL, Baltimore, Md.
ST. JOSEPH'S CATHEDRAL, Buffalo, N. Y.
ST. JEROME'S CHURCH, New York City.
CHURCH OF THE REDEEMER, Brooklyn, N. Y.
SEABOARD NATIONAL BANK, New York City.
CORN EXCHANGE BANK, New York City.
WILLIAMSBURG TRUST CO., Brooklyn, N. Y.
LEONORE HOTEL, New York City.
GRAND OPERA HOUSE, Cincinnati, Ohio.
TRENT THEATRE, Trenton, N. J.
ORPHEUM THEATRE, Brooklyn, N. Y.
AMERICAN THEATRE, New York City.
RESIDENCE, 1006 Fifth Avenue, New York City.
RESIDENCE, 811 Fifth Avenue, New York City.
RESIDENCE, 39 West 53d Street, New York City.
RESIDENCE, Roselawn, Greenwich, Conn.

1906

future. Listed in the same advertisement are domestic interiors completed by the firm, such as the Church of the Redeemer, Brooklyn, and the American Theatre, Manhattan. From the outset, most of the firm's commissions were executed in large public spaces.

One might expect a predominance of local work for such a new firm in a highly competitive field, but facts prove otherwise. One also wonders how such a new firm could successfully gain commissions as far afield as Cincinnati and locations in Canada. A possible, but as yet undocumented, source of work could have been a relationship with the Irish immigrant, Brooklyn-based builder-architect Patrick Charles Keely (1816–1896). Between 1848 and 1896 this prolific designer created hundreds of churches throughout the United States and Canada. Ironically, his masterpiece of a cathedral, reserved for his adopted borough, Brooklyn, was never finished. The 334-foot-long, dressed-stone foundation of this building was greater in dimension than James Renwick, Jr.'s Saint Patrick's Cathedral across the East River. Eventually Keely's cathedral was demolished. Frode Rambusch decorated many Keely-designed churches, including cathedrals in Erie, Pennsylvania; Buffalo, New York; and Halifax, Nova Scotia; to name just a few.

Frode converted to Catholicism in 1896 and was on good terms with several members of the clergy. These friendships most certainly were helpful. Until well after World War II, the pastor in Catholic parishes was in total control of his church's budget, design, and decoration. Today, by contrast, in most areas the Diocesan Building Commission controls the budget and the Liturgical Commission oversees designs for new churches and the renovation of aging ones.

Satisfied clients were, and remain, the firm's best source of new commissions. Early ledgers clearly reveal this emerging pattern. A job in a town was frequently, if not always, followed within a year or two by several others in the same vicinity. These and other reasons allowed business to prosper with commissions in the United States and Canada. Within the first decade of its existence, the fledgling firm received so much work that Frode hired a designer, countryman Knud Laub, who had also been trained at the Royal Danish Academy of Art in Copenhagen. It was quite natural that other recent Scandinavian immigrants would come to Rambusch looking for work. Names in early payroll records read like personae of the sagas: Axel, Kai, Knud, Leif, Per. In fact, Danish was the language of the design room in the early years. In contemporary times, Spanish and Ukrainian are often heard in the workshops. The more recent influx of highly skilled Polish metalsmiths has brought their language to the workplace.

Following the inexorable movement uptown, in 1912, the firm relocated its design rooms to 2 West 45th Street. In the same year, at the annual meeting, Frode was voted president for the first time. There was also an increase in capital investment to $5,000. William Hencken waived his stock rights and Frode's son, Harold, was employed at $2,000 a year. As a point of comparison, a stock book in these years cost $1.71 and a seal press $2.00, both of which were purchased for the newly capitalized firm. By the end of the decade, Hencken was no longer actively associated with the Rambusch Decorating Company. In 1916, he commissioned his classmate John Russell Pope to build a house in Greenwich, Connecticut, which he dubbed "Merleigh Farm." But the interior of this home was decorated by the Rambusch firm.

Change and growth occurred in another area. The firm's first expansion resulted from the increasingly ubiquitous use of electricity by the 1920s—at least in urban areas. Murals, carefully decorated walls, naves, and sanctuaries were first often illuminated by a single suspended naked light bulb. The resulting glare shattered the ambience and hampered appreciation of the decorative scheme. The firm had begun to design lighting fixtures in 1908. Initially, it only designed them, with outside artisans fabricating the designs under the firm's supervision. Wiring, for example, was done at S. J. O'Brien's, whose owner was formerly a bicycle mechanic who turned his talents to the new energy source.

Soon a second expansion in company business took place, gradually responding to requests of patrons. By 1919, the firm began to design and fabricate accoutrements for churches: candlesticks, chalices, ostensoria, crucifixes, tabernacles, gates, and screens. These were made in wrought iron, bronze, copper, silver, gold, or sometimes combinations of these materials. The first forge and metal workshops were located in an old stable at 243 East 44th Street. Blacksmith Jose Bartel, a Spanish immigrant, was the first master craftsman of the metal workshop. Two of his elegant wrought-iron letter openers—one a dagger and the other embellished with a realistic gingko leaf—are held in the company offices today.

After Bartel's untimely death, Axel Larsen was the head of the workshops for many years (fig. 1-11). In 1926, the firm bought a four-story brick loft building at 332 East 48th Street. A photo of the metal workshop interior

1-11 *Rambusch craftsmen,* 332 East 48th Street, Manhattan, at left: Axel Larsen, foreman; front row, from left: [first two men, unidentified], Joe Bisso, Alphonse Moe, [unidentified]; second row: Aage Pontoppidan, Ejner Rasmussen, [unidentified], Henry Olsen; third row: [first four unidentified], Louis Hansen, [unidentified], ca. 1928. **1-12** *Workshop interior, showing, at center, wrought-iron frames for Plumbob lighting fixtures,* 332 East 48th Street, Manhattan, ca. 1930.

1-13 *Advertisement, showing unified design rooms and workshops at 40 West 13th Street*, Manhattan, 1947. **1-14** *Past company presidents*, left: Viggo Frode Edvard Rambusch, president, Rambusch Decorating Company (1961–1963); president, Saint Ansgar's Scandinavian Catholic League (1937–1988); right: Harold William Rambusch, president, Rambusch Decorating Company (1924–1961 and 1964–1969); Knight of Dannebrog (1953), 1968. **1-15** *View of sanctuary*, Saint Raymond's Church, The Bronx, 1908; ca. 1930; 2008; and 2022.

of this building shows craftsmen working on several projects (fig. 1-12). The company remained at this location until 1947, when the design rooms and workshops were unified in one building at 40 West 13th Street (fig. 1-13). There, three blacksmith forges were installed in the metal shop in 1947. Over the years, the men who could use them died, and technology and taste changed. Reluctantly, the last forge was removed in 1985.

Frode's two sons, Harold William (1891–1981) and Viggo Frode Edvard (1900–1996; fig. 1-14), both worked for the firm in their youth and into adulthood. Harold, born in 1891, was apprenticed as a painter-decorator during summers and graduated in 1911 from Pratt Institute. After a journeyman's stint in Europe, Harold joined the firm officially. His first job in 1914 was as a foreman on the decoration of the Jefferson Theatre on East 14th Street in Manhattan. Simultaneously, the firm was also decorating a theatre of comparable size uptown, which created a healthy and spirited competition between the seasoned foreman and the boss's young son. Even as an octogenarian, Harold was still proud of the fact that his crew won out, for they had made a higher profit for the firm.

Harold became president of the firm in 1924. His dynamism, creative energy, and business acumen fully realized the potential of the Rambusch Decorating Company. Under his leadership, the different craft workshops were fully developed and functioned symbiotically as parts of a whole. As an example, the baptistry of Our Lady of the Blessed Sacrament, Harrisburg, Pennsylvania, illustrates the unified results of all the Rambusch craft workshops working together, as does Saint Raymond's Church (fig. 1-15). He wielded a firm dedicated to the design concept that the interaction of different crafts and the continuity of the process from design to fabrication would yield a fine, economical result. After Harold married Olava Steen, two of their three children, William and Robert, became associated with the company.

Viggo Frode Edvard graduated from Columbia College in 1922 and was awarded his Bachelor of Architecture from the same university two years later. He then attended Catholic University and received a Master of Architecture degree. He, too, became a recognized expert in the field and worked tirelessly for the growth of the firm as exemplified in the design and creation of beautiful interiors—hundreds of them. Viggo married Gudrun Harriet Bech. In 1988, Catholic University named him the "dean of American church architects." Of

their three children, Viggo Bech Ansgar (b. 1931) served as president of the firm from 1970 to 1989 and also from 1991 to 2002.

Skill and length of commitment seem to be the leitmotif of Rambusch's employees' histories. Leif Neandross, employed for sixty years, was chief designer for fifty of them. His mother had come from a family of Danish mural artists and his father, although born in the United States, was a European-trained sculptor who worked for Tiffany Studios, Stanford White, and the American Museum of Natural History. Several years before, Trygve Hammer, a Rambusch designer, notified Leif's father Sigurd that a position as office boy and apprentice had opened up. The elder Neandross brought in his son, who was then making models in the bronze-casting firm, William H. Jackson Company, for an interview. Leif was hired as office boy and apprenticed to work under Hammer.

With prodigious natural talent, Leif completed his schooling in mathematics, art, and archaeology by attending night classes at the General Society of Mechanics & Tradesmen, two blocks from the office. With an insatiable curiosity, he later regularly attended Saturday classes at the Art Students League. His talent, discipline, and skill of observation and facility for drawing, combined with an encyclopedic knowledge of historic styles and a complete command of the color spectrum, allowed his seemingly inexhaustible imagination to extend freely and easily. He also became a skilled ceramicist and enamelist and a Fellow of the American Water Color Society. The fruits of all his talents remain a glorious legacy to the firm.

Leif had none of the preciousness often encountered in some present-day designers, such as a rigid adherence to a particular style often due to a lack of knowledge. Later reminiscing about his career, Leif said: "Some people make dresses. We make architectural and artisanal crafts. It is in our genes." Leif was eventually joined by his two brothers who also were apprenticed to the firm. Knud became superintendent of the Painting and Decorating Shop and George became production manager.

The need to control all physical aspects of an interior, thereby creating an integrated design wherein light, color, and furnishings conceived as a whole complement each other, resulted in the opening of yet another workshop at Rambusch: the Stained-Glass Studio. It opened in 1930, above the metal shop on East 48th Street. This studio is still busy today, in a different location, creating both new designs and windows as well as restoring old ones, including those by Louis Comfort Tiffany, D. Maitland Armstrong, and John La Farge.

Costs, labor, and lack of skilled local artisans were a problem in a different area—namely, wood carving and working in marble. To obtain the best talent at the best prices for its clients, Rambusch opened an office in Florence, Italy, in 1924. Its management for more than thirty years and supervision of all projects was ably carried out by architect Mario Liccioli. With this Italian office, the firm could have its designs fabricated to its specifications in Europe for a fraction of the cost and in a superior manner than if they only were operating out of New York.

From 1948 to 1971, the firm maintained its own wood shop on 13th Street under the direction of Wilhelm Funke. Upon his retirement in 1971, the shop was closed. Now the firm works with such independent artisans as S. Diehm Company—just as it did half a century ago. Also, from the late 1940s until 1953 the firm had its own needlework workshop where custom-made altar cloths and hangings were made of imported silk and velvet.

Mosaic and marble were the materials through which Rambusch helped another immigrant realize his dream of owning his own business. V. Foscato (also known as Fascato), a New York–based Italian marble and mosaic firm, had a foreman with superior skills as an artisan. Costante (also known as Constante) Crovatto launched his own firm in 1953 with the promise of commissions from Rambusch and free use of their designers for his own projects. Stephen Miotto took over Crovatto Mosaics and renamed the firm Miotto Mosaic Art Studios, which is going strong today and still makes time to execute Rambusch commissions.

With the swift advance of lighting technology arose a demand for new and inventive solutions. Edward Vilhelm August Rambusch (1896–1978), a Danish-born cousin, joined the firm in 1924. He was a graduate from the Copenhagen Engineering School in 1915, and in London he studied gas engineering at the Battersea Polytechnic. A brilliant engineer, he headed the lighting division from 1925 until his retirement in 1966. He is credited with several US patents for lighting fixtures. Most popular is the Downlite. His original design of 1934 has been improved four times to adapt to newer and more powerful lamps, such as the halogen Mark IV Downlite. Edward designed and opened the in-house lighting laboratory to test newly invented fixtures. Rambusch is the only firm of its size to maintain its own

laboratory for scientific testing of precise, custom-made solutions for projecting the elusive medium of light.

Edward was also a dynamic and energetic salesman. He was invited to utilize the sales force of DayBrite, a manufacturer of standard fixtures for the exposure of Rambusch's custom work. He thereby inaugurated the Rambusch national sales force. H. C. King & Associates, Cincinnati, Ohio, is the longest standing associate since 1922. As early as 1927, Edward was writing articles for the Illuminating Engineering Society about the principles of good church lighting based on the coordination of the "specific requirement and viewpoints of the engineer, the architect, the clergyman and his congregation." Now the firm had its own independent national sales force trained to make available to architects and engineers Rambusch fixtures and custom-engineered lighting solutions. In addition to custom work, the firm had, and still has, several lines of patented fixtures, each of which has infinite adaptability. Downlite, Lite Paks, Shovelites, Pan-a-lux, Annulites, and Classic Lanterns are all made to original Rambusch designs and specifications in its workshops.

1-16 *Edwin Peter, Martin Viggo, and Viggo Bech Rambusch examining the Trinity Dome model for the for the Great Upper Church, Basilica of the National Shrine of the Immaculate Conception,* photograph, 2015.

After World War II, with increased interest in, and dominance of, Bauhaus principles in American architecture, light became an important and vital element in stark interiors, and it defined—even sculpted—the space and sharpened the lines and planes of an interior. Higher levels of light were also demanded and invisible sources were considered imperative. All these criteria could be met by the Downlite. Designers such as Gordon Bunshaft of SOM used Rambusch's Downlite in the ground-floor ceiling of the trend-setting Lever House on Park Avenue. Ironically, the firm's response to these demands for design austerity through the mid-1970s allowed it to remain solvent even as other traditional craft workshops were shrinking and disappearing. Applied ornament and decoration were anathema to the new architectural mode.

Rambusch clung tenaciously to the idea of creating completely integrated interior environments and maintained stained-glass, art-metal, decorating, and painting studios. It seemed there were always just enough churches where these traditional crafts and skills were needed to keep work going in each of the specialized areas.

What had begun in 1898 for independence combined with competence, skill, talent, and simple hard work continued to grow and expand into a third generation. Harold's son, Robert Edward Rambusch, worked for the firm until he resigned in 1984. Viggo Frode's eldest son, Viggo Bech Rambusch, was apprenticed as a painter during summers. After graduating from St. Michael's College within the University of Toronto, between 1953 and 1955, he served in the US Army Corps of Engineers in Germany and France as Military Occupational Specialty (MOS) cartographer. Then he embarked upon a journeyman's trip to Europe. Much to his delight, he was hired without a letter of introduction by the Royal Court painters in both Copenhagen and London. He returned to the United States after a year and was awarded his Master of Fine Arts degree, with a major in architecture, from Catholic University before joining the firm in 1957. He headed the lighting division from 1966 to 1970. He is a Fellow of the Illuminating Engineering Society and served as president of the firm for thirty years, from 1970 to 2002, with a two-year break in that span, between 1989 and 1991. The fourth generation, his twin sons, Edwin Peter and Martin Viggo (fig. 1-16), both now run the firm.

The Rambusch family members are both the leaders and stewards of the extraordinary talents and diverse and varied skills of hundreds of designers, craftspeople, and staff, whose joint common contributions over the years have become the tradition of the company. Longevity affords perspective. A chronicle of 100 years of the Rambusch Decorating Company serves the purpose to elucidate common threads of experience. Trends and changes in American taste are revealed in examining the firm's myriad commissions. The dynamics of client relationships and the changing role of the architect in American building practice are discernable. Names and wages on payroll ledgers exemplify patterns in immigration, business, and labor trends. Comparisons of job costs are a lesson in economics. In reviewing lighting fixture designs fabricated by the firm since the first decade of the twentieth century, one can see how they represent milestones of advancing lighting technology in the United States.

Given the present business climate and the state of commerce in the United States, the Rambusch Decorating Company is healthy and vital; yet, it is an anachronism. It is a survivor of the atelier tradition, with work patterns predicated on a philosophy and practice that seem at odds with a mass-produced, disposable culture.

In the United States today, there is a heartening growth of independent craftspeople and artisans who operate unencumbered by union regulations. And, in the larger business context, there is a discernable, seemingly inexorable, trend to rigidly separate design from fabrication. Furthermore, the bidding process, dominant in architecture as it is now practiced in America, is frequently destructive of integrity and excellence. The Rambusch Decorating Company works against these trends, holding fast to its original principles of creating integrated art and design. As a design/build firm, Rambusch clings to the notion that a cooperative, organic interrelation of design, fabrication, and installation is the most effective, economical, and ultimately satisfying for both the craftsperson and the client. With nineteenth-century processes embracing twentieth-century techniques, better results are possible. And it all started with the flip of a coin.

2-1 *Model of Baptistery*, Saint Bartholomew's Episcopal Church, Manhattan, 1988.

CHAPTER II

Church Interior Design and Decoration

Building God's house, to beautify and enrich a place of worship, was considered a part of a parishioner's privilege and duty. America's late-nineteenth- and early-twentieth-century religious edifices are among the nation's forgotten treasure houses of art and interior decorative design. No matter the diversity of religious practices, or the size and wealth of congregations, methods and techniques of painted interior decoration are relatively straightforward. Before a painter is able to work, a plasterer had to prepare the wall—first with a scratch coat, then with a brown coat, and finally with a third, or finish, coat of plaster. The painter would often sand the plaster to achieve a smooth surface on which to apply primer, then the second, final coat of paint. At this last stage, the painted surface decoration would be applied. The simplest form is plain painting. Specially mixed colors to meet the tonal requirements of the sketch or rendering are usually applied to the wall as a large sample, in situ, for the approval of the client—priest, pastor, rabbi, architect, or church committee.

Finishing methods can vary. Glazing is the application—usually with a brush of another contrasting color—after the plain-finish coat is dry. The glaze is wiped off by hand with a rag while the paint is still wet, leaving a residue and a hint of the other color. More or less of the glaze remains, according to the desired effect. In contrast to the subtle effect gained by glazing, stippling gives a textured effect to the surface. A brush with stiff hairs is struck repeatedly on a tacky surface. A crude variation in the finished effect occurs when using crumpled paper or a sponge instead of the stipple brush.

Decoration on plain or glazed surfaces can be applied in several ways. In stencil decoration, a series of patterns are cut on specially prepared waxed and stiffened paper, and one stencil is used for each color of the design. The stencil is positioned on the wall and color is applied, perhaps with a special, stiff boar's-hair brush onto the wall through the perforations in the paper. The stencil is carefully removed and the paint allowed to dry. The procedure is repeated until the multi-colored border or wall decoration is complete. In a complex design, as many as fifteen stencils might be required. The visual result is a repetitive, measured, two-dimensional design.

Stencils cut to simulate the tiny half-inch-by-half-inch mosaic tesserae are often used in ecclesiastical design. Gold or bronze can be painted through the stencils, one tessera abutting the other, to create rows of mosaic-like borders or entire fields. This technique was used as late as 1988, when Rambusch painted the baptistery ceiling of Saint Bartholomew's Episcopal Church in Manhattan. The firm created a model (fig. 2-1) to study the design issues of this decision. The final result of the painted and decorated ceiling represented a measure of economy because executing a true mosaic ceiling was deemed too costly.

Another decorative technique that results in a freer, more fluid, sweeping design is the pounce method. It utilizes a full-size drawing, or template, of a design made on a piece of paper cut to the size of the space to be decorated. First, the paper is attached to the wall. Then a metal wheel, with sharp, pin-like projections on its circumference, is run along the outline of the design, piercing the paper and leaving tiny pin holes. A bag of pounce, containing chalk powder or charcoal dust, is dabbed along these dotted lines. When the paper is removed, the outline of the design is visible on the wall. These dotted lines are a guide for both outlining the overall design and understanding its scale. Then the decorator is able to

paint directly on the prepared wall, filling in the design with shadows, highlights, and color, giving it a three-dimensional quality. Sometimes, parts of it are highlighted with Dutch metal, which is composed of brass and other elements, or even true gold leaf. Other special free-hand techniques can also be used. Marbleizing and woodgraining are but a couple of the other options in the repertoire of a competent, well-trained decorator.

A common feature of all these techniques is that paint is applied to a dry wall. Creating a traditional "buon fresco" in the Renaissance tradition of such masters as Paolo Uccello (1397–1475) or Benozzo Gozzoli (ca. 1421–1497) necessitates painting directly on wet plaster, with specially ground dry pigments or tints dissolved in lime water. These are absorbed by the surface as it dries, penetrating the wall and becoming part of it: the pigment and the wall essentially become one. Before World War II, Rambusch craftsmen executed a number of church interiors in this true fresco technique, a most demanding job.

The vaulted ceiling loggia at the Rochester Art Museum was done in true fresco for architect George Gade. Saint Patrick's Church, Bay Shore, New York (fig. 2-2), designed by Gustave E. Steinback, is another example. The mosaic at Saint Clement's in Rome was

2-2 Johannes Morton, *Chancel mural*, fresco, Saint Patrick's Roman Catholic Church (Gustave E. Steinback, architect), Bay Shore, NY, 1919. **2-3** Gustave Wraae, designer; Johannes Morton, artist; *Apsidal mural*, fresco, Holy Name Church (Edward A. Ramsey, architect), Columbus, OH, 1928.

the inspiration for the traditional fresco decoration executed by Johannes Morton. At Bay Shore, to guard against moisture seeping into the apsidal semi-dome, copper sheathing was installed before laying on plaster and lathe. A working model of the apse was shown in the exhibition of 1925 at the Architectural League in New York. Woven in with the S and C scrolls are such symbols of new life as the peacock. Note the small, dark bronze light shields on each side of the chancel with repoussé images of the angels.

Still other examples of Rambusch frescos can be seen at the Holy Name Church, Columbus, Ohio (fig. 2-3), designed by Edward A. Ramsey. A sketch for these frescos was included in the exhibition of 1930 at the Architectural League. The Scandinavian American Steamship Lines also commissioned two frescos for its New York offices in the late 1920s. One was of the skyline of Copenhagen and the other of New York, so passengers would see them when arriving in, or departing from, port.

During the period from about 1930 until after World War II, many commissions were completed using "fresco secco" techniques. Related to true fresco, it requires the same binder—lime—but the colors are applied to dry mortar or a dry surface that has been moistened with a solution of lime water. With either technique, the irregular surface of the mortar-covered walls or ceilings enhance color compositions with a subtle, penetrating vitality. No gloss or sheen is evident as with oil-based paint. Johannes Morton, a trained artist, was the meticulous master of both buon fresco and fresco secco at Rambusch.

Saint Agnes Church (no longer extant), Cleveland, Ohio, was a masterpiece of Gothic revival design by architect John Theodore Comes of Pittsburgh. It was completely decorated in the fresco secco technique. Harold Rambusch, fresh out of art school, had designed and painted approximately thirty shoulder-length portraits of saints in the spandrels between the arches in the nave. At the Annunciation of the Blessed Virgin Mary Church, McSherrytown, Pennsylvania (fig. 2-4), an older church, Comes oversaw a phase of redecoration in fresco secco. Saint Pancras Church, Glendale, Queens (figs. 2-5

and 2-6), was decorated in 1927 under the direction of architect Gustave E. Steinback in both types of fresco. In the earlier rendering, the essential elements of the nave are outlined, with Plumbob lighting fixtures prominently hanging from the ceiling. The later rendering, further embellished by Leif Neandross, shows a warm, golden color in the nave and aisles. The sanctuary ceiling was blue, and its heavy timbers were stained a light silver gray, with the woodgrain still visible. Richly ornamented, polychromed stenciling was added between the beams. The walls were painted deep red, with the lower portion depicting a trompe l'oeil drapery design. These colors and designs remain today.

In addition to decorative and non-figurative painting, simple compositions and single portraits of saints and angels—even monumental-sized figures of Christ—were sometimes painted at a site. More complicated compositions, murals, or series of related scenes of large dimensions were likely to be done on canvas in the studio and then mounted in a church. In the early days, Rambusch gave this sort of work to independent artist Hans Peter Hansen. He taught at the Art Students League and maintained his own studio. Also, artist Francis Helving executed some of the more exacting commissions in oil on canvas for the firm.

On occasion, small oil sketches would be prepared and shown to a client. One, from 1905 (fig. 2-7; see also fig. 1-10), is in the Rambusch archives. The work is competent and fairly representative of the academic tradition of the period both in America and abroad. Although often derivative, such academic approaches honored the use of historic prototypes. An advertisement of the firm underscores that this approach was respected at Rambusch because the artist "gained inspiration from acknowledged masterpieces." Before World War II, a good deal of western European religious art was imported into the United States. It would seem that every monsignor who traveled to Europe returned home with the spoils of his own religious-inspired Grand Tour. By 1930, the firm had its own mural studio, staffed with Gustave Wraae, Alfred Tulk, Hugo Ohms, and, finally, William Campbell Walsh as designer-artists.

The craft techniques and the execution of them were only the means. Equally important was what the techniques depicted in a church: elaborate and dense levels of meaning and iconography that could be conveyed through symbols that would be recognizable to parishioners. Although the Roman Catholic Church had erudite roots in the early years of the American Republic with Bishop John Carroll (1735–1815) of Baltimore, in large urban centers of the late-nineteenth and early-twentieth centuries, it had become predominantly an immigrant, and often barely literate, church. Decoration and instruction were the dual purposes of many ecclesiastical interior schemes. The truths of the faith, ejaculatory prayers, phrases from scripture, and Latin responses to the mass were carefully lettered and treated as integral parts of overall decorative designs. This kind of reminder or teaching was not limited to ecclesiastical interiors of the period. A lettered border of axioms sometimes would be painted around the cornice line of rooms, as it was in Andrew Carnegie's tiny office in his vast Fifth Avenue mansion of the early twentieth century.

Symbols were also significant and evocative teaching devices. Wheat and grapes symbolized bread and wine of the Eucharist; the lily and fleur-de-lis symbolized the Virgin Mary; the dove represented the Holy Spirit;

2-4 *Sanctuary: interior*, Annunciation of the Blessed Virgin Mary Church (John Theodore Comes, architect), McSherrytown, PA, ca. 1920, from *American Architect* 121, no. 2385 (January 18, 1922): 77.
2-5 Birch Burdette Long, renderer; *Sanctuary: interior*, rendering, and **2-6** Birch Burdette Long and Leif Neandross, renderers; *Sanctuary: interior*, watercolor sketch, Saint Pancras Church (Gustave E. Steinback, architect), Glendale, Queens, 1928.
2-7 A. Thomas, *Mural study*, oil on canvas, Basilica of the Assumption, Baltimore, MD, 1905.

2-8 *Advertisement, showing pelican vulning*, ca. 1925. **2-9** *Sanctuary interior*, Saint Martin of Tours Church, Brooklyn, 1922. **2-10** Alfred Tulk, designer and artist; *Jesse Tree*, ceiling mural, Saint Ann's Church (Haskell & Considine, architects), Hornell, NY, 1935. **2-11** Rambusch designers, *Sanctuary: interior redesign*, Church of Saint Louis (William A. Koehl, architect), Louisville, OH, late 1940s; lighting fixtures renovated as LEDs, 2020.

the triangle the triune God, the Father, Son, and Holy Spirit; the eye of God—a symbol popular in the Eastern Church—sometimes was identified in this country with Freemasonry. A frequently used symbol in the early years of the twentieth century, one that virtually disappeared by the late 1940s, was the pelican. This creature was traditionally shown piercing its breast to feed its young with its own blood (fig. 2-8), and was symbolic of Christ's care for the Church. Also used for didactic purposes were easily recognizable scenes from scripture. These, as well as likenesses of saints, provided inspiration for a congregation. Saintly portraits, sometimes full-sized faces or larger-than-life-sized figures, bespoke the virtues of true-life heroic men and women.

Just as it is revealing to read old inventories about period trends, or to know what books were part of a particular library, it is also instructive in the history of ecclesiastical interior design to examine the decorative program of a church. Saint Martin of Tours Church, Brooklyn (fig. 2-9), was decorated by Rambusch in 1922. It typifies the knowledge, study, and careful planning that were an integral part of these intricate, complete design programs—both decorative and didactic. The Jesse Tree ceiling mural, Saint Ann's Church, Hornell, New York (fig. 2-10), portrays the ancestry of Jesus and also interspersed symbols of the Litany of Loreto. A miniature painting of the church façade was even included in its decoration. At this church, designer and artist Alfred Tulk also incorporated angels into the tapestry-like background. This work, in addition to the decorative scheme of Church of Saint Louis, Louisville, Ohio (fig. 2-11), offers a further example of such complex approaches by Rambusch.

At Saint Martin of Tours (see fig. 2-9), an embellished, painted, framed mural states the Ten Commandments. Not surprisingly, the portrayals of Saint Patrick and Saint Boniface in the transept ceiling satisfied the then-recent Irish-German immigrants of the parish seeking Christian guidance through imagery. Latin-Mass responses also ringed the dome. The nave ceiling pairs several portraits of golden-haloed saints. Saint Ambrose and Saint Augustine, who are shown together, were both leaders in the diocese concept. Ambrose was the first Bishop of Milan and Augustine; his protégé, who converted to Christianity and was inspired by the magnetism and power of Ambrose's sermons, became the first Bishop of Hippo. Saint Jerome and Saint Gregory, another pairing, were individuals who contributed to the development of scripture and law. Jerome translated the Vulgate Latin Bible and Gregory was Pope and promulgated the

Gregorian calendar. Saint Benedict and Saint Francis, a third pairing, were highly respected monks. Benedict founded Western monasticism in the sixth century and Saint Francis reformed it in the twelfth century. Then, finally, there is Saint Ignatius and Saint Dominic, both Spaniards, who were teachers and missionaries, and founders of the Jesuit and Dominican orders, respectively. In the transept closest to the altar, smaller portraits are presented to the viewer: Saint Stephen, the first Christian martyr; Saint Agnes, the first female martyr; Saint Lawrence, deacon; and Saint Cecilia, patroness of musicians.

The pendentives supporting the dome hold full-length likenesses of the four evangelists and their appropriate symbols: Matthew is represented by a man; Mark, a lion; Luke, an ox; and John, an eagle; all of which are related to the opening text of each gospel. On the end walls of the truncated transepts, framing an arch, are very small portrait roundels of Old Testament prophets and other figures. These include, on one side, Moses, Elias, Abraham, Samuel, and Jeremiah, and, on the other, Saint Jeanne d'Arc, Saint Olaf, Saint Columbia, Saint Elizabeth, and Saint Ansgar. Taken together, they complete a richly decorative, scholarly, and instructive interior design program.

At the Church of Saint Peter, Staten Island, a remarkable amount of the original design and decoration executed in 1904 by Frode Rambusch remains largely untouched. Close examination reveals methods of painting techniques and use of iconography, and also what might be called a Rambusch Style. That is, there is a distinctively recognizable manner of artistic design and execution, which is quite representative of the firm's ecclesiastical work from the first quarter of the twentieth century. Robust, vine-line scrolls, organized in S and C curves, often plaited with naturalistic tendrils, fill the apse over the chancel. This building originally served an Irish congregation, and not surprisingly, shamrocks are included with traditional symbols of wheat and grapes. Centered in the apse is a full-length figure of Christ in a mandorla. The robes of the figure are red, providing a contrast to the background which is decorated in gold and green. The soffit of the sanctuary arch is filled with medallion portraits of the saints, each carefully identified. Profiles and three-quarter views are skillfully painted against a gold background, reminiscent of the Russian icon, Western Byzantine, and Gothic traditions. Each portrait is bordered by three concentric circles of alternating red and gold squares, creating a mosaic-like

2-12 Russell Joy, *Floor mosaic: detail*, Saint Andrew Avellino Roman Catholic Church, Flushing, Queens, 1990.

frame. Executed boldly in a flat and angular style, paired angels fill the spandrils of the sanctuary arches.

Most remarkable in the Staten Island church is the small vaulted, octagonal baptistery, a true gem with decoration that was, in 1998, virtually untouched. The decorative program is enhanced by gilded creatures of the sea done in relief. Above oak wainscoting, blue-, green-, and sand-colored zigzag lines suggest the sea in which fish and water lilies coexist. The lines of these elements are both painted on and incised in the plaster, which suggests the use of traditional fresco. Above the water design, large areas of the wall are decorated in an abstract design, highlighted with raised, embossed gold leaf and jewels. The cornice band in the small room includes arbor-like, painted decorations from which, at regular intervals, water-like cascades pour down to join the aquatic lower border. The overall imagery symbolizes the rite of baptism, which, by washing away Original Sin, reunites humans and God. The ceiling is decorated with raised and gilded plaster circles, enclosing four pointed stars. These and other decorations on the walls and ceiling catch light and give a sense of vitality to the whole. The total effect is one of a bucolic, airy enclosure. The robust painted decoration might be termed a Nordic version of Art Nouveau, injecting classical antecedents, with nature as its inspiration. A related work, the mosaic baptistery floor that was designed by Russell Joy at Saint Andrew Avellino Roman Catholic Church, Flushing, Queens, portrays marine imagery in vivid colors (fig. 2-12). A triune group of fish provides a central focus over a cross that is articulated with shells and abstracted waves in each corner.

Rambusch studios and workshops have always been identified with church interior design and decoration. Since its incorporation, the firm has worked for congregations of every religious tradition. Early company ledgers show a breakdown of the following categories under general billing for church work: Roman Catholic, Russian Orthodox, Jewish, Methodist, Episcopalian, Eastern Orthodox Rite, Swedish Baptist, and Reform Presbyterian. All these and more, in a wide ecumenical range, were clients within the first decade of the firm's incorporation.

Churches are often cited for their conservative approach toward renovations, partly due to the cost of erecting scaffolding for such work. But in studying the ecclesiastical interiors designed and executed by Rambusch over time, one can see that they reflect the very same changes and trends evident in secular American architecture. As noted, the firm has worked for congregations of almost every religion and sect, ranging from small modest chapels to vast, elaborate, landmarked cathedrals. For ease of comparison and study, mostly churches in the Roman Catholic tradition will be examined in this book.

In the early years of this century, the internal arrangement of most churches in this tradition can be characterized by a strict separation of the congregation from the celebrant or priest. This spatial organization was symbolized and effected by an altar rail, which separated the chancel from the rest of the nave. Although these rails were often made of bronze or marble, or sometimes even solid onyx, many were plain or carved in wood. All performed the same purpose. A gate provided limited access to the chancel, and it usually was aligned with the main aisle. As an example, one can see this detail in the Church of Saint Louis (see fig. 2-11), where an overall redecoration was completed by Rambusch in the late 1940s.

In this church and others, the main or high altar was placed against the back wall of the sanctuary, as far away as possible from the congregation. The altar was an assembled arrangement of Gothic architectural elements of precious marbles and painted wood. In other cases, this material could be gilded wood or a carpenter's Gothic fantasy of stained wood. Usually, the altar contained niches for statues of angels or saints, and the tabernacle was a part of the whole construction. The presence of the latter was marked only by a decorated door in the center. Mass was celebrated in Latin by the priest at the altar with his back to the congregation. On either side of the main altar, nearer to the congregation but still behind the altar rail, were often two smaller altars, usually dedicated to the Virgin Mary and Saint Joseph. This typical spatial arrangement changes over time, as does the type and iconography of associated interior decoration.

One tends to think of liturgical reform coming in the years after the Second Vatican Council, also known as Vatican II (1962–1965). The decrees and edicts issued by this body are credited with such reforms within the Roman Church. However, at the turn of the twentieth century, Cardinal Herbert Alfred Henry Vaughan of England (1832–1903) initiated a collection of laws and rules gleaned from the missals and the Ceremonial of the Bishops. This anthology, *Directions for the Use of Altar Societies and Architects*, was published in 1912 after his death. It dealt with every aspect of interior liturgical design and ceremony, and even included illustrations for the proper cut of a priest's vestments. Among other reforms, it called for a free-standing tabernacle, one of the most sacred and valuable objects in the Catholic tradition. This harbinger of change did not find acceptance for several decades. However, Rambusch notably was making free-standing tabernacles as early as the late teens. The company was also designing free-standing altars, waist high, for church interiors by the 1920s. To provide the effect of nobility and visual dominance, the baldachin was introduced in many church interiors in the United States.

While these changes were gradually being made in physical appointments, the decorative treatment of Roman Catholic churches remained much the same. Dense, overall wall decoration and richly embellished ceilings—some with very elaborate compositions depicting scenes from scripture—were executed in the manner of Giovanni Battista Tiepolo (1696–1770) and others from his era. Some ceilings had simpler stenciled decorations of stars or geometric forms interwoven with appropriate symbols. Others were timbered with restrained, stenciled borders of plain decoration on the chamfered sides of the beams. An earlier, diffuse type of Gothic-inspired decoration gave way to accurate detailing, correct scale, and a certain type of ornament. This was the same mentality that demanded academically correct details for great Beaux-Arts buildings.

The years after World War II saw many changes. In existing church interiors, the church, clergy, and designers restudied arrangements. There was a trend toward simplification of, as well as a new emphasis on, the chancel area, especially with a free-standing, centralized altar. The removal of side altars, or their relocation to an area outside the altar rail, was common practice. The altar rail remained, but it became lighter in articulation and the gate was often replaced with a catenary or an open area. The strict separation of celebrant and congregation was officially dissolved by the proclamations of Vatican II.

Suburban expansion necessitated the construction of many new churches. Colonial style rose in popularity. One wonders if this harkening back to eighteenth-century roots was an expression of an invigorated nation: with much the same spirit that motivated the neo-colonial revival decades earlier. Also, the principles of the Bauhaus exerted an increasingly strong influence in American architecture. Many new churches reflected its principles. Unfortunately, a diluted version of high

2-13 *Tabernacle niche*, Cathedral of Saint Ignatius Loyola (Harold Sekinger, architect), Palm Beach Gardens, FL, 1984.

modernism often became a euphemism for inexpensive building, which accounted for many modest churches built during this period. The amount of painted decoration in church interiors was now minimal. As in secular buildings, an interest was evident in the reintroduction of such materials as marble, mosaic, and polished bronze. Emphasis was often on form and line—not ornament. Several efforts experimented with new spatial arrangements in the church nave. One example was the introduction of fan-shaped congregational seating.

Some congregations rushed to implement the new edicts, stripping their churches of what was once thought necessary to arouse devotional sentiment, but now was considered shallow, distracting accretions. Murals were painted over, shrines and side altars torn out. This mentality was similar to that which led to the demolition of Pennsylvania Station in Manhattan, and the destruction of countless other distinguished buildings, criticized derisively by avid practitioners of the International Style.

Other parishes wisely waited. They chose to study and interpret the edicts of Vatican II to gain perspective before implementing changes. The unadorned altar of sacrifice was given primacy in a central location. The tabernacle, which less than a half century before had featured a small door embedded in the high altar, was now placed by itself in a separate space. The congregation could now cluster around the altar, no longer sequestered from the celebrant by the demarcation of altar rail.

It would seem that purity of line of the 1960s and 1970s was not enough. In ecclesiastical interiors, as in secular decoration, some softening occurred with a desire for some decorative enhancement. Echoes of communal identity and parish history were incorporated into designs for new worship spaces. Freed from subservience to past themes, the church felt more respect for the past, using historical materials common to the parish to evoke memories that would enrich ritual and communal worship and participation, thus providing a lively blend of the old and new.

Perhaps the change and evolution in Roman Catholic interiors in recent decades can be most dramatically demonstrated by the examination of the treatment of the tabernacle. Used to store the undistributed consecrated bread from the Eucharist, the tabernacle was often originally called a tabernacle house in the ancient church. It was always a free-standing, three-dimensional object, though sometimes was small enough to be carried. In mid-nineteenth-century America, the tabernacle had become merely a small, embellished door in an elaborate architectonic structure built into the back wall of the sanctuary. By 1985, most tabernacles returned to their original form as a singular, free-standing element, placed in its own space, away from the central altar.

A Rambusch commission of 1984 shows how far this concept had evolved. At the Cathedral of Saint Ignatius Loyola, Palm Beach Gardens, Florida, the tabernacle was housed in a hexagonal, stained-glass, reliquary-like, jewel-colored space (fig. 2-13). Situated in the wall of the cathedral, the stained-glass enclosure simultaneously projects into the church interior and through the outside wall. Parish visitors can see inside to the tabernacle, which is set on a coral-stone pier surrounded by flickering candles, making it a glowing feature. In addition to the tabernacle design at this cathedral, Rambusch executed a full-size statue of St. Francis of Assisi (figs. 2-14 and 2-15).

In contrast to the tabernacle, whose design and placement have come full circle back to its ancient origins, the motif of the angel, once a part of every early church interior decorative scheme, has now largely disappeared. An examination of several Rambusch commissions where angels were an integral part of the interior design reflects a similarity in execution to general style trends of the period. In the Church of Saint Peter, Staten Island, the painted angels in the spandrils of the sanctuary arch are flat, soft-edged, and stylistically consistent with Art Nouveau and the Book of Kells. Full-size angels in the flat dome of Saint Jerome's Church, the Bronx, are reminiscent of the idealized creatures of the Aesthetic movement. Those in the dome of Saint Martin of Tours, painted in 1922 and cleaned by the firm in 1947, are full-size with portrait-like faces, filling the dome in varied compositional groups. They have fluid, loose-flowing garments, in contrast to the regular, almost static, placement of those at Saint Jerome's. The ceiling of Our Lady of Good Counsel Church, Brooklyn, in which angels play a less dominant role, portrays them as supernatural creatures from the medieval triptychs. In the Church of Saint Louis, angels are a part of the overall decorative scheme and iconography (see fig. 2-11). They are attenuated, sinuous, and stylized almost in the Mannerist tradition. As late as 1950, Rambusch was using angels in decorative schemes. But angels, like hell, seem to have vanished from the frame of reference of the present-day churchgoer.

In completing more than 10,000 church interiors (including more than 100 cathedrals) and creating thousands of objects used in religious services, the firm has embraced a philosophical ethos regarding ecclesiastical

2-14 *Sculptor modeling clay for statue of Saint Francis of Assisi*, and **2-15** *Saint Francis of Assisi, detail*, marble sculpture, Garden of Cathedral of Saint Ignatius Loyola (Harold Sekinger, architect), Palm Beach Gardens, FL, 1984.

The American Architect, May, 1932

BANKS
CHURCHES
CLUBS
SYNAGOGUES
HOTELS
RESTAURANTS
THEATRES
PUBLIC BUILDINGS

Painted Decoration

To have had a part, under the supervision of the architects, in the development and execution of so many outstanding interiors, speaks well for the Rambusch organization. A representative list is presented for your information.

Empire State Building . . . New York City
(Public Lobbies and Observation Tower, 86th Floor)
SHREVE, LAMB AND HARMON, ARCHITECTS

New Waldorf-Astoria Hotel . . New York City
(Main Foyer, Lobby and Appurtenant Rooms)
SCHULTZE AND WEAVER, ARCHITECTS

The Nebraska State Capitol . . Lincoln, Nebraska
(House of Representatives Ceiling—House Lounge Ceiling)
MAYERS, MURRAY AND PHILLIP, ARCHITECTS
HILDRETH MEIERE, DESIGNER

The Ohio State Office Building . . Columbus, Ohio
HARRY HAKE, ARCHITECT

Westchester County Office Building . White Plains, N.Y.
(Hearing Room)
MORRIS AND O'CONNOR, ARCHITECTS

Club Boca Raton . . . Boca Raton, Florida
SCHULTZE AND WEAVER, ARCHITECTS

Syracuse Lighting Company Building . Syracuse, N.Y.
BLEY & LYMAN, ARCHITECTS
MELVIN H. KING, SUPERVISING ARCHITECT

Childs Restaurant (R. C. A. Bldg.) New York City
PRUITT AND BROWN, ARCHITECTS

Willow Cafeteria . . . New York City
CHARLES N. WHINSTON & BRO., ARCHITECTS

Horn and Hardart Restaurants (3) . New York City
F. P. PLATT AND BRO., ARCHITECTS

Vassar College . . . . Poughkeepsie, N. Y.
(Belle Skinner Music Building)
ALLEN AND COLLENS, ARCHITECTS

National Title Guaranty Company Bank . Brooklyn, N.Y.
CORBETT, HARRISON AND MacMURRAY, ARCHITECTS

First National Bank of Ithaca . . . Ithaca, N. Y.
UFFINGER, BOOKWALTER AND FOSTER, ARCHITECTS

Roxy Theatre . . . . New York City
WALTER W. AHLSCHLAGER, ARCHITECT

Fox Theatre . . . . . Hackensack, N. J.
THOMAS W. LAMB, ARCHITECT

St. James' Cathedral . . . Chicago, Illinois
MAYERS, MURRAY AND PHILLIP, ARCHITECTS

St. Catherine of Sienna's Church . . New York City
WILFRID E. ANTHONY, ARCHITECT

St. Gabriel's Church . . . Washington, D. C.
MAGINNIS AND WALSH, ARCHITECTS

RAMBUSCH

Painting, Decorating, Murals & Mosaics

2 West 45th St. New York City

interior decoration. Beginning in the early 1940s, principals of the firm published articles urging the implementation of prescriptions from the Congregation of Sacred Rites and the Ceremonial of Bishops, especially the revision of spatial arrangements, to facilitate communal liturgical celebrations. Even more important, the firm forged the idea that a church interior, with all its varied elements, should and must be considered as an organic whole. Spatial arrangements, painted decorations, lighting, stained glass, sanctuary furniture, stations of the cross, shrines, and all the individual parts, are to be effective and harmonious functional parts of the whole.

Although the language of an advertisement from 1930 is a bit stilted, it succinctly expresses the philosophy of the firm, one still being practiced today. It states:

> To complete the interior of a church successfully, with paintings and statues from catalogues, to say the least is very difficult. Before our commercial times, our forefathers obtained their wonderful results in ecclesiastical art not only by individual work on the part of the men who actually executed the objects, but by harmonious combination of all concerned, Bishops, Priests, Architects, Sculptors, Painters, etc.
>
> Decoration is a broad field, for it really covers all that goes to produce the effect of a church interior. We have tried to carry it out to its last detail . . . all the things that can be made by draftsmen and that give the church an atmosphere which can be created only when one feels that every detail has been carefully thought out and painted, carved or wrought to its most perfect finish. . . .

Talbot F. Hamlin, in his article, "A Collaborative Alteration, Saint John's Church, Sharon, Pennsylvania," published in *Architectural Forum* in May 1932, discussed the work of Theodor Carl Muller, a designer at Rambusch. Muller had carried out work under the direction of Warner and Mitchell, architects. After extensive examination and discussion of the concepts, the purpose of the design changes in the square-towered, Romanesque revival church; the fabrication of objects; and the use of decorative ornament; Hamlin concludes why the result was successful:

> Perhaps the old Victorian church, beautified and altered from time to time, as best it can be done, achieves a humanity, a warmth, a quiet dignity, impossible in the brand-new edifice, however brilliantly designed in the current fashion. After all, it is not a matter of stylisms, of being in this, that, or the other type of Gothic, or in this, that, or other school of modernism—all eclecticisms are lazy men's routes, much traveled but strewn with moribund bodies. It is a matter of composition, of harmony, of consistency, and of using materials in ways that are natural and in accordance with the thinking of today.

These characteristics were not only evident in the churches Rambusch designed, but also in various building types. An advertisement from the early 1930s suggests the range of work across the spectrum (fig. 2-16) as does the Blessed Sacrament Chapel, Cathedral Basilica of Saints Peter & Paul, Philadelphia, Pennsylvania (fig. 2-17). But first, before exploring this facet, the next chapter will examine the company's work in art metal, and consider how this specialty is created and also how the trends evident over time are reflected in the company's work.

2-16 *Advertisement, listing examples of painted decoration,* from *American Architect* 141, no. 2607 (May 1932): 93. **2-17** *Blessed Sacrament Chapel,* Cathedral Basilica of Saints Peter & Paul (Eggers & Higgins, architects), Philadelphia, PA, 1970.

RAMBUSCH
DEC CO.
ART
METAL

CHAPTER III

Art Metal: Techniques, Trends, and Styles

The hand working of metal, along with that of painting and decorating, has been a consistent craft activity at the Rambusch Decorating Company. Almost from the beginning of the firm's incorporation, in addition to its production of lighting fixtures, the firm designed and fabricated liturgical and other objects in iron, bronze, copper, brass, silver, gold, and such exotic metals as Monel, a nickel-copper alloy. Metal objects can be raised in repoussé (figs. 3-1 and 3-2) and worked from a single sheet. Or, they can be formed, as in the case of a silver pitcher (fig. 3-3) or a wedding present (fig. 3-4) made for individual clients. Still other objects can be cast. Large-scale commissions have sometimes necessitated the use of castings. These have been executed in conjunction with local foundries.

Fabrication of a cast metal object involves many steps. First, the object is designed, then shop drawings are made to scale. From these drawings, a slightly oversized wood pattern is carved by hand in fine-grained wood, such as maple or birch. An example of such patterns can be seen in carvings for light fixtures at the US Capitol (fig. 3-5). In addition to decorative details, special attention is given to overflow channels, where molten metal can escape. When especially crisp, fine detailing is required, a metal pattern is made from the wooden one. In turn, it is "chased" by hand, meaning that designs are refined in metal with a sharp tool and mallet. The final, or finished, casting can then be made from the metal pattern. The fifteen-foot-high monumental gates (fig. 3-6) that close each night on the four exterior vestibules of the North Building of the Metropolitan Life Insurance Company, Manhattan, were cast in Monel, a material that resulted from a Rambusch collaboration in the 1930s. This alloy, with high nickel content, carries a high sheen on the surface. The plant-like motifs in the gate were so striking to the building's architects that they repeated the motifs in the stone grills over the windows. Lighting fixtures of the late 1950s by the firm for the US Capitol in Washington, DC, also employed castings. The company's archive holds a multitude of patterns, signed off in red ink by architect Alfred Easton Poor.

In 1982, a new entrance for the American Security and Trust Company, Washington, DC, was designed by Swanke Hayden Connell Architects. They wanted to flank it with exterior lamp standards like those cast in 1901 by William H. Jackson Company for the main entrance (fig. 3-7). But there was less available space for the base of each standard. Rambusch was commissioned to remove the originals and clean, rewire, and use them as a pattern for the new pair, while also adjusting the base to fit the smaller area (fig. 3-8). So true is the quality, detail, and attention to scale that only a trained eye can tell the difference.

The firm's art metal workshops have made several hundred objects in cast bronze, but modern technology and cost factors have usurped age-old metallurgical processes. Now, often large commissions fabricated in solid bronze are considered too costly, so designers use an epoxy amalgam, bonded bronze, in which thousands of particles of real bronze are suspended. Less costly, lighter, easier to work with, and impervious to the deleterious effects of environmental pollutants, this material offers many good qualities for fabricators and clients.

3-1 *Sign*, repoussé bronze, 1925, photograph from ca. 1981–1982. **3-2** *Fleur-de-lis sheets*, bronze worked to show the repoussé process, 1948. **3-3** Knud Laub, designer; Peer Smed, craftsman; *Pitcher*, hammered silver, 1920, photograph from ca. 1981–1982. **3-4** *Wedding present*, silver, 1930.

PATTERNS

From working or design drawings, patterns of wood, usually maple, mahogany, or walnut, are carved by the pattern maker. They are made slightly oversized with special attention to draft and piping. Wood patterns are used by the foundryman to make metal shapes. For smaller shapes, when finer detail is needed, the "lost wax" technique is usually used. For larger pieces, French sand casting is employed, whereby the wooden pattern is used to make a negative impression in the fine sand. Into this impression molten metal is poured. The resulting casting is ground down, cleaned and polished. Sometimes, when especially crisp detail is needed, it is then hand chased. The forms are then assembled to make a candlestick, lighting fixture or other decorative art objects.

3-5 *Carved wooden patterns used to fabricate lighting fixtures for the US Capitol*, 1958, from *Technology & Conservation*, Winter 1981.
3-6 *Gates*, Metropolitan Life Insurance Company North Building (Everett Wald and Harvey Wiley Corbett, architects), Manhattan, ca. 1931.

3-7 *Bronze lamp standards*, from the *William H. Jackson Company Catalog* (1901), American Security & Trust Company (York and Sawyer, architects, 1904–1905), Washington, DC.

3-8 *New entrance: detail of bronze lamp standards*, American Security & Trust Company (Swanke Hayden Connell, architects), Washington, DC, 1982.

In 1979, Rambusch executed, in bonded bronze, an eight-foot sculpture of Neptune, designed by Michael Ducar. This figure is the decorative ornament in a fountain at Busch Gardens, Williamsburg, Virginia.

Three commissions, designed and fabricated before World War II, illustrate the range in technique and materials still employed today with non-cast metal objects made in the art metal shop. Designer Edward Ferlin and fabricator Alphonse Moe designed a gold ciborium set with amethysts (fig. 3-9) in 1926 for the Church of Saint Paul the Apostle, Manhattan. On its quatrefoil base, four scenes are engraved from the New Testament: the visit to Mary and Martha, the raising of Lazarus, the washing of the feet of the poor, and the Last Supper. Faceted gems float in rectangular settings around the rim of the cup. The cast finial of the ciborium's cover is a full-length figure of Saint Paul.

When silver and gold are considered too costly, bronze, also a noble metal, can be a useful option. Other options can include plating lesser metals, as in the Ambry (or Holy Oils), Cabinet of 1919 that was constructed of repoussé silver-plated copper (fig. 3-10) and made for the Reverend Joseph H. McHamon at the Church of Our Lady of Lourdes, Manhattan. In this object, silver plate was oxidized to give contrast and the illusion of texture to the metal. Inside, a candlestick carries both realistic and symbolic elements on its base: a fish and deer alluding to Psalm 42:1, "As the hart panteth after the water brooks, so panteth my soul after thee, O God."

Also of bronze but utilizing an entirely different process of ornamentation, are a set of stations of the cross designed in 1929 by Alfred Tulk (figs. 3-11 and 3-12) for architect Charles D. Maginnis, who designed and built Christ the King Church, Rutland, Vermont. Cloisonné is a technique whereby thin bands of copper are adhered to the metal surface and molten enamel made from powdered, ground glass is poured into the resulting tiny reservoirs. The entire bronze sheet is fired in the ovens of the company's stained-glass studio, and a vitreous enamel forms in the depressions. A sample of this technique was exhibited at the Metropolitan Museum of Art, December 1930.

Though the metals and techniques in the Rambusch art metal shop are varied, it is helpful to examine a particular form and the shapes and styles that form took over an extended period of time. That form is the candlestick, which is used in virtually every place of worship as a vessel to hold—and sustain—a flame. Candlesticks designed and made in the Rambusch art metal workshops over the course of the last half century display not

only a difference in materials and techniques, but they also indicate changes and trends in American decorative arts during these years (fig. 3-13).

Two pairs candlesticks and a matching crucifix were made in 1919 for Our Lady of Lourdes Church, Manhattan (see fig. 3-13, grouping second from right). They conform to and exemplify the philosophy of John Ruskin's Arts and Crafts movement. Composed of simple, functional shapes, the solid, heavy bases give stability, and their flared metal bobeche is of ample proportion to catch every drip of wax. The decoration consists of applied bands of silver-plated repoussé copper, an ancient technique that in the years of its creation was pressed into service because of the scarcity of metal. Worked in a repetitive soft wave-like design, the metalwork is reminiscent of the borders in Norwegian medieval stave churches. Not surprisingly, church interiors of the early-twentieth century were executed by Scandinavian-trained craftsmen at the firm. The original finish of the set is painted in green enamel over wood. It matches exactly the semi-precious, pointed oval cabochon stones set in the band midway up the round shaft. Distinctive and unlike any other Rambusch commission discovered to date, perhaps they may have been painted to blend with, or provide an accent to, the overall, now-painted-over

3-9 Edward Ferlin, designer; Alphonse Moe, craftsman; *Ciborium*, gold and amethysts, made for the Church of Saint Paul the Apostle, Manhattan, 1926. **3-10** *Ambry (or Holy Oils) Cabinet*, repoussé copper with silver plate and moonstones, made for the Church of Our Lady of Lourdes, Manhattan, 1919. **3-11** Alfred Tulk, designer; *Designs for the Stations of the Cross*, drawing, Christ the King Church (Charles McGinnis, architect), Rutland, VT, 1929. **3-12** Alfred Tulk, designer; *Stations of the Cross*, bronze and vitreous enamel, made for Christ the King Church (Charles McGinnis, architect), Rutland, VT, 1929.

3-13 From left: *Candlestick*, bronze, designed and made for Cathedral of Saints Peter and Paul, Philadelphia, PA, 1964; *Candlestick*, bronze and enamel, Church of Saint Vincent Ferrer, Manhattan, 1927; *Candlestick*, bronze, Church of the Epiphany, Manhattan, 1966; *Candlestick*, wrought iron, Saint Francis School, Athol Springs, NY, 1929; *Candlesticks and crucifix*, painted wood, silverplated, repoussé copper, semi-precious stones; Church of Our Lady of Lourdes, Manhattan, 1919 ; *Candlestick made during WWII*, glazed ceramic, ca. 1943; photograph from ca. 1981–1982.

decorative scheme of the interior. Although inexpensive materials were used, the scale and proportion of the candlesticks' components give a substantial and almost monumental quality to the entire altar set.

By the 1920s, the preferred style for church architecture in America was inspired by Gothic precedents. Rambusch responded with a set of four wrought-iron candlesticks designed by Viggo F. E. Rambusch, 1929 (see fig. 3-13, one is right of center, with spike), for Saint Francis School, Athol Springs, New York, with clear medieval qualities—a tour de force in the way the iron has been worked, stretched, pierced, twisted, incised, and glazed. Three ball feet accent the boldness of the design. The shaft floats on a pierced circular base.

Architect Wilfred A. Anthony designed a set of six cast-bronze candlesticks in the late 1920s for Church of Saint Vincent Ferrer, Manhattan (see fig. 3-13, one such candlestick is second from left). Characteristics of late Gothic ornament are reflected in the light, lacy detail that sheaths the slender six-sided shaft. Halfway up is affixed a foliated, four-inch shield that holds a vitreous enameled cartouche in red or blue. Made specifically to be placed on the high altar of the academically correct and beautifully detailed Gothic interior designed by Bertram Grosvenor Goodhue, the set enhances and reinforces the ambiance of the context in which it is used.

During World War II and for some time afterward, metals such as bronze, and even iron, were scarce or not even available. Rambusch was constantly called upon to supply candlesticks; therefore, the company designed and created a series of ceramic ones. They could be glazed in a range of colors or in a metallic finish that resulted in a warm, shining gold color. Two styles were created to meet clients' needs for modern or traditional interiors. The single low stick had a quilted diaper pattern on the shaft and a bold, gadrooned top. The design for the taller sticks utilized classical motifs and were created in interchangeable parts; bases, bobeches, and shafts, all could be assembled in different configurations to produce sets of candlesticks of varying heights.

In the middle of the twentieth century, another new material prompted a Rambusch design. The Aluminum Corporation of America (ALCOA), in an attempt to introduce new ways to use its product, in 1953 commissioned Rambusch to design a series of candlesticks and altar furnishings. Called the New Kensington Collection, it was manufactured and sold by ALCOA for many years. This was the first—and only—time that Rambusch participated in any mass production of ecclesiastical furnishings.

After World War II, the church was often conservative and frequently retained ideas about older architectural and decorative forms, even amid the impact of the International Style. As late as 1964 Rambusch made a set of six cast and chaste bronze candlesticks (see fig. 3-13, one is at far left) weighing more than 200 pounds each for the Cathedral Basilica of Saints Peter and Paul, Philadelphia, which originally had been designed by Napoleon LeBrun (1821–1901). Made to complement the classical design of the building, Otto Eggers, architect and consummate renderer, designed these candlesticks and supervised their fabrication. A reeded shaft sits atop a trefoil base ornamented with volutes, an oval cartouche with a fleur-de-lis, and the monogram of the cathedral's patron saints. It would be many years before Rambusch would be called upon to fabricate similar classically inspired designs.

By contrast, the Church of the Epiphany, Manhattan, built in 1967, was one of scores of churches that bore the stamp of Le Corbusier's masterpiece at Ronchamp. Asymmetrically placed clusters of windows illuminate the glazed-brick interior. Its free-standing altar is composed of hand-textured, white Vermont marble. Flanking the altar, standing directly on the floor, are six forty-eight-inches-high, acid-etched, cut-bronze candlesticks (see fig. 3-13, left of center) designed by Leif Neandross and executed by Stefan Scheidling. The shape and line of these candlesticks are defined solely by three vertical elements that support the shallow bobeche and candleholder. The only decoration is the subtle etched surface of the bronze, which catches light and creates delicate shadows.

In a similar modernist mode, the candlesticks and crucifix made in 1978 for the Episcopalian Church of the Heavenly Rest, Manhattan (fig. 3-14), are in use in a small daily visiting chapel. The design of the cross, by Harold W. Rambusch and again executed by Stefan Scheidling, presents the vertical and horizontal members of ebony, the ends of which are set with a brilliantly faceted lead crystal. The metal for the base and corpus is sterling silver.

Taken together, these candlesticks and earlier ones from a half century ago show the use of modest and precious materials. Their simplification in form and decoration over the course of decades speak volumes about trends in American ecclesiastical arts, which itself was mirroring changes in taste in general design. This trajectory can also be seen in designs of an object used in Roman Catholic liturgical celebrations since the fourteenth century: the ostensorium. This object holds the concentrated bread, or host, which is venerated for exposition and adoration of the Blessed Sacrament.

Some of the gold and gems in the ostensorium (fig. 3-15) made for Saint Raphael's Church, Pittsburgh, Pennsylvania, in 1926 were donated by members of the parish, then a common practice. Edward Ferlin's design, executed by Alphonse Moe, allowed for the incorporation of these donated gems, which are varied in size, color, and value. They are worth a fortune, including flawless diamonds donated by a member of the Mellon family. The diamonds were set as rays emanating from the center where the host is placed. The eight-sided base rests on a pierced gallery, reminiscent of the ciborium base made the year before for Saint Paul's Church, Manhattan. Two years later, an ostensorium (fig. 3-16) was created for Saint Michael's Church, Jersey City, New Jersey. Architect Wilfred A. Anthony had purchased jewels of the same type, size, and cut as the Mellon diamonds. In a similar design for the Jersey City parish, Ferlin created an ostensorium which, like its predecessor, drew upon the visual ideas of the Disputata in the Raphael frescoes for the Borgia Apartments in the Vatican. The shaft in both of Ferlin's objects could be removed from its base so that the ostensorium could be used in ritual processions.

After the Depression, the use of precious metals and gemstones declined sharply even in the fabrication of the most sacred vessels. Although exceptions occurred, generally, ostensoria made after World War II show an ever-increasing simplification in design, lack of applied ornament, and use of less-costly materials—all characteristics of trends in secular decorative arts in this period. An exception to the trend was an ostensorium made in 1946 for Eugene Kennedy, a partner in the firm of Maginnis, Walsh and Kennedy. The liturgical article was made for Saint Clement's Eucharistic Shrine, Boston, Massachusetts. The design was inspired by a fourteenth-century Spanish model, and it resulted in an architectonic contribution of exquisite Gothic detailing, made of sterling silver with gold plating. In its niches, small three-dimensional silver figures of saints raised out of sheet sterling were inserted. Diamonds, emeralds, sapphires, rubies—many in their original setting of rings donated by the faithful—were incorporated in this four-and-a-half-foot-tall object.

Still other objects in this realm used precious materials. The ostensorium designed by Joaquin Santos and made by Herman Scheurle for Saint Agnes Church, Arlington, Virginia, is gold-plated bronze with a corona of turned-ivory pieces. Edward Ferlin designed the polished-bronze ostensorium for the Church of the Immaculate Heart of Mary, Scarsdale, New York. There was no applied ornament. The decoration was achieved by incising and working the metal itself.

It is important to note that the needs of a cathedral are quite different from those of a parish church.

3-14 Harold W. Rambusch, designer; Stefan Scheidling, craftsman; *Candlesticks and crucifix*, ebony, sterling silver, and crystal, made for Church of the Heavenly Rest, Manhattan, ca. 1979. **3-15** Edward Ferlin, designer; Alphonse Moe, craftsman; *Ostensorium*, gold and precious stones, made for Saint Raphael's Church, Pittsburgh, PA, 1926. **3-16** Edward Ferlin, designer; *Ostensorium*, gold-plated bronze and precious stones, made for Saint Michael's Church (Wilfred A Anthony, architect), Jersey City, NJ, ca. 1928.

3-17 Frederick W. Christian and Viggo B. Rambusch, designers; *Ostensorium*, bronze with gold plating, made for Cathedral of Saint Joseph (Eggers & Higgins architects), Hartford, CT, 1968, photograph from ca. 1981–1982. **3-18** Knud Laub, designer; *Baldachin*, watercolor rendering, made for Saint Boniface Church (Link, Weber & Bowers, architect), Pittsburgh, PA, 1922. **3-19** *Detail, Bishop's crosier*, wrought iron, part of the altarpiece of the pilgrimage church of Saint Wolfgang, St. Wolfgang im Salzkammergut, Austria, from Robert Stiassny, *Michael Pachers St. Wolfganger Altar*, Vienna, 1919.

The ostensorium (fig. 3-17) for the Cathedral of Saint Joseph, Hartford, Connecticut, supervised by architect Apollinaire (Paul) Osadca of Eggers & Higgins was constructed in two pieces. To catch, and focus, the attention of the large congregation in the vast contemporary interior, a separate disc-shaped corona, five feet across, was set with thin rectangles of bronze (either satin-finished or polished), brass, and copper. The deepest part of the disc was unornamented and painted a warm matte Swedish red. It was against this background that the ostensorium itself was placed, made of dozens of gold-plated bronze squares varying in size from one-quarter to three-quarters of an inch across. Each one was held from behind on its own bronze wire. These were bent to cluster around the center where the host was displayed. Designers Frederick Christian and Viggo Bech Rambusch amassed and contrasted different metal textures and shapes to catch, hold, and break the light, thereby creating an aura of mystery and sacredness. A half century ago this effect was achieved by the use of intrinsically precious metals.

The art metal shop has produced a vast range of objects, from delicate portable sizes to architectural structures fifty feet high. From the 1920s through the 1960s Rambusch designed, fabricated, and installed nearly 100 baldachins. The idea of differentiating, and thereby making sacred, the space where liturgical rituals are performed is an ancient one. In the Western world probably the most famous example is the monumental bronze baldachin under the dome of Saint Peter's Basilica, Rome, designed by Gian Lorenzo Bernini (1598–1680).

In the early- to mid-twentieth century, baldachins were installed with increasing frequency in Roman Catholic churches in the United States. This was due, in part, to changes in the sanctuary and specifically the increasingly popular placement of a free-standing altar in the center rather than against the rear sanctuary wall as had been customary for centuries. The purpose of the baldachin was to draw attention to the altar. By its very nature, a baldachin is monumental and can be made of wood, metal, and stone. Rambusch worked outside this norm and even designed and fabricated one in terra cotta at one point in its history. The structure can be largely decorative in performing its purpose or it can be functional. In the case of the latter, lighting and sound amplification systems can be incorporated in its canopy.

Since its beginnings, the firm has maintained its own extensive research library with periodicals, scrapbooks, folios, and books to educate and inspire. Surely,

one of the sources in 1922 for designer Knud Laub in the earliest Rambusch baldachin (fig. 3-18) for Saint Boniface Church, of the Benedictine order, Pittsburgh, Pennsylvania, was a newly arrived book in the firm's library. Published in Vienna in 1919 by Robert Stiassny, *Michael Pachers St. Wolfganger Altar* consisted of two profusely illustrated volumes about the famous medieval Benedictine church in Austria. The wrought-iron medieval bishop's crosier (fig. 3-19) appears to have captured Laub's attention, for his design of the completely wrought-iron and bronze structure shows the four supports of the free-standing baldachin terminating in precisely this type of crosier.

Gustave Wraae, another Rambusch designer, envisioned a different baldachin (fig. 3-20) in 1924 using an unusual combination of materials: bronze, copper, and glazed terra cotta. From four dark, reeded square pedestals sprang spiral columns of blue and gold surmounted by cushioned capitals emblazoned with winged angel faces. The arch of the baldachin supported a straight molded entablature. Its cost was more than $14,000. The Federal Seaboard Terra Cotta Corporation of Perth Amboy, New Jersey, owned by the Danish Mathiasen Brothers, made the terra cotta parts. On an elaborate eighteen-foot terra cotta base sat a pierced repoussé copper dome supported by four ribs of bronze, with the whole surmounted by a cross. This most distinctive

Abb. 23. Pedum des hl. Benedikt vom Hochaltar.

baldachin, perhaps without compare in American ecclesiastical design, was destroyed by fire in 1981. It was part of the elaborately decorated, richly furnished Holy Trinity Lithuanian Roman Catholic Church, Newark, New Jersey. This church was considered the mother church of Lithuanians and especially central to the life and community of recent immigrants from the Baltic region who came to the United States.

Sheathing wood with repoussé sheets of silver or silver-plated copper was a medieval technique. Rambusch employed this method to fabricate a baldachin (fig. 3-21) for the House of the Good Shepherd, Troy, New York. The program presented by architects Morgan and Milliman called for a building plan with a spoked design: three naves for different congregational groups (the public, the cloistered nuns, and the nuns from order of the Good Shepherd), each entirely separate from one other, all simultaneously facing the altar. Rambusch's design for the baldachin was made of wood overlaid with repoussé bronze sheeting, identical on three sides (fig. 3-22). An extensively illustrated article in 1930 in *American Architect and Architecture* discusses the design, the remarkable technique, and the craftsmanship with which this commission was executed:

> The idea of applying hammered metal to a wood base is not a modern method of decoration, for it can be traced to ancient medieval times. It is frequently observed in the works of Spanish and Italian craftsmen. However, it has not generally been employed in this country and its adaptation here is therefore all the more interesting.

The original design sketch in the mid-1940s for the Franciscan Monastery of the Holy Land in America in Washington, DC (fig. 3-23), shows a canopy suspended from the ceiling of the vast church. This idea eventually evolved into one of the most elaborate baldachins designed and fabricated by Rambusch (fig. 3-24). The final version was constructed of cast bronze. Gleb Derujinsky sculpted four uprights, with three-and-a-half-foot, full-length figures of the twelve apostles. The soffit of the ceiling was enameled and contained lighting and a sound system. It was installed in 1950.

Shifts in taste, as with the development of stylistic changes in candlesticks and other liturgical objects, can be seen with baldachins as well. At Holy Cross Church in Omaha, Nebraska, the baldachin (fig. 3-25), designed by Joaquin Santos in 1953, is streamlined and more

3-20 Gustave Wraae, designer; *Baldachino*, in *American Architect* 126, no. 2462 (December 31, 1924): 632, Holy Trinity Church, Newark, NJ, 1924. **3-21** *Baldachin*, graphite rendering, and **3-22** *One face of three identical tympana*, wood sheathed with repoussé bronze, House of the Good Shepherd (Morgan & Milliman, architects), Troy, NY, ca. 1930. **3-23** *Early sketch showing altar proposal and the decorative color treatment of vaults, pendentives, and dome coffers*, watercolor, and **3-24** Joaquin Santos, designer; *Baldachin, as built*, Franciscan Monastery of the Holy Land in America, Washington, DC, 1950.

RSAN & MILLIMAN ARCHITECTS.
HIGH ALTAR AND BALDACHINO
HOUSE OF GOOD SHEPHERD TROY.
RAMBUSCH DEC. CO. 2 W. 45 ST. N.Y.

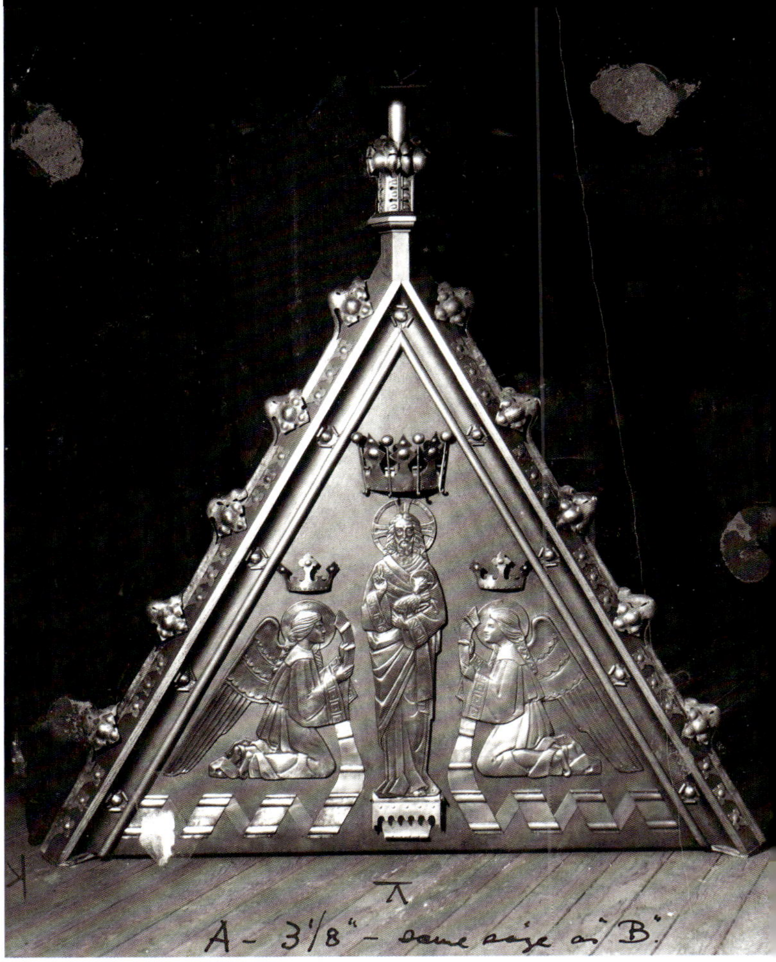
A - 3 1/8" - same size as "B".

evocative of modernist ideals. While straight posts replaced elaborately decorated columns, an underlying classical vocabulary still echoes in the anthemion-like termination of these members. Made of cast bronze, it used a traditional material for this structural form. But the sweeping canopy was employed to suit then-contemporary needs by concealing a light and amplification system. The changing church was evolving through technology and its applications for worship. Novelty, coupled with a sharper break with tradition, seems to have governed the design for the baldachin (fig. 3-26) made for Saint Mary's Church, Rockville, Maryland, 1962. It seems to hover, fluttering over the altar, while also responding to the upside-down, catenary arches of the sanctuary walls.

At Saint Joseph's Cathedral, Hartford, Connecticut, the firm developed and installed a baldachin (fig. 3-27) according to the requirements of Eggers & Higgins, the building's architects. This baldachin employed new materials and a new design concept. It has three upright supports symbolizing the Trinity. The trifoliate canopy of the structure is enamel on copper, with a symbol of the Trinity and the Holy Spirit. Lean and streamlined, the baldachin, juxtaposed to the highly decorated bronze baldachin made half a century before for Saint Boniface, is a vivid indicator of the revolution in American decorative arts that has occurred since then. The dramatic changes in liturgical celebration of the Roman rite made the original purpose and function of the baldachin obsolete. However, as an art form, and as examples of craftsmanship, they remain treasures within the evolving traditions of the church.

Although ecclesiastical commissions historically have been Rambusch's most prodigious field of work, the firm has continually produced unusual secular commissions utilizing all art metal techniques during its history. Cartier, the well-known jeweler on Fifth Avenue, Manhattan, in 1927 purchased two bronze showcases from the firm for $1,984, which would be equivalent to nearly $35,000 in 2023. They remained in the store and subsequently they were sold at auction at Park-Bernet Galleries.

In 1929 Rambusch was commissioned to decorate the boardroom suite in the Chanin Building, 42nd Street, Manhattan. Alfred Tulk designed and decorated this lavish suite, which included a private theater. The full-size working (or shop) drawings, more than eighteen feet long, with sinuous, reed-like lines serving as guides for the craftsmen are all that remain of these Art Deco

3-25 Joaquin Santos, designer; *Baldachin*, Holy Cross Church (Leo A. Daly, architects), Omaha, NE, 1953. **3-26** Joaquin Santos, designer; *Baldachin*, Saint Mary's Church (Donald Johnson, architect), Rockville, MD, 1962. **3-27** Joaquin Santos, designer; *Baldachin*, Cathedral of Saint Joseph (Eggers & Higgins, architects), Hartford, CT, 1962.

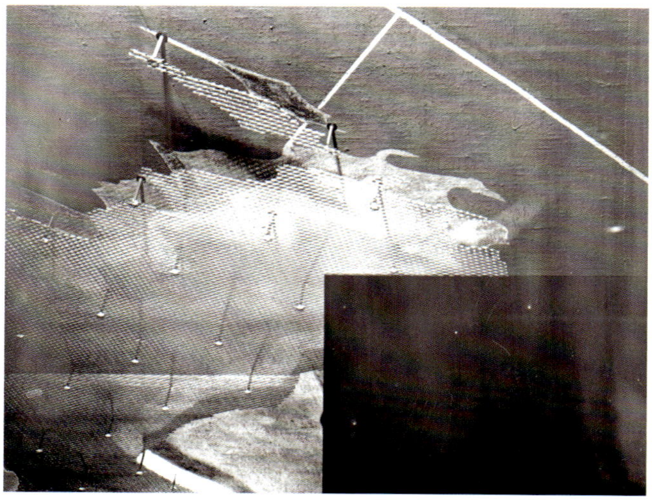

3-28 *General Assembly Chamber: Map mural*, United Nations: Early Headquarters (Skidmore, Owings & Merrill and Aymar Embury, architects), Lake Success, NY, 1946. **3-29** *General Assembly Chamber: detail of mesh*, United Nations: Early Headquarters, Lake Success, NY, 1946. **3-30** Peter White, designer; *Raintree Fountain*, model, cast and formed aluminum with anodized leaves, and **3-31** Peter White, designer; *Raintree Fountain*, five-foot sculpture in bronze and enamel, period postcard, Sterling Forest Gardens (Robert Dowling, developer), Tuxedo, NY, ca. 1959.

grills, the bill for which was $3,114. The theater was subsequently removed and the space utilized for other purposes.

The forty-eight-foot metal mural (fig. 3-28) commissioned in 1946 by Skidmore, Owings & Merrill and architect Aymar Embury for the early headquarters of the United Nations, Lake Success, New York, is an illuminating case study in Rambusch methodology and adaptability. The architect's program called for a map to be installed on the long wall behind the podium of the General Assembly Chamber. The world's land masses were to be made of woven wire "as diaphanous as a lady's hairnet." Only the finest materials were to be used. Rambusch designed a hand-woven mesh of brass, bronze, and aluminum. At its presentation to the client, Rambusch cautioned that unless each metal cutout had its shadow painted in another color on the wall, the metal mesh land masses would not be visible beyond the first few rows of the Assembly. The architect dismissed the advice and cancelled the project on the grounds that it was too costly. Rambusch countered that machine-made, commercially available metal mesh (fig. 3-29) could be cut, shaped, and painted to give the same effect as the costly hand-woven wire mesh originally specified. The architect responded that if the map could be delivered and installed in three weeks, Rambusch could have

the job. Completed on time, the metal mesh land masses were indeed scarcely visible on the wall. An additional contract was given to Rambusch to paint the wall in a darker shade, following the contours of the metal mesh shapes. The map remained in place until the United Nations moved into its current location in Manhattan, where it officially opened in 1952.

Architects consistently have awarded commissions to the Rambusch Decorating Company. With such architectural firms as Leo A. Daly; the Eggers Group; Gaudreau, Inc.; Swanke Hayden Connell; and Paul C. Reilly; by 1998, the company had entered a third generation of collaboration. Also, many commissions come directly from individual clients. Real estate developer Robert Dowling was a case in point. In the late 1950s, having purchased a 22,000-acre tract in Tuxedo, Rockland County, Dowling embarked on a three-part development plan: corporate and industrial parks, individual dwellings, and Sterling Forest Gardens—America's answer to Keukenhof Gardens, outside of Amsterdam. In fact, a symbolic first tulip was planted in 1959 at Sterling Forest by Princess Beatrix, from the Netherlands. A world traveler, Dowling had been enchanted by the magnificence and whimsy of Catherine the Great's gardens at Peterhof on the Gulf of Finland. In addition to classic garden themes such as a canal, a cascade, and a geyser, playful trick fountains were also part of the plan. In one, an innocent, inviting garden seat would spray the unwary sitter. Rambusch was commissioned to create a fountain that would include this element of surprise. To that end, designer Viggo B. Rambusch and designer Peter White proposed the Raintree (figs. 3-30 and 3-31).

The wrought-bronze "tree" was five feet high. Situated on a rocky island in a small pond, its hollow trunk and branches were threaded with capillaries of tubing that carried water under extreme pressure. As the visitor approached this inviting spot, a lever under the path triggered a current which released the water through hundreds of tiny holes. The result was a delicate fine mist that enveloped the leaves and branches and gently bathed the vitreous-enamel leaves. With serendipity and bright sunlight from the right angle, a visitor could be treated to a rainbow. So popular was the Raintree that a second version, ten feet high made of aluminum with baked enamel leaves was ordered, fabricated, and installed. This project and another reflect Rambusch's artmetal work for logos. The Raintree was immediately adopted as such for the Sterling Forest Gardens. Another logo, the Prudential Insurance Company's Rock of Gibraltar, was a Rambusch commission. In 1954, Kemp Bunch & Jackson built the first skyscraper for Jacksonville, Florida. On a nineteen-story limestone

wall—the focal point of a three-block plaza—Rambusch mounted a twenty-foot stainless-steel sculpture of the Rock, made of hand-hammered repoussé sheets.

Although a great deal of Rambusch art metal work is commissioned for public spaces, some special commissions have been fabricated for individuals. Samuel Lionel "Roxy" Rothafel, a long-term client, had a pair of wrought-iron gates (fig. 3-32) made for the arch between the entrance hall and living room in his apartment in New York City. Composed of musical notations, and male and female dancing figures, the gates epitomize the syncopated rhythm of the Jazz Era. These gates were included in the annual exhibition of 1931 at the Architectural League. Another special commission came from Adolph Zukor, the Hungarian-American movie producer who lived in the Savoy-Plaza Hotel and was a partner of Frederick Loewe. Zukor was a long-time client. He wanted his suite to be distinctive, and he commissioned a pair of bronze doors. Quite the opposite of Roxy's fanciful set, these doors depended upon symmetry and a vocabulary of traditional statements for impact. They were fabricated of cast and hand-worked bronze. The door of his dressing room was also overlaid with a bronze grill, creating a lavish effect.

As an indication of how far a client might be willing to go with elaborate and expensive metal work, consider the cast and hand-chased bronze casket designed in 1963 by Edward Ferlin. It was suitable to house the jewels of a Medici. The restrained elegance and historical overtones of the piece were intentional. Actually, it was a receptacle created to hold the ashes of the client's beloved poodle, and was labeled, "Our Darling." The casket eventually was placed surreptitiously in a niche of the family's section in a large mausoleum.

Two commissions from 1985 exemplify the continuing strains of ecclesiastical and secular art metal work. The tabernacle designed by Mario Locsin, Rambusch's chief designer, for Cardinal Law's private chapel in Boston, Massachusetts, utilizes a tabernacle door that was formerly embedded in the original, half-century-old altar. This element, rich with history, was thus incorporated into the new design. Freestanding and made of bronze, the new tabernacle sits in a niche in a small, refurbished chapel, where mass is televised to thousands of home-bound viewers each day.

An armillary sphere was a device used by late-medieval and early-Renaissance astronomers to prove that the earth was the center of the universe. It had a ball in the center representing the earth. Bands around it represented the trajectories or paths of the sun and planets were suspended around the central ball. Over time, the firm has designed and made several. Four such spheres, each weighing about 1,000 pounds, five feet nine in diameter, were fabricated in bronze for the Nassau Street Annex to the Federal Reserve Building, downtown Manhattan. A model at one-quarter size (fig. 3-33) was constructed as the project evolved.

Rambusch has thus produced a kaleidoscope of art metal objects, from those held in one's hand to freestanding, sixty-foot-high structures. Fashioned in gold, silver, bronze, iron, stainless steel, or aluminum, they have been cast, raised, repoussé, chased, acid-etched, or enameled in technique and process. Private rooms or public places, the range and diversity have two central, unifying characteristics: each object is individually designed and each one is custom made. This was true in 1919 and it is still true today.

3-32 *Pair of wrought-iron gates*, made for Samuel Lionel "Roxy" Rothafel House, Manhattan, ca. 1930.

3-33 Viggo Bech Rambusch, *Model of armillary sphere, one-quarter size,* Federal Reserve Bank—Nassau Street Annex (Johnson / Burgee, architects), new arcade, Manhattan, 1989.

CHAPTER IV

Lighting Fixtures: Innovation, Technology, and Design

Humankind's command of fire, and thereby early artificial illumination, remained essentially the same from prehistory until the late nineteenth century. But Thomas Alva Edison's successful experiment and subsequent inventions transformed man's control of the environment. It was in his laboratories in Menlo Park, New Jersey, on New Year's Eve, 1879, that electric illumination began a new era in history. The Edison lamp and the harnessing of electrical energy allowed humans to control darkness and, eventually, accurately and precisely control the quality and quantity of light. Ever since Edison's groundbreaking discovery, a direct relationship has existed between the development of fixtures that house lamps and the manufacture of them. The development and design of lighting fixtures has been heavily determined by technical advances made by lamp manufacturers.

Early electrical lamps operated on very low wattage, producing only two to four lumens per watt. In other words, only a small amount of light was emitted—equivalent to illumination just slightly brighter than a candle flame. In a domestic setting, these lamps often were grouped or cascaded to produce attractive highlights for interiors. Louis Comfort Tiffany, as well as others, designed fixtures in this mode. The pinpoints of lights were not irritating. Indeed, they added bits of brilliance. Tiffany today is well known for creating a skirt for the single lamp, or a clustered group, with richly colored stained-glass domes, inspired by nature, to diffuse the light. A few decades later, Frank Lloyd Wright shielded lamp lights using a similar technique but with different results. He created geometrically ordered, textured, leaded-glass shades that were subtlety shaded.

Non-domestic settings presented other problems, especially with the increase in intensity, or number of lumens, emitted. The naked light bulb produced light and glare. The Rambusch Decorating Company was the first in America to systematically engage in the invention, design, and fabrication of church lighting fixtures. The firm took this step because it wanted to control and protect its painted church decorations and murals. When Frode C. V. Rambusch visited his murals in the Cathedral of Saints Peter and Paul, Philadelphia, his view was hampered by a single incandescent lamp that was suspended in front of each mural. It impaired his appreciation of the mural. He considered this problem, learned about the physiology of the eye, and especially how the ocular lens worked. Soon he realized the need for a diffuser that would address the irritating point source of light. Take, for example, a light shield illustrated in company archives (fig. 4-1).

As early as 1908, the Rambusch company designed lighting units that were fabricated in small workshops throughout the city. The fixtures were then taken to S. J. O'Brien, a bicycle manufacturer-turned-electrician, for wiring. Peer Smed, an extremely tall Danish immigrant with red hair who also was an accomplished metalsmith, had a shop in the backyard of his Brooklyn home. Smed would work on some of these fixtures, too. Even though for decades, the majority—if not all—of Smed's work was commissioned from Rambusch, he steadfastly refused to join the firm as a salaried employee because he wanted to maintain his independence. Indeed, it was he who developed and fabricated a silver helmet pitcher made to celebrate a family occasion (see fig. 3-3).

4-1 *Light shield for a one-bulb lamp*, drawing, ca. 1920.

The first Rambusch lighting fixtures were simple repoussé metal shields, hung in front of a suspended single bulb. Made of iron and copper, the fixtures were often polychromed and sometimes gilded. The repoussé design could be a fleur-de-lis symbol of Mary, a heraldic device of a bishop, or a purely fanciful and decorative motif (fig. 4-2). After discovery of the x-ray in 1895 by German physics professor, Wilhelm Röntgen, researchers and commercial entities began to explore the invention and manufacture of radiation reflectors. The development of corrugated, parabolic-shaped mirrored-glass reflectors became quite useful in the lighting industry. Rambusch developed various types, including one version (fig. 4-3), which shows the reverse of a mounted lamp shield, with corrugated, parabolic-shaped mirror reflectors. The actual object has an ornate front (fig. 4-4). As lamps became more powerful and were amplified by these shields, Rambusch produced larger shields for lighting uses. These were constructed of repoussé metal, and sometimes anchored on the side of a sanctuary arch, allowing the lamps to be hidden but directed at the altar. The purpose thus was to diffuse as well as direct light. A favorite repoussé decoration in Rambusch fixtures was the figure of a saint, often with Saint Peter on one side and Saint Paul on the other.

Rapidly developing technology that resulted in ever-increasing lumen output necessitated another invention that would allow for more than only one-way, accent light. This development required that a light source be shielded on all sides. To meet this need, the Rambusch firm designed the Plumbob fixture (fig. 4-5), so called because it resembled an engineer's surveying tool. It was a lantern cage made of metal, usually from hand-wrought iron, holding translucent, pale, amber-colored glass plates, thereby providing a shield for the eye from all sides and from any angle. These fixtures were hung at regular intervals down the nave of many churches. The glare-free light was quite satisfactory, and the rhythm of the free-hanging units accented the architecture. Various versions of them were developed by the company, such as one design that held a corona of "candles," lit by electricity (fig. 4-6), to add sparkle and also provide a counterpoint to the textured glass. Rambusch designs could also respond to the style, often Gothic revival, of many a church. After a hiatus of half a century, in 1985, Rambusch began fabricating these elongated, elegant pendant fixtures again.

By 1919, Rambusch had its own metal shop at 343 East 44th Street. The first lighting commission designed and fabricated in the Rambusch workshops was for the Cathedral of Saint Peter, Scranton, Pennsylvania. By 1926, the firm had outfitted fifty-nine major churches with Plumbob fixtures. Some were even designed for exterior settings that were either secular or religious (fig. 4-7). Now many are for sale in antique shops and on websites owing to their distinctive design and fine craftsmanship.

Though difficult to fabricate and hard to relamp, the Plumbob lantern was nonetheless the progenitor of a long line of hanging lantern fixtures (figs. 4-8 to 4-13), made to specifications, in an endless variety of designs and materials. One of these designs (see fig. 4-9) was stylistically inspired by Byzantine ideas, and was fashioned so that holes in its rounded top allowed heat to escape. The cost in the 1930s was pegged, not surprisingly, to size: $100 for a 200-watt, eight-inch cylinder, $125 for a 300-watt, ten-inch cylinder, and $150 for a

4-2 *Lighting fixture with shield*, wrought iron, 1931. **4-3** *Wall-mounted lamp shield: reverse*, drawing, and **4-4** *Wall-mounted lamp shield: front*, bronze and wrought iron, 1911.

4-5 *Plumbob lighting fixture in a church nave*, 1911. **4-6** *Plumbob lighting fixture*, with a corona of electric candles, 1915. **4-7** *Exterior bracket-mounted Plumbob lighting fixture*, repoussé bronze, 1935.

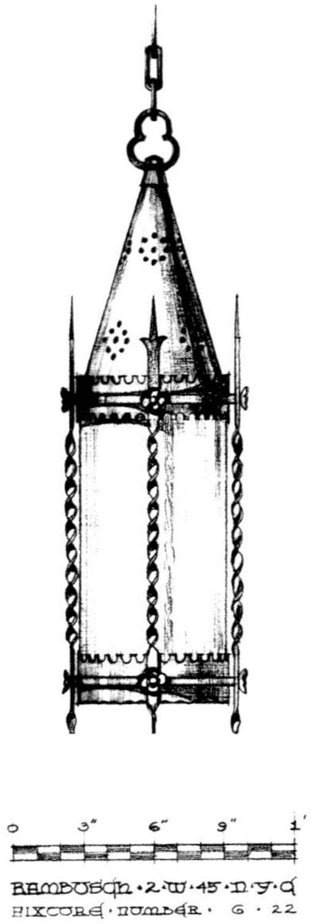

4-8 *Lantern light fixture*, scale drawing, ca. 1930. **4-9** *Byzantine-inspired lantern*, scale drawing, ca. 1930. **4-10** *Cluster lantern fixture*, watercolor scale drawing, ca. 1930.

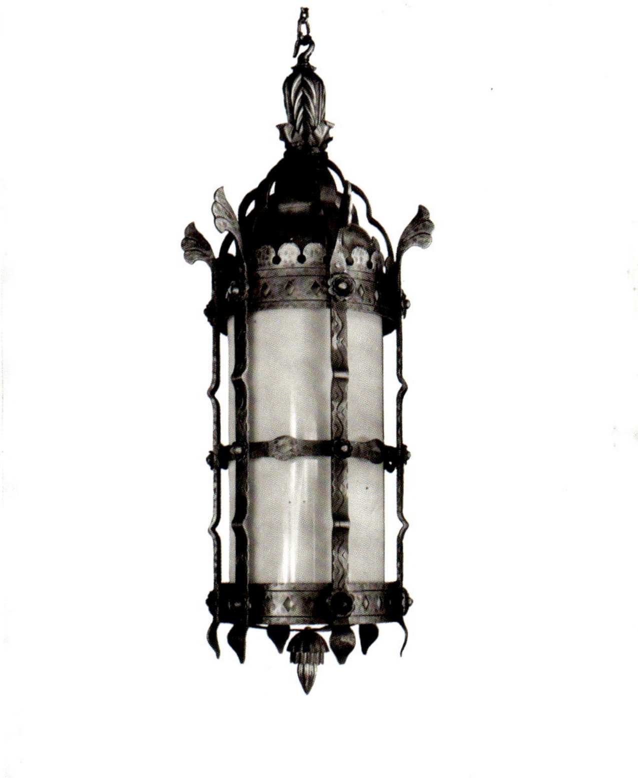

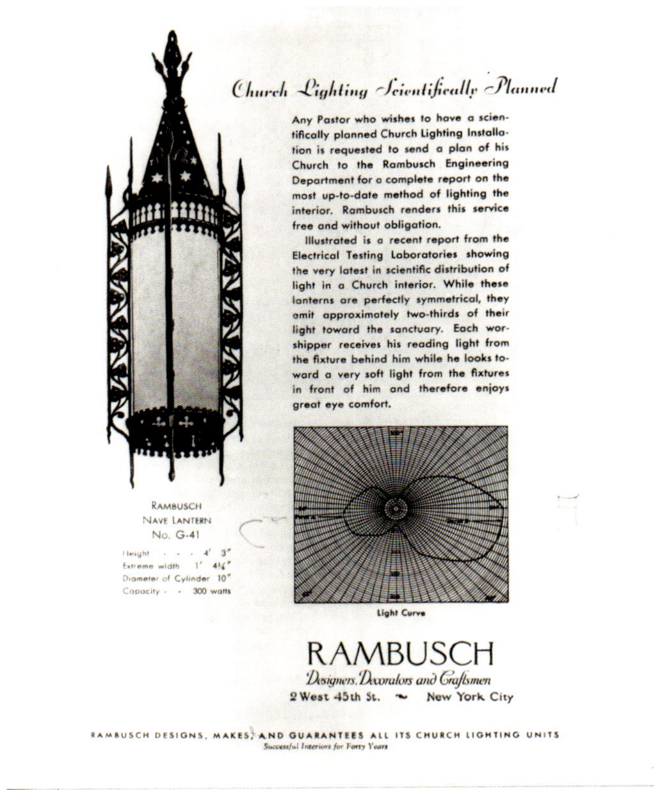

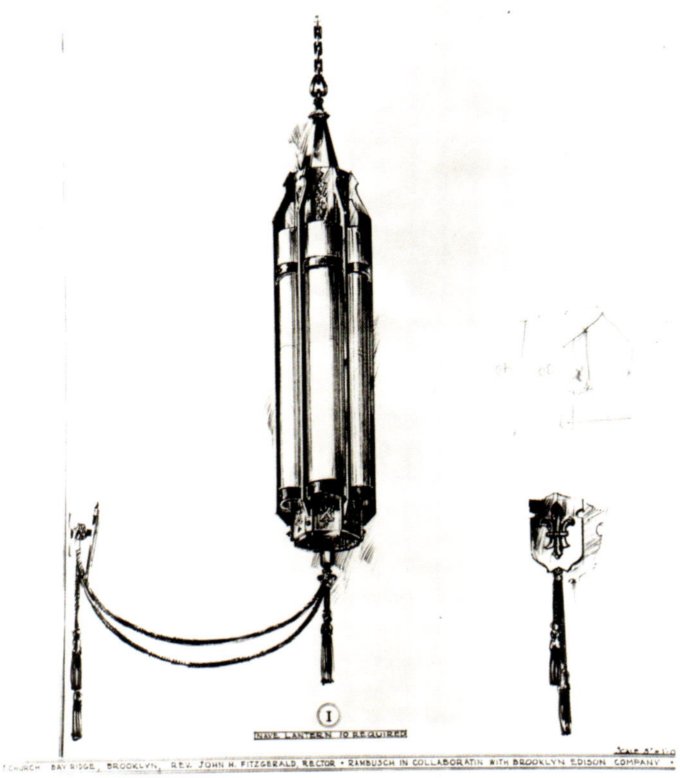

4-11 *Lighting fixture*, wrought iron, made for Saint Vincent de Paul, Bayonne, NJ, 1930. **4-12** *Advertisement, describing church lighting*, ca. 1940. **4-13** *Elongated lantern fixture*, scale drawing, 1934.

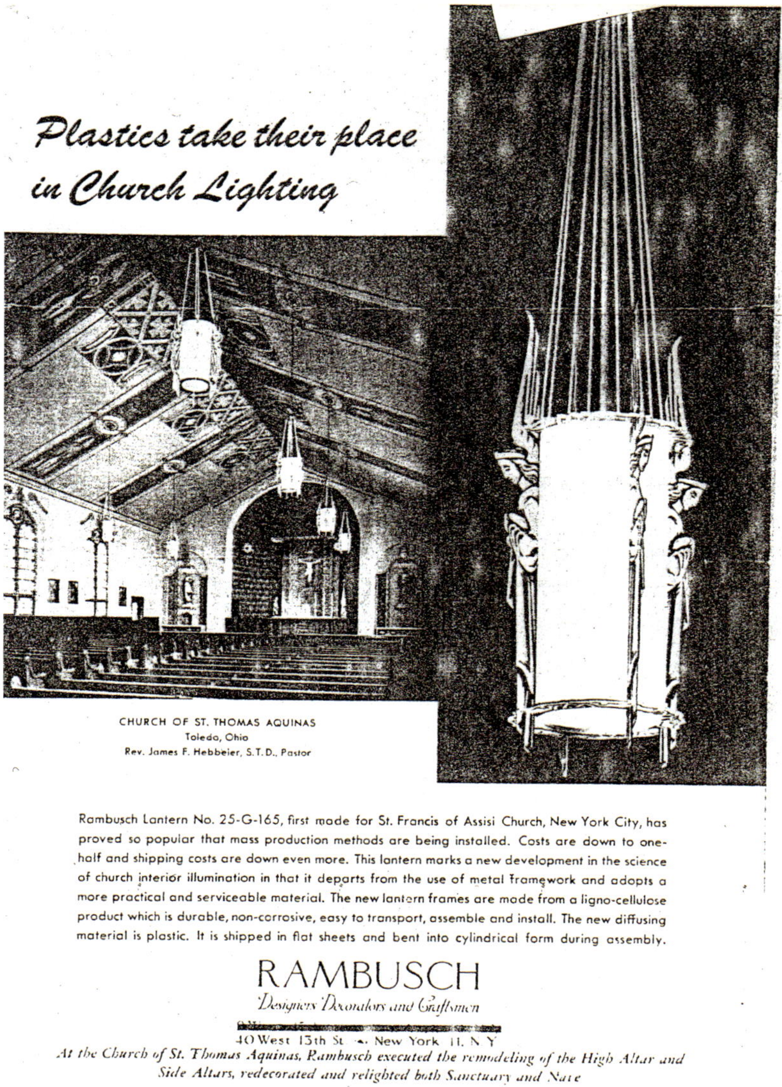

500-watt, twelve-inch cylinder lantern. During World War II, when metal was scarce, embellishments in alternate materials on lanterns, such as angels (figs. 4-14 and 4-15), were even composed of Masonite, painted gold, and then stenciled. Advances in design replaced the typical eight pieces of flat glass in the fixture by a single glass cylinder fastened in a metal cage by the 1950s. Bulb replacements in newer designs became a simple procedure. Further developments with cylindrical-shaped fixtures could accommodate a cluster of bulbs inside the cylinder, thereby providing higher levels of illumination and output.

Because of renewed interest in traditional, classical antecedents, Rambusch reintroduced these types of lanterns in the early 1980s. The Classic lantern series of 1985 was based on the old designs simplified and fabricated by modern manufacturing methods and procedures. Thus, they were more readily available than were their hand-wrought, iron or cast-bronze, and chased predecessors. Commissions for the earlier, more elaborate and handmade fixtures still come to the firm and are completed.

In the first quarter of the twentieth century, owners of large public spaces that did not lend themselves to illumination by lanterns—particularly theaters and movie houses—came to Rambusch for lighting solutions. High levels of illumination were not generally necessary. A more subtle effect was often desired. Rambusch designed a wall-mounted fixture for just a single lamp. The first theater fixture, #1 in the job files, was made for the Strand Theatre on Times Square in 1920. This prototype is now in the collection of the Museum of the Moving Image. The shell-shaped reflector was hammered out of copper and gold plated. The resulting textured surface fractured the rays of light producing a soft, diffused effect. The simple reflector also served as a decorative element in

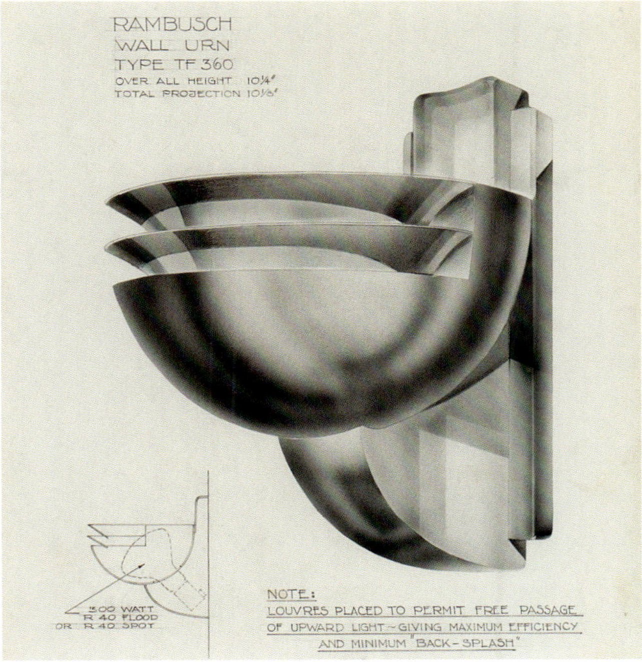

the design. It was held in place by wrought-iron scrolls (see fig. 4-20). A decade later, Rambusch engineered and fabricated a more complex wall unit (figs. 4-16 and 4-17). The illumination, still produced by a single lamp, was thrown onto the wall or ceiling after passing through a series of precisely engineered baffles. The result was a soft, even light from a single, but much stronger, lamp than that of the unit of previous years.

With recent interest in Art Deco art and architecture, this light, Theatre-Fixture 360, also known as the TF-360, was reissued in 1983. Today, this fixture is in the collections of the Metropolitan Museum of Art. Notably, despite the much more powerful lamps being used today, these reissued fixtures are fabricated from the original molds. The engineered design dating back to 1930 does not have to be altered. It is also important to note that the driver in illumination is not the fixture designer but the lamp manufacturer. Gas-discharge lamps (fueled by metal halide or sodium vapor) were not mass produced until the late 1930s, although they had been developed in 1904 by Peter Cooper's son-in-law Abram Hewitt.

Rambusch began experimenting with hidden sources of illumination in the early 1930s. Lantern design had been evolving as brighter lamps became available in the 1920s. These lamps produced not only more light but also more glare. One solution was to raise lanterns higher, out of sight from the congregation that was seated in pews, viewing liturgical ceremonies. Reflectors were introduced to push more of the light down, and baffles were placed on the congregational side to protect viewers' eyes from glare. This design development was utilized especially in units placed over choir and chancel areas. Over time, it became more difficult to replace, or "relamp," the units as they were installed higher up from the floor. Ultimately, the solution was to place units in the attic, or plenum, areas under the church roof. Because most large churches had vaulted ceilings with these interstitial spaces, these areas were a natural site for the installation of light fixtures and wiring. When lighting maintenance was needed, the lamps could easily be replaced from catwalks, which usually existed in these spaces. By 1934, the Rambusch Downlite was born and was awarded a US patent.

Edward Rambusch and optic engineer Victor G. Anderson pursued continual testing and refinement in the firm's in-house testing laboratory, which resulted in the Downlite where the housing, the reflector, and all the electrical wiring were completely recessed in the ceiling (figs. 4-18 to 4-20). The only visible part of the fixture was a flat face plate projecting less than one-eighth of an inch from the surface of the ceiling. When painted the color of the surrounding area, this plate was almost invisible. The ellipsoidal reflector, which shaped light rays and channeled them down and out of the small ceiling aperture, was contoured so that glare was reduced significantly.

4-14 *Advertisement, showing plastics in church lighting*, ca. 1942. **4-15** *Angel*, painted and stenciled Masonite on plastic light cylinders, ca. 1942. **4-16** Joaquin Santos, *TF-360 Theatre Lighting Fixture*, drawing, ca. 1935. **4-17** Joaquin Santos, *TF-360 Theatre Lighting Fixture*, bronze, ca. 1935.

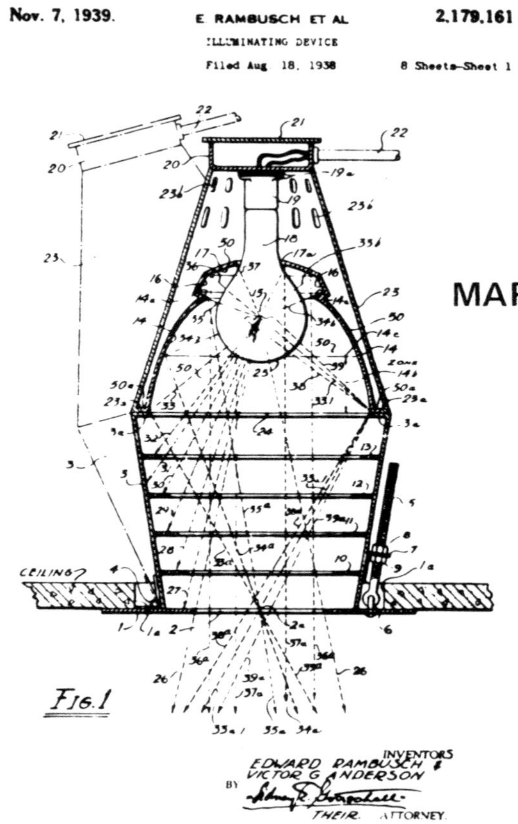
Nov. 7, 1939.
E. RAMBUSCH ET AL
2,179,161
ILLUMINATING DEVICE
Filed Aug. 18, 1938
8 Sheets-Sheet 1
CEILING
FIG. 1
INVENTORS
EDWARD RAMBUSCH &
VICTOR G. ANDERSON
BY
THEIR ATTORNEY

MARK I

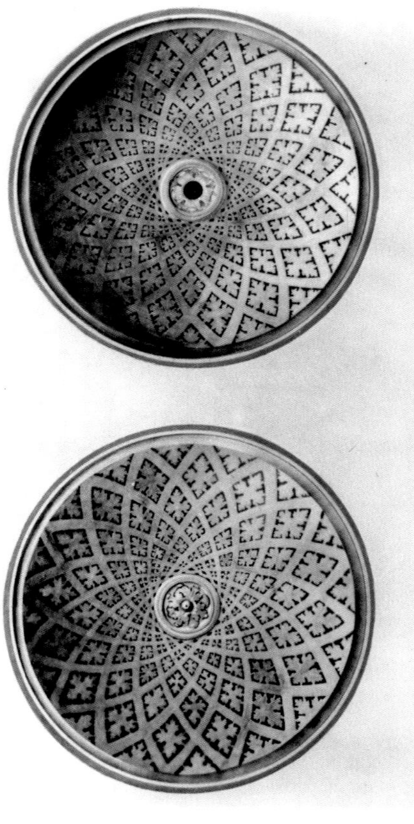

Only if one stood directly under the unit did a viewer experience any such effect.

Ever since the Downlite was first produced, Rambusch has continued to refine the original patent. As newer and more powerful lamps were invented, the firm's lighting engineers and designers responded with new units to fit the more powerful lamps. The Downlite, now in its fourth permutation dubbed the Mark IV, was designed by Peter White. It utilizes the tungsten halogen lamp. In the earliest units the reflectors were electroformed galvanic castings. Heavy and unyielding, they were plated with rhodium, or even on occasion, with gold. For the theater division of Warner Brothers, Rambusch gold-plated a version of these reflectors in order to create a warm light that the company desired. Today, the reflectors are formed in lightweight aluminum. More flexible and precisely engineered in this adaptable material, a reflector can be shaped to channel light at virtually any angle. These can be compared to examples of earlier versions of fixtures (fig. 4-21). Vast public spaces can be exactly and evenly lit from the invisible Downlite or wall washers, such as the atrium space at the National Gallery of Art (fig. 4-22), where a wall 360 feet long by sixty feet high was washed with light, with no obvious fixtures in the space.

Downlites can be installed as single units or as part of a complete, engineered lighting solution. For example, they were used in the Turbine Room of Consolidated Edison's Waterside steam plant and in Lever House designed by Skidmore, Owings & Merrill. In 1970, they were clustered in the Great Hall of the Metropolitan Museum of Art (figs. 4-23 to 4-25) for architects Kevin Roche and John Dinkeloo, and museum director Thomas Hoving. The project was overseen by Arthur Rosenblatt, director of architecture. This multi-lamp Downlite was composed of twenty-four 1,000-watt incandescent lamps, clustered in each of the three oculi above the main floor. The composite unit measured more than five feet in diameter and eight feet high. For this project, Rambusch received the first of a remarkable series of Lumen Awards. These accolades are the Illuminating Engineering Society's equivalent of the Academy Awards.

Mercury-vapor lamps, bluish in tone, although invented and produced in the early years of the twentieth century, were not commercially marketed until

4-18 Edward Rambusch and Victor G. Anderson, designers; *Patent drawing: Mark I Downlite*, November 7, 1939. **4-19** *Downlite: detail of installation*, 1938. **4-20** *Downlite installed in dome: single unit replaces rosette at center*, 1938. **4-21** *Three different lighting fixtures*, from left: *Lite Pak, Theatre Fixture #1, Downlite*; 1981, 1920, and ca. 1980, respectively, photograph from ca. 1981–1982. **4-22** Peter White, designer; *Lighting for East Building: Atrium*, National Gallery of Art (I. M. Pei, architect), Washington, DC, 1974–1978.

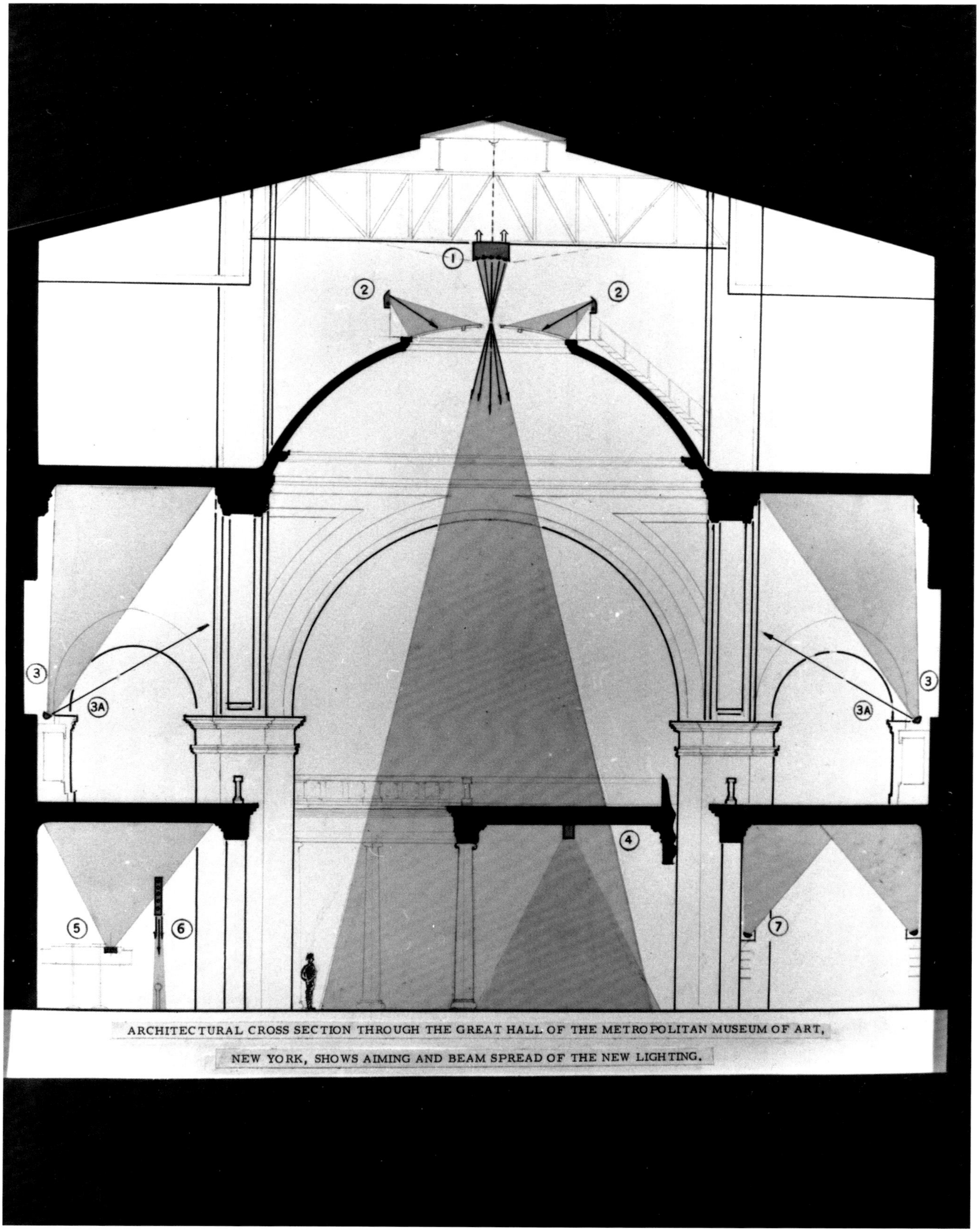

4-23 *Cross section of new lighting system for the Great Hall,*
Metropolitan Museum of Art, Manhattan, 1970.

three decades later. Such lamps give off strong light, generating several times the lumens per watt of an incandescent light source. In the late 1950s and 1960s, even more powerful levels of illumination were available from high-intensity discharge (HID) lamps.

Wall-mounted units for single lamps or pendant fixtures did not meet the demands after World War II. During the 1960s and 1970s, several factors conspired to require higher levels of illumination from an invisible source. These included the increasingly strong influence of the International Style in American architecture, the desire for uncluttered spaces where architectural design alone was central, and increased wattage and power of the new lamps.

By the mid-1970s energy efficiency became an important consideration in any large-scale lighting program. The Main Concourse in Grand Central Terminal was illuminated by approximately 400 incandescent lamps, which required a tremendous amount of electricity. In the original Warren & Wetmore, Reed & Stem design, the great windows had initially flooded the vast space with natural light. But with neighborhood development over time, this type of light became blocked by nearby tall buildings. Commissioned by William M. Aston of the MTA, the purpose of the Rambusch lighting program was to return the then-dingy space to its original ambience. Individual uplights were mounted behind each pier to

4-24 *Two of three clusters of Multi-lamp Downlites, foreground and background, above the Great Hall*, Metropolitan Museum of Art, Manhattan, 1970. **4-25** *Single cluster of Downlites for the Great Hall*, Metropolitan Museum of Art Manhattan, Manhattan, 1970.

4-26 *Main Concourse: new lighting scheme*, Grand Central Terminal, Manhattan, 1976.

provide ambient light in the side bays. Eighteen special fixtures were positioned under the hall's ten dormers and huge end windows (fig. 4-26). These lights, which were more energy efficient, had a distinctive combination of metal halide and high-pressure sodium lamps that combined to produce a Kelvin rating close to daylight. (Such a rating is used to indicate the "temperature," or whiteness, of light according to industry standards.) The cost of the new installation was paid for within an astounding twenty-eight months because of the savings on electricity, to say nothing of the drop in maintenance with the new system.

Largely unchanged to this day is the shape of the original incandescent lamp. Fluorescent lighting introduced commercially in 1938, with its unusual tubular form, had an immediate appeal to designers. Many such fixture designs are in the firm's files. One in particular (fig. 4-27), by Theodor Carl Muller, made of aluminum and plate glass, was exhibited in the annual exhibition of 1931 at the Architectural League of New York: it was no. 695 lighting fixture with tubular lamps. The sleek line of tubular fluorescent and neon lighting, as this example shows, was readily applicable to the Art Moderne, a style that became popular in the 1930s. The Aura lighting fixture (fig. 4-28) illustrates this trajectory: a ring of Lucite encircles an anodized aluminum core and seems to float above and around it. Both uplight and downlight emanate from this streamlined, elegant design.

A commission much farther afield in the early 1930s included work for the Brewer family, who were among the original missionaries in Hawaii. They created a trust and built an office building in Honolulu. Rambusch was asked to create special lighting fixtures for the public spaces of this building, including the lobby (fig. 4-28). The sconces and pendant lights that the firm designed were, like the Aura light, heavily influenced by Art Moderne ideas of the period as well as Polynesian elements. The Hawaii designs were also shown in the Architectural League exhibition in this period.

Another advance in lamp technology—the manufacture of a small quartz lamp able to produce twenty lumens per watt—was met by Rambusch designer Peter White. He and Viggo Bech Rambusch patented the Lite Pak in 1981. The fixture is two by four by six inches and evenly spreads a broad fan of light from a small source. The intense heat of the lamp is dissipated through the ridged radiation at each side of the fixture. Originally designed for track or wall mounting, a special request led to its being mounted on a yoke with a stationary

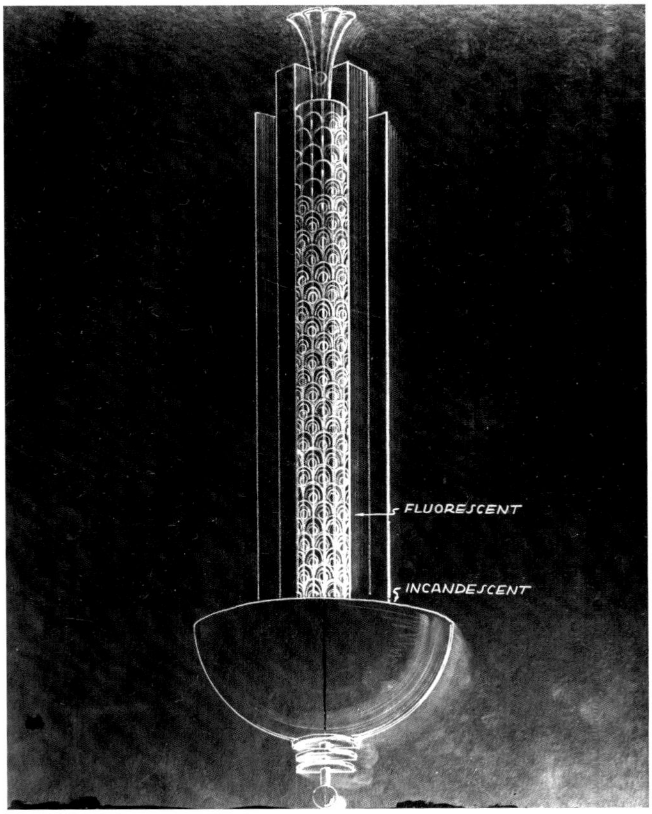

4-27 Theodor Muller, designer; *Sconce with fluorescent and incandescent lamps*, blueprint, ca. 1934.

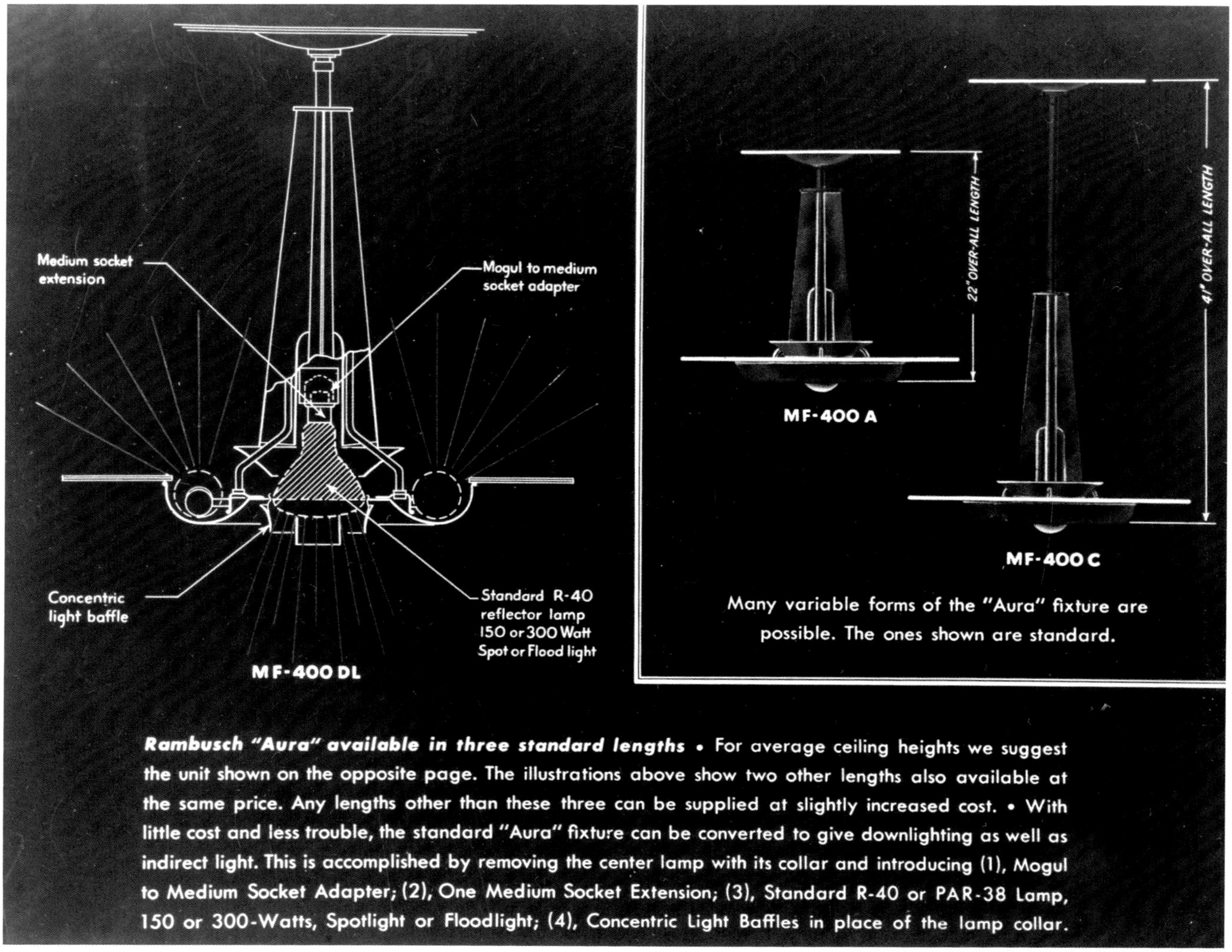

4-28 *Aura lighting fixture*, now in the Fixture Collection, Smithsonian Museum of American Art, Washington, DC, ca. 1950. **4-29** *Lobby interior, with pendant light fixtures*, Brewer Building, Honolulu, HI, early 1930s.

base (see fig. 4-21, fixture at left). This fixture has been introduced very successfully in historic interiors. It can be hidden on top of a case, bathing a room with warm illumination from a seemingly invisible source.

Despite the changes in fashion and architectural styles, it would appear that certain lighting needs remain constant. The wall unit of the TF-360, designed in 1932, has its 1985 cousin in the form of the Pan-a-lux, a version of which was used many years later in the lobby of the New York Academy of Medicine (fig. 4-30). This fixture has simple lines enclosing the housing for an HID lamp that can effectively emit eighty to 120 lumens per watt, in contrast to the much lower output of eight to twelve lumens years ago.

Ever since Edison's invention, the change in lighting technology has been swift. Demands for increasingly higher levels of illumination frequently resulted in the removal of early lighting fixtures. As a point of reference, a bill from 1931 indicates the Brooklyn Edison Company was charged $100 for "remodeled fixtures." To be sure, some original fixtures still remain in such stately interiors as the Reading Room of Cass Gilbert's Battle Hall at the University of Texas of 1910. However, the common pattern and general tendency in renovations was, and still is, to update to the ideals of prevailing taste, which leads to the removal and disposal of what is considered "outdated."

Mid- to late-twentieth-century interest in restoration and preserving material history has resulted in the creation of a special division of Rambusch Decorating Company. This division is devoted to the accurate re-creation of old fixtures, some of which have been discarded from renovations, and the refabrication of appropriate, period fixtures to be installed in interiors. Restoration is addressed in more depth later in this book (see chapter XI). But a couple of examples here reflect the general orientation of this type of work. In 1959, under the direction of the Architect of the Capitol and Alfred Easton Poor, Rambusch designed and made more than 100 fixtures of cast and chased bronze, crystal, and carved alabaster for the East Front Extension of the United States Capitol. Adelbert Potter of the distinguished, but no longer extant, Edward F. Caldwell & Company was the Rambusch project director on this commission. These new fixtures were created in a manner suitable to the decor of the interior. Lighting consultant Sven W. Bruun described the challenge of this large commission in *Illuminating Engineering* in November 1963, when

4-30 *Pan-a-lux lighting*, Lobby, New York Academy of Medicine, Manhattan, 2000.

4-31 Peter White, designer; *Ceiling lighting*, Lobby, Buchanan Center for the Performing Arts, University of Wyoming (HGA architects, 1979), Laramie, WY, 1982.

PIERCE
PAINTS
PHILCO

he wrote, "To provide twentieth-century engineering facilities within the ornamented framework of eighteenth-century architecture accepted by architects and engineers alike; the finished result [was] of interprofessional collaboration in a mutual challenge." All the stakeholders in the project were pleased with the outcome.

Curiously, the documentation for an entire set of fixtures fabricated for the Alabama State Capitol came from a doodler. In 1852, an inattentive state senator sketched the chamber and a wall sconce. His notebooks were found 132 years later in the state archives. Using this miniature reference, Rambusch designer Jesus Gonzalez-Rio made scale drawings, specifications, and shop drawings from which the fixtures were made.

Small-scale settings have not been the only contexts for their lighting work. In 1978, Rambusch was asked to create a strong decorative feature without sacrificing floor space because of the need to accommodate crowds in a new building that had been constructed at the University of Wyoming. The Art Center held two theaters under one roof and shared a narrow lobby. Rambusch's solution (fig. 4-31) was to utilize the entire ceiling. A horizontal grid exactly the size of the ceiling was made. Variously shaped, four-sided pieces of brass, copper, and bronze were suspended from the grid at regular intervals. Each piece was hand hammered and either polished or given a satin finish to reflect the uplight from nearby wall-mounted units. The highly polished, trapezoidal shapes hung on a two-point suspension, and they ranged in size from two to two and a half feet. This method of suspension allowed for slight, though restricted, movement, creating a subtle shimmering, scintillating effect.

The way in which light is emitted imparts a distinctive character to the illuminated space. It also determines what we see and how we see it. Light can be categorized according to the atmosphere it creates. Task lighting provides illumination for completing a job such as assembling parts, looking at a work of art, or reading a hymnal. Architectural lighting, often produced by recessed fixtures, compliments the architectural features of a room and defines a space. Festive light, resembling the sparkle or flicker of a candle, can often be produced by the introduction of chandeliers. Special lighting refers to unusual situations that call for high levels of illumination, such as television filming, movie making, disco dancing, and particular requirements of gambling casinos.

Early ledger books confirm that from its outset, Rambusch designed and fabricated fixtures that produced all these types of illumination. Files of the firm's lighting division, begun in 1919, are revealing on several levels. They reflect trends in the technology, inventions, design materials, manufacturing processes, and fabrication techniques. They show a range of aesthetic approaches, varying types of lighting solutions, and social and historical developments in architecture as well as preservation and restoration. These threads constitute a whole cloth, with technical, practical, and artistic outcomes, showing that Rambusch lighting is an innovative industry leader committed not only to art but the needs of its clients.

One can even turn to the developments of Edward V. A. Rambusch, for examples of how some lighting was used in the context of public space in New York. In the late 1940s he developed a design for a special program of Consolidated Edison to supply even lighting of entire sidewalks, with the added feature of being able to replace lamps without scaffolding (fig. 4-32). The units operated until 2008. These examples illustrate the multifaceted lighting solutions that the company has been able to pursue in public and other spaces, which is addressed further in chapter X.

4-32 *Edward V. A. Rambusch, with his design for the Consolidated Edison Sidewalk Lighting Program*, 1948.

CHAPTER V

Stained Glass: Techniques and Styles

Windows filter natural light and are a significant element in controlling the atmosphere of an interior, especially an ecclesiastical one. As the previous chapter explained, Rambusch entered the lighting field to control artificial illumination. In a sense, it opened its own stained-glass studio for much the same purpose—to create and maintain complete control of the interior environment.

As early as 1896, before the Rambusch firm was even incorporated, Frode Rambusch designed stained-glass windows. Early records of Gibson Art Glass and Decorating Company, where he had been an employee, link him to the windows of Saint Michael's Monastery Church, Union City, New Jersey. Sadly, the windows were destroyed when the building was demolished by fire. But in 1898 when Frode Rambusch and William Hencken incorporated the Rambusch Decorating Company, the articles of incorporation read, for "the manufacture and sale of stained glass, the execution, manufacture and sale of ecclesiastical and domestic decorations for churches, houses and other buildings, and of sculpture, relief and mosaic work." Clearly, Frode and Hencken wanted to make stained-glass work central to their new company.

Yet, despite this goal, for several decades no windows were fabricated by Rambusch. The bulk of glass used in American church interiors at this time was imported: some glass came from England and most came from Germany. The German studios, producers of realistic and highly detailed painted work, were large and well managed. They had streamlined the complex process necessary for the completion of a stained-glass window to a series of specialized tasks. Within a single, large studio, one worker might paint only grisaille canopies, or hands and faces. Conversely, some smaller studios produced only a few such elements and then supplied them to larger studios where they were incorporated into a completed window. Because of their size and the availability of cheap, but skilled, labor, European studios could produce windows at a very reasonable price. As late as 1954, in the summer issue of *Stained Glass*, Karl Barre Lamb lamented: "Our situation is rapidly becoming desperate . . . over 60% of the stained-glass windows installed in the . . . New York metropolitan area during the past twelve months came from Europe. The price of our product depends on the price of labor, and we cannot, therefore, compete with low European rates."

Desirous of controlling all the decorative elements in a church interior as well as the budget, Rambusch's initial entrance into the field of stained-glass design was tentative. Before 1929, three large commissions were designed in New York by a German émigré, Gustave Bernhardt, a Rambusch employee. His designs were then fabricated in a Berlin studio and subsequently installed in the locations for which they were destined: Saint Agnes Church, Tonawanda, New York; Saint Stephen Church, Winooski, Vermont; and Church of the Assumption of the Blessed Virgin Mary, Detroit, Michigan (fig. 5-1).

Even though a great deal of glass was still being imported, 1930 seems to have been a propitious year for the founding of the Rambusch stained-glass studio. Several large church interior commissions called for glazing, or creating windows for, an entire church. Indeed, although the original program for the Cathedral

5-1 Gustave Bernhardt, designer; Puhl-Wagner-Heinersdorff, Berlin, Germany, fabricator; *Virgin Mary, with Saints,* stained glass, Church of the Assumption of the Blessed Virgin Mary, Detroit, MI, 1928.

5-2 William Haley, designer; *Saint Mark and Saint John*, stained glass, Saint Agatha's Church, Brooklyn, 1939. 5-3 William Haley, designer; *Noah's Ark: detail*, stained glass, 1953. 5-4 *Rose window, South Gallery*, stained glass, Basilica of the National Shrine of the Immaculate Conception (Maginnis and Walsh, 1919–1939; Maginnis, Walsh and Kennedy, 1954–1959; architects), Washington, DC, 1970.

of Saint John the Divine, Manhattan, stipulated that no American stained glass be used in the edifice, this stipulation was later rescinded. As such, it was becoming apparent that more American glass should be utilized in American buildings for economic, practical, and artistic reasons.

Other Americans had already blazed the way. As a result of an international competition, William Willet and his wife Ann Lee Willet gained attention in 1910 when they won the commission for the chancel window of the Cadet's Chapel at the United States Military Academy, West Point, New York. They beat out such competitors as Louis Comfort Tiffany and other prominent designers. Subsequently, their son, Henry Lee Willet, opened a stained-glass studio in Philadelphia that continued his parents' tradition of charting a new path for art-glass design. Also located in that city was the prosperous D'Ascenzo Studios. In Boston, Charles J. Connick was rapidly gaining a reputation for the exquisite coloration of medieval-inspired windows. Otto Heinigke's studio in Manhattan and independent artists such as Harry Goodhue were also being awarded commissions.

The salary envelope of Per Bergethon for the third week of June 1930 documents the opening of the Rambusch Stained Glass Studio. He was a talented designer who had come to the firm several years before as an office boy. Bernhardt and Bergethon were the first two Rambusch stained-glass studio employees. The latter eventually handled one of the most challenging commissions in the history of the firm: the Mapparium in the Mary Baker Eddy Library of the Christian Science Publishing Society, Boston, Massachusetts (see fig. 5-20), a five-year project. Rambusch artists at this point began to draw full-size designs (also known as cartoons), for stained-glass projects. Within a very short time, workers possessing all the skills necessary for stained-glass window fabrication were hired. On East 48th Street, Lucien Rinaldi managed the shop, located on the top floor over the metal workshops. In 1931, some of the first commissions to be completely designed and fabricated in the studio were for Kirkleigh Villa, Baltimore, Maryland, and Holy Child Jesus Church, Richmond Hill, Queens. Soon after, in 1932, Rambusch was awarded a commission in an international competition for the Indianapolis War Memorial. It was indisputable that the studio had become an excellent choice because of its impressive early track record.

Completion of the staff occurred with the arrival of William "Bud" Haley, a designer and stained-glass

artist who had trained in Buffalo and Boston. He joined Rambusch in 1931. Among his many designs are those for the windows he produced for Saint Agatha's Church, Brooklyn, in the late 1930s (fig. 5-2). He also designed a detail of Noah's Ark (fig. 5-3) that was inspired by an eleventh-century stained-glass fragment from Durham, England, of a similar subject. Peter Gibson, superintendent of The York Glaziers Trust, in the same country, in 1980, generously shared with the firm an image of this fragment.

In 1949, Stephen Bridges—orderly, scholarly, and masterful—was both a highly respected iconographer and dean of the studio until his retirement in 1971. By that time Rambusch had completed more than 2,000 commissions. Some projects with Bridges were for a single small window, as in the Carroll House Chapel, Washington, DC. Others were for more complex results, such as the three rose windows for the Basilica of the National Shrine of the Immaculate Conception, Washington, DC, each almost thirty feet in diameter (one, from the South Gallery, is depicted in fig. 5-4).

Still other commissions were for sets of windows, each with an individual subject that contributed to a coherent, thematic whole. Some schemes were fabricated one by one over a period of time until the whole church was glazed, following the original schematic program. More often, entire sets of windows were made and installed together. All were team efforts, with each member of the studio contributing his or her talent. Records show that within a decade of its opening, female designers, painters, and cartoonists were regular employees in the stained-glass studio.

In the early years until after World War II, the studio strictly adhered to the guild system and the inherent

5-5 *The Doctors of the Church*, drawing study for stained-glass windows, 1950 and 5-6 *Te Deum window*, stained glass, Saint John's Cemetery, Brooklyn, 1946.

apprenticeship structure that had been practiced in since the medieval era. Today, in Europe, this system is still rigidly enforced. For example, a five-year indentured apprenticeship is common in England. Yet, in the United States the orderly guild structure has gradually eroded and fallen out of favor. The industry now lacks the ability to test or enforce strict levels of craftsmanship. Gone are training manuals and empirical standards against which individual skills are tested or matched. Gone are the spirited competitions between apprentices of various Manhattan studios. And gone are the days of creating a masterwork, literally a work of art in paint, metal, or glass that by its excellence in execution attested to an individual's distinction as a master of the trade. Now, in the United States, the test appears to be a combination of time and ability of a studio to consistently produce windows in which art and practical expertise come together for lasting success.

One aspect of the old medieval system, however, has remained the same: that of an itinerant artist who spends time in one studio and then another, according to the flow of work or the temperaments of the artisan and his or her colleagues. Since World War II, some artists who have worked in this vein at the Rambusch studios include Albinas Elskus, Father Arnold Johannes Wilhelmus (Marcolino "Marco") Maas, Richard Millard, Joep Nicholas, Robert Pinar, Abraham Ratner, Robert Sowers, Leandro Velasco, and Marco Zubor.

Because of diverse client needs and the fecundity of the many artists who gravitated to the studio, Rambusch never developed what could be termed a "studio style," as was the case with Connick Studios, one of its competitors. Rambusch has, and still does, produce a wide variety of work, both in artistic style and technique. The examples in this chapter illustrate the diversity of these aspects. Rambusch has executed countless windows in the traditional manner, ranging from acutely realistic rendering to suggestive figural treatments, and from dense painting with extensive use of grisaille to broad, loose approaches of painting on glass. Saint John's Cemetery, Brooklyn, is one such example of traditional work (figs. 5-5 and 5-6). In a large commission from 1946–1958, one can see the complexity of the program by merely looking at the subject matter in just one section. Erudition and knowledge of iconography is a necessity for the designers and viewers in this realm.

In the Chapel for the Sisters of Saint Martha, Antigonish, Nova Scotia, in 1966, abstracted figural forms accentuate the verticality of the window openings

THE GLORIOUS CHOIR OF
THE APOSTLES
WE PRAISE THEE
O GOD
WE ACKNOWLEDGE THEE
TO BE THE LORD
ALL THE EARTH DOTH
WORSHIP THEE

(fig. 5-7). These utilized large pieces of glass and no paint. It is through the symbol that the saint is identified rather than through human features or written title. In economic terms, obviously a window of this type is much less costly than those that had been completed for the Saint John's Cemetery.

Perhaps due to a resurgence of patriotism, Colonial Revival became a popular post-World War II architectural style for churches. Traditional stained glass, with its irregular, random lead lines, was deemed unsuitable. Architect Charles D. Maginnis challenged Rambusch studios to create a solution that was fitting for these newly designed churches. Rambusch's response was to develop a style of colored glass windows where mullions and muntins were filled with rectangular sheets of specially made glass suitable for a Colonial-inspired building. After extensive experimentation, the glass company Blenko developed for Rambusch a type of glass that was blown and then rolled in order to trap and incorporate many air bubbles. These irregularities caught the light and produced the desired effect of translucency. The glass was made in lightly tinted, pastel hues, and the classically inspired borders of the windows were painted in grisaille, with highlights in silver-nitrate salts. When fired, these salts produced a yellowish, translucent highlight on the gray background. The Church of Our Lady of Victory, Manhattan, provides a good example of this type of window (fig. 5-8). A commemoration, lesson, or painted scene was often enclosed in a cartouche inserted in the compositional field. Here, varied stronger colors were introduced. Other times, an entire scene would fill the window, as in one of the stained-glass windows at the Valley Forge Military Academy (fig. 5-9). In either case, the entire overall effect was of a delicately colored window, emitting diffused light that was complementary to, and not competitive with, its architectural context.

Quite a different technique was developed with the artist Hildreth Meière for Saint Bartholomew Episcopal Church, Manhattan. The original glazing, installed under the direction of architect Bertram Goodhue, was monochromatic light-gray glass with no subject matter. The effect on the interior had been one of subtle, diffuse, and mysterious light. In the new windows, the effect was to be the same, except with subject matter replacing the simple geometric forms found in the original version. The solution lay in the use of lead cames—soft and bendable boundaries for the glass. Inexpensive commercial gray glass was used as the base. Over it, the design was fabricated with lead cames of varying thicknesses. This unique solution allowed the windows to be "read" both by day and by night. It introduced topical scenes while at the same time retaining an aura of mystery within the sanctuary.

By the late thirties, glass block was a widely utilized building material. An early attempt to break the traditional masonry wall, this type of block became the visually penetrable boundary between indoors and outdoors. It was often used in church basements being turned into worship areas, allowing natural light to filter in while simultaneously providing structural support. Rambusch developed a technique to transform this ordinary commercial material into an artistic and decorative element involving grisaille. The form of decoration is an age-old technique of painting on glass with metal oxides. When properly fired, the oxides fall into the softened surface of the glass and the two materials become one. After lengthy experiments in their own kilns, Rambusch developed and perfected a technique of grisaille painting on hollow-core glass blocks. It was patented and called Bloc de Cor. One project that utilized these blocks was the crypt of Saint John the Evangelist Chapel at Saint John's Seminary, Brighton, Massachusetts. Along its walls are a series of altars where Mass, before Vatican II, was celebrated each day by the priests of the seminary. Above each altar is a rectangular group of fifty-four glass blocks. The twelve blocks in the center of each group hold grisaille portraits of a saint. A duplicate of the likeness of Saint Thomas More was sent to Rome in 1950 for an exhibition at the Vatican.

Using age-old techniques, such as grisaille painting, on new materials produced decorative and affordable results. The same method of painting was used to produce purely decorative blocks, some designed within the confines of a single block. Others, such as the Morning Glory design (fig. 5-10), were conceived to spread over several blocks. This particular design mimics the naturalistic forms of actual morning glories, which have vinelike tendrils that extend and intertwine as they grow upward.

5-7 Frederick W. Christian, designer; *Mary Magdalene and Claire of Assisi: cames pattern*, study, Chapel, Sisters of Saint Martha, Antigonish, NS, 1966. **5-8** *Stained-glass window*, watercolor sketch, Church of Our Lady of Victory (Otto Eggers, architect), Manhattan, ca. 1960. **5-9** *Abraham Lincoln window*, stained glass, Valley Forge Military Academy, Gettysburg, PA, 1950. **5-10** Margarete Overbeck, designer; *Bloc de Cor: Morning glory design*, stained glass, ca. 1958.

Acid etching of flashed glass provided yet another dimension for the artist designing colored-glass windows. To fabricate flashed glass, the blower first collects a gather—a ball of molten glass at the end of a blow tube—then dips the clear gather into a pot of molten, colored glass that immediately fuses with the clear glass. The artisan subsequently blows out the gather into a hinged mold which, after cutting, becomes a flat sheet. This overlay, or flashing, is fabricated in such primary colors as blue, green, or yellow. Sulfuric acid is then applied to the areas that are to be "read" in the design: the top layer is eaten away and the design appears in the base glass as clear white, or whatever is the color of the base glass. The commission for Saint Francis of Assisi Church, Neligh, Nebraska, is an example of this type of very precise and demanding design, with its ruby-flashed glass showing through as an underlayer (fig. 5-11).

In 1940, Rambusch decorated thick plates of clear glass in an unorthodox manner at the Saint Thomas More Chapel, Yale University, for architect Douglas W. Orr. These figures and their garments were carved with jets of high-pressure water and sand, which produced a soft, muted effect. Then the faces and hands of the

5-11 *Saint Francis of Assisi: detail*, flashed glass, golden amber flash with a ruby underlayer, Saint Francis of Assisi Church, Neligh, NE, after 1963. **5-12** *St. Francis of Assisi*, etched glass, Saint Thomas More Chapel (Douglas W. Orr, architect), Yale University, New Haven, CT, 1940. **5-13** Richard Millard, artist; *Portrait of Pia Zadora*, detail of full-size cartoon, 1983. **5-14** Robert Sowers, designer; *Stained-glass window*, American Airlines Terminal, John F. Kennedy Airport, Queens, 1964.

figures, including those in the portrait of Saint Francis of Assisi (fig. 5-12), were carved by hand, using special, electric copper wheels and drills to create these details. The result is a window with sparkle, vitality, and clarity, reminiscent of a finely cut crystal goblet. The reflective quality of glass carved in this way is remarkable.

The invention and general availability of epoxies in the sixties had a dramatic effect on the fabrication of stained-glass windows because pieces of glass could be held together without lead cames. Earlier, in the 1930s, pieces of glass—painted or mirrored—were adhered to a solid background and framed to make an opaque or reflective glass mural. Rambusch made several windows in this technique. With new epoxies, the whole composition could be transparent. Two rather unusual Rambusch commissions used this technique. One was the headboard for the bed of the twin sister of the last Shah of Iran, Ashraf ol-Molouk Pahlavi. Like a splayed tail of a peacock, colorful pieces of glass were glued to a mirror, and they added vitality and a reflective quality to the colors. The second was for Meshulam Riklis, movie mogul and promoter, who wanted to give his then-wife, Pia Zadora, a distinctive gift. He commissioned Rambusch to make a four-by-six-foot stained-glass portrait (fig. 5-13). No lead lines were permitted. Relatively large pieces of colored glass were cut and laid edge to edge on the clear plate-glass base. Artist Richard Millard, who had spent four years in the formal apprentice program at the Rambusch studio, created the likeness of Zadora by building up matted overlays on the glass. In the darker shadowed areas, as many as sixteen layers were needed.

Another twentieth-century technical development in stained-glass window fabrication was the process of embedding chunks of thick, colored, and cast dalle de verre in cement or a cement-like matrix. This technique created the effect of a rugged, translucent mosaic. As technology progressed, epoxy compounds increasingly replaced cement to hold the pieces of glass in place. This technique first was invented in France in the 1930s and became popular in the late 1940s. Although very effective in some settings, it did not lend itself to many traditional fenestrations. Rambusch fabricated many windows using this technique, but the firm also refused several commissions because it felt this technique was incompatible with the architecture of the structure in which it was to be installed.

Just as the International Style of architecture purged interiors of applied decoration and allowed asymmetrical fenestration patterns, its effect can be seen in

stained-glass design as well. Although Rambusch has always made, and continues to make, representational windows, during the 1960s and 1970s, pure color, texture, and line alone were enough to attract and please clients. No longer was it deemed necessary to depict historical or religious events; didactic considerations were forgotten. Rambusch during this time executed many commissions in abstract stained glass. For American Airlines, at Kennedy Airport, independent artist Robert Sowers designed a window to connote movement (fig. 5-14), which his Rambusch studio colleagues fabricated at 40 West 13th Street. Sowers had received this commission largely due to serendipity and his friendship with Viggo Frode Edvard Rambusch. Sowers had been working on another project for the firm when Robert Jacobs of Kahn and Jacobs, the architects of the American Airlines Building, came in one day. Their interaction led to his obtaining the job, underscoring the significance of professional relationships with the Rambusch firm. For several years after its installation in 1964, the wall of glass panels was listed in the Guinness Book of Records as the largest stained-glass window in the world.

Similarly, Lovers Lane United Methodist Church, Dallas, Texas (fig. 5-15), is a building with walls of colored glass. Architect Thomas E. Stanley designed the structure to simulate a jewel box. Taking more than a year to fabricate, the windows cover nearly a quarter of an acre of non-representational stained glass, emphasizing pure color and line. The two-sided walls, which were installed in an accordion pattern for acoustical reasons, have a rhythmic flow of movement, directing one's vision toward the interior chancel and altar. The Rambusch designer for this commission was David Wilson.

5-15 David Wilson, designer; *Nave window*, stained glass, Lovers Lane United Methodist Church (Thomas E. Stanley, architect), Dallas, TX, 1978. **5-16** Leandro Velasco, artist; *The Life of Christ* (center section), **5-17** Leandro Velasco, artist; *The Life of Christ* (left section), and **5-18** Leandro Velasco, artist; *The Life of Christ* (right section), stained glass, Saint Stephen's Episcopal Church (G. Milton Small, architect), Durham, NC, 1976.

In 1976, a commission for Saint Stephen's Episcopal Church, Durham, North Carolina (figs. 5-16 to 5-18), which was designed by the well-known Columbian artist Leandro Velasco, combined the nuances and vitality of pure, colored glass with caming patterns and painting. The result was a triptych twenty-five feet high with a combined length of eighty-five feet. Velasco portrayed the life of Christ in twelve scenes from scripture. The building was designed by G. Milton Small, a student of Ludwig Mies van der Rohe. After it was completed, transparencies of this triptych were displayed on the legendary Kodak billboard, now gone, in Grand Central Station, Manhattan, for Christmas in both 1978 and 1979 (see fig. 4-26). Subsequently, the Field Museum of Natural History, Chicago, used the transparency as the focal point for its holiday celebration in 1981. Velasco's work was also recognized by *Time* magazine, when his stained-glass work was selected for the cover of an issue in 1971 (fig. 5-19), the first time the medium had been celebrated accordingly.

A truly significant commission, completed half a century ago, still holds the attention of those who experience it as well as those who created it. It is the Mapparium (fig. 5-20) in the Mary Baker Eddy Library, Boston. Conceived by architect Chester Lindsay Churchill, its successful completion involved solving many complex problems. Bergethon led the Rambusch design and fabrication team. The challenge was to make

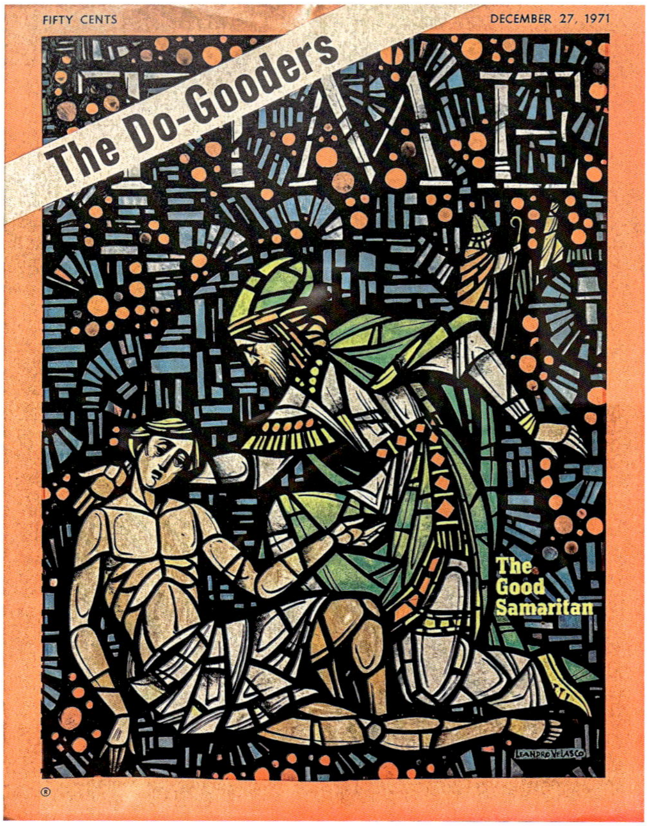

5-19 Leandro Velasco, artist, *Cover of* Time, December 27, 1971.
5-20 *Mapparium*, stained glass, The Mary Baker Eddy Library, (Chester Lindsay Churchill, architect), Boston, MA, 1932–1935.

a globe or spherical room through which a visitor could walk and view the world as if standing inside the earth. The larger project team was made up of Picklington Glass, who formed the curved panels; Rand McNally, who provided cartographic information; and Rambusch, who applied enamel color and text to the panels and then fired them at high temperature. The firm then installed and lighted the 608 panels of tempered and individually molded glass. Each panel represented ten lines of longitude and latitude of the globe. At a scale of twenty-two miles to the inch, a world map of was painted on the inner surface of all the panels. Land masses, political subdivisions, and geographical data required accurate and precise representation.

Subtle gradations in color were achieved after lengthy experimentation. Vitreous-glass enamel, usually used in such situations, would not work. Blues and greens when fired for the third time turned white. In the last phase of trials, the firm discovered that special powders—not paint—produced the desired effect. Red was fired first at 1,359 degrees Fahrenheit, then greens and blues at 1,100. Each panel of glass was fired in its own special cradle, ensuring that the glass would not lose its curved shape at high temperatures.

Each completed panel of glass was then set in a specially made bronze frame, assembled on site in a three-story room, and illuminated from the outside. The architect insisted upon no "hot" spots of light. After days of effort, the work glowed evenly from the illumination of 300 bulbs. It was like an enhanced view from outer space. In the words of the architect in an interview on opening day, November 27, 1935:

> The concave surface represents exactly the whole surface of the earth as it appears in its true spherical shape on the outside of the great ball which we know as earth . . . The Mapparium lends to its geographical service a quiet permeative, although unvoiced, sense that after all, the earth is a simple, intimate place, rightly designed for friendship and unity.

Although hardly performing one of its original tasks of providing accurate geographical information, even now the Mapparium is viewed by approximately 200,000 people each year.

As restoration has become an increasingly significant facet of work at Rambusch, so too has been the case with the stained-glass studio. In relatively recent history, two windows by Louis Comfort Tiffany and one by John La

Farge, both of whom were Frode's contemporaries, could be found on studio workbenches while being expertly conserved. Quite different in scale are several dozen leaded-glass domes that have been removed from their various original locations in railroad stations, state capitols, libraries, or board rooms brought to the studio to be cleaned, repaired, and reinstalled. It is not uncommon that some of these stained-glass works measure more than thirty feet in diameter. A contemporary commission in the Baltimore Penn Station attracted national attention. Three forty-five-foot-diameter saucer domes that had been designed to pour natural light into the main concourse had been covered with a thick layer of tar during World War II as a precautionary measure when blackouts were required. Rambusch succeeded in not only removing the tar but they also replaced broken pieces, recamed weakened leads, and replaced others. This work allowed the skylights to fulfill, once again, their graceful, original purpose. As a result, in 1984, the studio was recognized for "outstanding public service and exceptional craftsmanship" from the US Department of Transportation and the Advisory Council on Historic Preservation.

Two Baltimore projects stand out in the firm's history. The first was a commission of 1985 that necessitated both restoration and re-creation on a grand scale. The Clarence M. Mitchell Courthouse is a magnificent palace of justice in the Beaux-Arts tradition that had opened in 1898. Above the two staircases were four-sided, twenty-four-by-twenty-four-foot domes of stained glass. In each quadrant sat a monumental female figure. These four figures symbolized Fortitude, Charity, Justice, and Prudence, and each was seated on an entablature flanked by two potted, topiary trees. As time went by, the courthouse was renovated, and the domes were concealed under a false ceiling. A restoration of this magnificent space was spearheaded by Judge Joseph Kaplan and supervised by architects Kann & Ammon. Subsequently, an investigation revealed that the domes held less than ten percent of their original glass. Rambusch removed the one quadrant that was almost fully intact. Using this quadrant as a master pattern, along with additional information from period photographs and written accounts, the other seven quadrants were refabricated to match the original. After doing so, the intact quadrant was restored and reinstalled. The second commission was to restore the approximately thirty-six-foot stained-glass dome at the offices of Alex. Brown & Sons (fig. 5-21), which offers an expansive and stately crown to one of the company's central spaces.

In addition to restoration, the Rambusch stained-glass studio continues to design and fabricate new ecclesiastical and secular commissions in many styles and techniques. As in the past, this reflects the diverse talent and skill of its craftspeople. The files of the Rambusch stained-glass studio, with more than 2,000 commissions, read like a textbook of stained-glass techniques and history. The executed work speaks for itself although even commissions less than twenty-five years old have already been lost to damage and demolition. Some of the churches or chapels for which the projects were commissioned are now used for other purposes. Stained-glass windows in more than a few cases have been taken out, dispersed, or destroyed.

Perhaps the greatest contribution of the stained-glass studio to the history of the craft in the United States is quite simply its continued existence. It has always attracted talented designers and craftspeople. Much work has emanated from this fulcrum. The irony is that it has become such a good training ground that it has created a good problem. Staffing records indicate several stained-glass artisans first got their start at the Rambusch studios before striking out on their own to set up specialty workshops.

5-21 *Dome restoration*, stained glass, Alex. Brown & Sons, Baltimore, MD, 1980.

CHAPTER VI

Hotels, Restaurants, and Shops

From the very beginning of the firm's existence, Rambusch has decorated public rooms of hotels and restaurants. In 1906, the firm's advertisement in *Sweet's Indexed Catalogue of Building Construction* lists the Lenore Hotel, Manhattan, as one of its completed commissions. The interior decoration of some of the company's early hotels and restaurants showed a marked similarity to the style and execution of its church interiors of the same period. This common ground is not surprising because Frode Rambusch and designer Knud Laub were responsible for all these areas of work. These designs are characterized by robust fullness and a free, bold effect. Frode and Laub frequently favored heavy, dense borders incorporating naturalistic forms, stylized designs, and geometric shapes. The overall result seems to have been based on both Nordic and Art Nouveau precedents. It is also similar in feeling to the early pieces of then-contemporary craftsman and fellow countryman, Georg Jensen.

Although often directly commissioned by a client, the firm has always worked for architects. In the early years there were many commissions from architect John J. Petit, a partner in the New York firm of Kirby, Petit & Green. In subsequent years, architects Hubbell & Mink, Lee and Eugene Schoen, and others, also commissioned work, as this chapter will illustrate. This discussion will also include the wide-ranging aspects of the company's hotel work, including that for the new entrance to the Waldorf-Astoria in 1930 (fig. 6-1).

Company ledgers and account books indicate that Rambusch decorated many grand and ornate spaces in Manhattan and the metropolitan area. In ledgers, such names as the Union League Club, Century Association, Harvard Club, and the Stork Club are just a few of the many well-established organizations who were clients. A similar scan of Rambusch account books from this period indicates the range of services the firm supplied to Petit for his clients in both Manhattan and other locations, such as New Jersey and Connecticut. John Petit commissioned work at the Hotel McAlpin in Manhattan after 1912, when the first phase of building had been completed. Rambusch decorated a small screen for $7 and three desks were painted, glazed, varnished, and gilded for a total of $129. The firm was paid $435 for "ripping and reversing blue fabric, cutting and stenciling borders, and stenciling valences free hand." In 1918, Petit commissioned Rambusch to decorate several Tiffin tea shops. One of these, at 42nd Street, Manhattan, was painted and decorated, with the "walls prepared and hung with canvas, per contract for $3,165." At another Tiffin shop, a bill for $55 was rendered "for the cleaning, touching up and painting of storefront and entrance and the repairing of decoration and big sign." The relative value of these commissions can be gauged by the daily wages of a standard painter and master painter-decorator at $7.50 and $11, respectively. Later, in 1920, the Claridge Hotel in Manhattan received extensive decorative treatment, consisting of "gilding, glazing, making and graining Circassian walnut," on the walls.

The decoration of Reisenweber's Restaurant on the West side of Manhattan was a further commission gained from Petit in the same year, this time at a cost of $4,000. Heavy beams were "combed, to create the effect of a loosely wood-grained appearance, in a suggestive trompe l'oeil manner." The edges of naturalistic

6-1 Leif Neandross, renderer; *The New Waldorf-Astoria: Park Avenue entrance*, watercolor sketch, Manhattan, 1930.

The Main Restaurant

borders—with birds, animals, and stylized forms—were softened by a bird's tail and the tendrils of a vine projecting below the border edge. Such projections penetrated into the plain wall surface at regular intervals around the room. In one historic photograph, two portly chefs, seemingly almost caricatures, inhale the aromas wafting from their casseroles. These fragrances filled the spandrels of the arch in the grill area. The services that Rambusch thus provided to Petit more than 100 years ago ranged from decorating a screen to decorating a whole restaurant.

Completed in the summer of 1920, the Elks Club, Brooklyn, represented another sizable commission for the company, although not related to Petit's architectural work. Like other projects of this period, the interior exhibits a blending of naturalistically derived forms and geometric decorative devices that were used repetitively. The work was precise, restrained, and classical in concept and execution. The space included large murals with views of elk in their natural habitat.

Petit, at the turn of the century, had designed the sleek and vast Café Savarin (fig. 6-2), which filled most of the basement of the Equitable Building, 120 Broadway, downtown Manhattan, and he additionally conceived the decoration. The new mode—for an updated Savarin at a new location—cost $31,203.86 and was completed in 1923 after the architect's death. Illustrated in a promotional brochure, the café was self-proclaimed as "one of the places of interest in New York, the glorification of the American Grill." Management of the Savarin explained the new uptown venture in 1924 in this way:

> Many important big-business interests have established branches in the 42nd Street neighborhood. The Savarin management decided to follow this trend and provide Café Savarin services to these uptown offices and to the larger number of people using the transportation facilities centering near the Grand Central Terminal.

Scandinavian-inspired designs by Norwegian artists Trygve Hammer and Francis Helving contributed to the decorative scheme that Rambusch carried out for the entire restaurant. The restaurant was large, with several public and private rooms. Savarin's souvenir brochure continues:

> The supreme classics of art in the restaurant are the beautiful mural paintings on the side walls. On all sides, one views what appear to be most unusual and attractive oil paintings. These murals, however, are not made with oil and brushes, but of a new cement material called 'Morene[sp?].' This composition, in the consistency of an emulsion, is susceptible of being treated in colors and is applied with a towel. The paintings represent actual scenery in Norway. The last corner of the wall, left side of the room going in, shows Valdres, a typical landscape of Norway, in the mountainous section of the country such as would correspond to the Adirondacks of America.

It is likely that these environments struck a chord with the wave of Danish immigrants, who, as they gained a foothold in their new country, were also seeking nostalgic connection to what they had left behind.

By 1927, Hubbell & Mink architects commissioned Rambusch to decorate Schumann Sons Jewelry Shop, also in Manhattan. Pompeii and Herculaneum were design sources for the delicate painted decoration that covered the wall of the main salesroom. Mirrors were placed in such a way that customers were surreptitiously under constant surveillance. Perhaps as a metaphor to connect with wealthy customers, a private room for special clients was decorated in the manner of the Italian Renaissance: the deep, rich colors and heavy wooden trim recall a time when all of the arts were integrated at a high level for patrons of significant means.

Architects Lee and Eugene Schoen brought their discriminating client, restaurateur Louis H. Saltzman, to Rambusch in 1930. Saltzman wanted every room in his large, eponymous restaurant in Manhattan to have a different character. The cost of the painting and lighting design ultimately was $8,000. Downstairs in the restaurant, low arches supported by heavy round columns were decorated in a tight, repetitive, geometric Art Deco design with stylized rosettes (fig. 6-3). The shallow-vaulted ceilings had large-scale floral sprays springing from each corner. These gay, free-hand designs were reminiscent of traditional Scandinavian rosemaling painting techniques. Real roses were the inspiration for this stylized, but recognizable and artistic, interpretive rendering. The wooden floor was painted to resemble large, irregular stone slabs, simulating a terrace. All these details combined to create the atmosphere of a rustic country inn.

6-2 *Main dining room*, Café Savarin (John J. Petit, architect), Manhattan, 1924. **6-3** Leif Neandross, designer; *Downstairs dining room*, Saltzman's Restaurant (Lee and Eugene Schoen, architects), Manhattan, 1930.

The panache of then-contemporary Art Deco style characterized the entrance and the main upstairs dining room. Leif Neandross created a design in gray and black, with airy circles and angles interspersed with lithesome female figures, for large rectangular columns. These painted surfaces were illuminated by a sliver of light from a recessed ceiling trough, located just above the juncture of each column with the ceiling (fig. 6-4). This feature gave the illusion of a halo of light, making the capital glow. The center of the dining-room ceiling was decorated with an elaborate, paint-and-gold-leaf composition (fig. 6-5), using motifs popular during the period: angular forms juxtaposed to circular ones, along with clouds and signs of the zodiac. The whole was a study in contrasting shapes and tonal values, and was selected for the annual exhibition in 1931 at the Architectural League. Attesting to Saltzman's demand for fine detail was the monogram painted at the crest of the top rail of each chair.

Some hotel projects were wide ranging. The original Waldorf-Astoria Hotel, on Fifth Avenue and West 34th Street, which had opened on March 13, 1893, is a case in point. George A. Glaenzer (1848–1915) had been identified as the decorator and was one of the guests at the celebratory dinner, along with Henry J. Hardenbergh, architect of the project. Rambusch executed work in the hotel and business records indicate the firm participated in the original contract as a sub-contractor. In 1922, the firm refurbished the lobby, the roof garden, and the chef's dining room. This latter space was large, commodious, and elaborately decorated. The Waldorf-Astoria attracted famous travelers and clientele from New York's Four Hundred, the list of fashionable New York society. The hotel and the published recipes of its restaurant fare legitimized a trend that was to flourish in American society—namely, dining out.

In a time of many flamboyant characters, Lucius Boomer, manager of the Waldorf-Astoria, became a legendary figure. Two bills in the Rambusch archives predate his connection with the hotel. One was for work at the Hotel McAlpin in 1920 "for painting for Roof Garden as per order of Mr. Boomer, $250." The other, rendered to architect John Petit, was "for cleaning, touching up, glazing and polishing ivory furniture" for Boomer, in his apartment at 815 Park Avenue. He demanded the best for himself. Lucius Boomer would become an important Rambusch client.

As the fashionable district of the city moved uptown from midtown Manhattan, so did the hotels that catered to residents and visitors alike. The decision to erect a new Waldorf-Astoria Hotel on Park Avenue, north of Grand Central Terminal at 50th Street, was the brainchild of none other than Lucius Boomer. It was his chef-d'oeuvre. Schultze and Weaver were selected as architects and after several unsuccessful attempts to please Boomer, Rambusch was engaged by the architects to design the overall scheme and color styling. The second Waldorf-Astoria filled an entire city block. Rambusch set the color palette and designed and executed painted decoration for the entrance off Park Avenue (see fig. 6-1; fig. 6-6), all the lobbies and public rooms on the main floor, Peacock Alley, and the Norse Grill. Company ledgers show bills for March 1931, $29,200; June 1931, $4,184; July 1931, $973; September 1931, $85.50; and November 1931, $50; so work executed there was substantial and ongoing.

Lucius Boomer's wife was Norwegian, and she perhaps had a say in the decoration of the hotel's spaces. Peppered throughout the lobbies were Scandinavian decorative touches, including specially woven rugs that were a representation of the Norse-based Yggdrasil tree. The designs on the grills of the ventilation systems were based on those of the Stockholm town hall. The Norse Grill, on the Lexington Avenue side of the hotel, received special attention. Its columns, wainscoting, and fireplace were made of limestone. Heavy wooden beams traversed the ceiling in the manner of a great Viking banquet hall. Carved and polychromed elements decorated each beam. These were inspired by designs that had been discovered at Oseberg: especially animals and plant designs found on exhumed swords and artifacts from a funeral Viking ship. Even the flatware (fig. 6-7) was designed for this room by Rambusch. The west wall was dominated by a massive, carved-limestone fireplace. The mural above it portrayed a map of the environs of Manhattan and Long Island, with the locations of country clubs and golf courses highlighted. It provided the only, and oddly discordant, note in the room. For many years, while the hotel remained independently owned, Rambusch continued to carry out decorating projects for the Waldorf-Astoria. As late as 1959, they restored the Jansen Suite, patterned after the Maison Jansen, Paris.

Both the Rambusch Decorating Company and Boomer linked the old and new at the Waldorf-Astoria. Rambusch did so with their decorative design and Boomer did so in January 1940 with the installation of a special plaque in the east foyer of the new building. Made of bronze, it honored former employees who had worked at both locations. By that time, however, the original establishment at midtown was no longer

6-4 Leif Neandross, designer; *Main dining room: column detail*, Saltzman's Restaurant (Lee and Eugene Schoen, architects), Manhattan, 1930. **6-5** Leif Neandross, designer; *Main dining room: ceiling detail*, Saltzman's Restaurant (Lee and Eugene Schoen, architects), Manhattan, 1930. **6-6** Leif Neandross, renderer; *The New Waldorf-Astoria: Park Avenue entrance detail, vase made by Edward F. Caldwell & Company*, watercolor sketch, Manhattan, 1930.

6-7 Leif Neandross, designer; *Flatware: recto and verso*, made for the Norse Grill, The New Waldorf-Astoria, Manhattan, 1930.

extant. Nevertheless, then as now, the hotel's name evokes the apogee of luxury, consummate with Boomer's original plans.

It was not only in Manhattan, however, where the firm was awarded large hotel projects. For a period of several years, from the late 1920s to the early 1930s, Rambusch had so much work in Florida that they became incorporated in that state as well as in New York. Schultze and Weaver were the managing architects and designers of the Breakers, Palm Beach, the brainchild of Addison Mizner, who described the resort hotel as: "Bastard-Spanish-Moorish-Romanesque-Gothic-Renaissance-Bull-Market-Damn-the-Expense-Style." The Cloister Inn (fig. 6-8), now simply known as the Cloister, had every decorative painting technique lavished on its interiors. Authenticity was a priority. Tiles on the floors were cracked and then pieced together again to lend an air of age to the new building. The huge dining room, which Mizner informally referred to as the Chapel, had a deeply coffered ceiling that was gilded and polychromed. Arches that dominated the Mizner Room were painted to give the effect of a stonework arch. Vast plaster walls were all hand-palmed, instead of being finished with a trowel, in a soft gray. Leif Neandross was the designer on this project. In October 1929, a bill was rendered for $3,800; it was followed by one for an additional $25,000 in December of the same year.

Eating out was becoming increasingly popular after the Depression eased. Department stores had restaurants, and a new restaurant at Bamberger's department store, Newark, New Jersey, in the late 1930s, was decorated by the firm (fig. 6-9). This location was the headquarters for the retailer's regional stores. It offered an environment that made store goers comfortable. With classically inspired swags; Art-Nouveau-inspired floral roundels on the main columns; and a scenic view of a historic, urban street city plan; shoppers could think about past, present, and future as they relaxed over a midday meal. Consumerism was on the rise, as the nation moved toward the beginning of World War II.

Chains of restaurants, each catering to a different clientele such as Child's (fig. 6-10), Schrafft's, Morrison's, or Willow cafeterias, all had Rambusch decorate their restaurants in Manhattan and around the country. But it was at Horn & Hardart that interesting insights into the decorative and societal trends of three decades occurred. Horn & Hardart had introduced a new concept of complete self-service, an elaborate system imported from Germany and patented in this country as the Automat. Labor saving and practical, it also was in keeping with the streamlining and efficiency characteristics of the period.

A Philadelphia-based firm, Horn & Hardart entered the New York market with its first restaurant in July 1912. Although a self-service operation, Horn & Hardart wanted to provide a genteel setting to attract appropriate customers. From the outset, the firm was concerned with attractive decoration, extensive and excellent maintenance, and keeping everything up to date. Paintings, handsome lighting fixtures, stained glass, murals, and fine art metal work were included along with nutritious meals prepared in their own commissary. The central and dominant feature of the first Manhattan Horn & Hardart restaurant (fig. 6-11) was a massive central column, embellished with a confection of plaster. Stenciled patterns and free-hand painted decoration studded by single light bulbs were also part of its decorative scheme. About twenty years later, this restaurant interior underwent a renovation; the central column was stripped

6-8 Leif Neandross, designer; *The Cloister Inn: main lobby*, Boca Raton Hotel (Addison Mizner and Schultze and Weaver, architects), Boca Raton, FL, 1929.

The American Architect, November, 1932

6-9 *Restaurant: interior*, Bamberger's, Newark, NJ, ca. 1938. **6-10** *Advertisement, depicting mural at Child's Restaurant*, R.C.A Building (Pruitt & Brown, architects), Manhattan, 1932. **6-11** *Interior*, Horn & Hardart Automat, 1557 Broadway, Manhattan, ca. 1912. **6-12** *Interior*, Horn & Hardart Automat, 2712 Broadway, Manhattan, 1930.

of its plaster ornament and the single bulbs removed. Rambusch decorated several other locations, including the Automat that opened on 2712 Broadway, which, in 1930, was enlivened with geometric Art Moderne motifs (fig. 6-12).

Another Philadelphia company, D'Ascenzo Studios, supplied stained glass and some painting and decoration for Rambusch projects during the 1920s. So did the New York firm of Mack Jenny and E. F. Tyler. By and large, it was almost exclusively a Rambusch account, a business relationship that lasted until the 1960s. One particular ledger page for December 1933 shows three separate listings for Horn & Hardart jobs. New York architects were employed to build these restaurants in many locations in the New York metropolitan area; control for the interiors was firmly lodged in the hands of the Philadelphia house architect, Ralph Becker. Rambusch would create a decorative scheme and prepare large-scale samples or mock-ups in the restaurant. Becker would come up from Philadelphia, inspect, and request changes or give approval. Then work would proceed, often at night after the restaurant was closed. Rambusch designer Leif Neandross remembered designing a Spanish-style interior, especially at the request of Mrs. Hardart.

The evolution and diminution of Horn & Hardart work was characteristic of what was happening in most commercial interiors during the 1950s and '60s. Treatment of interiors became simpler and surfaces remained unadorned. Instead of colors being specially mixed or subtle glazes applied, off-the-shelf, stock paint colors were used by maintenance staff. Painted surfaces were covered with coated wall coverings that were washed down periodically to conform to the sanitary code. Instead of decorative painting in a series of original designs, scenic wallpaper was utilized.

After World War II, the genteel boarding houses of Manhattan began to disappear and the middle class began to move to the suburbs. Horn & Hardart attracted a different kind of patron, one interested in efficiency, anonymity, and low-cost, undistinguished meals. In response, strict utility prevailed in the interiors of these cafeterias.

Utility, low-maintenance, and more frequent but inexpensive decorative changes—often executed by house maintenance crews—constituted the trend in restaurants and hotels well into the mid- to late 1960s. Restaurant Associates' initial venture, the Forum of the Twelve Caesars at Rockefeller Center, was the first in 1957 of what was to constitute a slight reversal in that

COLD DRINKS
HOT DRINKS
CAKES

6-13 William Campbell Walsh, mural designer; Venetian Art Mosaic, fabricator; *Forum of the Twelve Caesars* (William Pahlmann Associates, interior decoration), mosaic of marble, Venetian smalti, and stone tesserae, 57 West 48th Street, Rockefeller Center, 1957. **6-14** Julian Zimmerman, designer; Ronald Millard, artist; *Mural*, made for L'Enfant Plaza Hotel, Washington, DC, ca. 1980. **6-15** Benjamin Baldwin, designer; *Reflections Restaurant*, Americana Hotel (Roger Ferri, architect), Fort Worth, TX, 1981.

trend. William Pahlmann & Associates, a renowned interior decorating firm of the period, requested Rambusch to design and create the full-size cartoon of a large mosaic. William Campbell Walsh did so, as head of the mural department in Rambusch Studios. Costante Crovatto's firm, Venetian Art Mosaic, which Rambusch helped form, fabricated the work out of imported marble, Venetian smalti (colored glass or enamel stones), and natural stone tesserae (fig. 6-13). Filling one wall of the restaurant, it provided a subtle richness to the interior. Waiters were dressed in reproductions of Roman legionnaire uniforms. Italian antiques were used as accents. A new trend was discernible.

Even as late as 1974, when Loews commissioned Rambusch to paint two original ten-by-eight-foot murals in the manner of Watteau (fig. 6-14) for their L'Enfant Plaza Hotel, Washington, DC, it was atypical. About this time, however, older hotels began to discover and take interest in refurbishing and preserving their handsome, often beautifully detailed interiors. In 1979 at Hardenbergh's mansard-roofed iconic building, the Plaza Hotel, Manhattan, Rambusch was commissioned to work in the Oak Room. The firm cleaned Everett Shinn's murals in the adjacent bar that had become dirty from accumulated grime and smoke. The molded ceiling was cleaned and oiled. Original bronze chandeliers were removed, cleaned, rewired, and fitted with uplight to provide more general illumination.

New restaurants and hotels with increasing frequency began commissioning fine custom work. In 1981, the Americana Hotel in Fort Worth, Texas (fig. 6-15), required polychroming and glazing to achieve the desired effect on several giant, tulip-shaped columns. Rambusch also installed a glass mosaic-lined reflecting pool.

In 1984, John Coleman, owner of the Ritz-Carlton at the edge of Central Park, Manhattan, needed a pair of large, distinctive, bronze, bracketed lighting fixtures for the exterior. He also had a very tight schedule. Rambusch, after settling with the client on a general shape and the type of detailing, went to its files and produced—in one day—a set of working drawings for a fixture designed and fabricated in 1937 for Saint Ignatius Loyola Church, Manhattan. With the knowledge and full consent of both parties, the original lantern was used as a pattern and the new fixtures were put in place for the opening of the hotel. Today, the Rambusch bronze bracketed lantern has become the trademark of the hotel. The interest in quality custom-made objects was proven, making this outcome a hallmark of what Rambusch can do.

In the early part of this century when Rambusch first offered its services for painted decoration, art metal, and stained glass, this work could have been supplied by innumerable craftsmen and art-craft studios. In the 1980s, Rambusch was perhaps the only survivor still able to render these multiple services. Rambusch had always been a union shop. Gradually, by this decade, it became impossible to compete with non-union pricing. As the senior-decorator staff died off, the decorative painting department closed. Along with offering restoration services, however, using skills and resources in the latter realm, the parlor of the Villard Houses (fig. 6-16), was restored to its Gilded Age splendor. The company is a mini conglomerate of sorts, with specialized craft artisans able to restore old objects and create new ones, a topic that is explored later in this book.

6-16 *Parlor: interior restoration*, Villard Houses, later the Helmsley Palace Hotel and now the Lotte Plaza Hotel (Joseph Morrill Wells of McKim, Mead & White, architects 1881–1885), Manhattan, 1975.

CHAPTER VII

Theaters and Movie Houses

Within the first decade of its existence, the Rambusch Decorating Company was embellishing theaters. That undertaking is not surprising because theaters have many characteristics in common with churches, a building type with which the firm had vast experience. In an advertisement of 1906 in *Sweet's Indexed Catalogue of Building Construction*, the Cincinnati Grand Opera House was listed as a completed commission. The driving force behind this spectacular project was the politician and businessman Mark Hanna. Borders, ceilings, and cornices were painted with Renaissance-inspired decoration. Frode Rambusch designed the pattern for yellow cut velvet that was specially woven and stretched, over a base of flannel, onto the walls of the opera house. Family lore has it that a yard or two of the fabric was brought home, and Frode's wife made a shirtwaist, with leg-of-mutton sleeves, which she wore on festive occasions.

By 1910 and soon after, several commissions came in closer to home, beginning with the Orpheum Theatre, Jersey City (figs. 7-1 and 7-2). Later, there were the Crescent, Fulton (figs. 7-3 and 7-4), Broadway, Empire, and Casino theatres in Brooklyn; the Alhambra (fig. 7-5), the American (with its famed roof garden), and the Colonial in Manhattan; and Percy Williams's Bronx Theatre in that borough. All were decorated by Rambusch. In Manhattan, theaters offering popular vaudeville shows were being constructed in the area around Union Square and on 14th Street. Entrepreneurs B. S. Moss and Sol Brill engaged Rambusch to design and decorate the interior of their flagship house, the Jefferson (fig. 7-6), located on East 14th Street. Moss and Brill owned a chain of theaters, each named after an American president. The Jefferson could be termed the first of these deluxe theaters—a vaudeville house catering to the carriage trade. The ceiling above the stage's proscenium arch once held an oval, cameo-like roundel where three Muses had been painted by Frode in 1913. But, sadly, their frozen attitudes of playful dance are now gone. The building, with its elegantly proportioned dome, was demolished in 2000.

The vitality and glamour of vaudeville was short-lived, pushed out by a rapidly developing motion-picture industry in nearby Fort Lee, New Jersey. First introduced as additions to live vaudeville acts, movies soon took over the whole stage. Just as the Jefferson was opening in 1913, Thomas W. Lamb was putting the finishing touches on The Strand, on Broadway between 47th and 48th Streets, for Mitchell and Moe Mark. It was designed specifically for showing movies: it was the first of the great movie palaces.

In less than two decades, film shorts that had originally been introduced as extra features would take precedence over vaudeville acts and eventually push those entertainers off the stage altogether. By the late 1920s, the Rambusch Decorating Company was creating sumptuous movie palaces for such architects as Lamb, along with Walter W. Ahlschlager, C. W. and George L. Rapp, and promoters Fox, Warner Brothers, William Brandt,

Top, left to right: 7-1 *Partial view of theater* and **7-2** *Proscenium arch: detail*, Orpheum Theatre, Jersey City, NJ, 1910. **Middle, left to right: 7-3** *Partial view of theater* and **7-4** *Proscenium arch: detail*, Fulton Theatre (William H. McElfatrick, architect), Brooklyn, before 1908. **Bottom, left to right: 7-5** *Partial view of theater*, rendering, Alhambra (originally known as the Harlem Auditorium, John B. McElfatrick & Son, architect), Manhattan, before 1905. **7-6** *View of stage and roundel above proscenium arch*, Jefferson Theatre (George Keister and Thomas White Lamb, architects, 1913), Manhattan, photograph from ca. 1955.

NOTHING BUT
THE TRUTH
STANTON
STANTON
DOUGLAS FAIRBANKS
IN "THE IRON MASK"
HEAR DOUG TALK
DYNAMIC/ DASHING/ DOUG

and many others. For the Loew's chain alone, the firm designed and decorated more than fifty theaters. With an expandable workforce, often the decoration of as many as ten theaters would be in progress concurrently. Historically, winter was a slack season for painting work, but so great was the pressure that for more than a decade records indicate that there was work for master decorators the year round—a most unusual situation.

The scope of Rambusch's involvement in these several hundred theater commissions varied—from total design control (as with the Roxy) to simply execution (as with Radio City Music Hall). Often, for simple neighborhood theaters, Rambusch presented a package that included decorating, lighting, carpeting, and drapery designs to the owner or architect.

A sampling of the firm's books from 1926 through 1932 reveals the geographic spread and wide price range of the firm's commissions for movie theaters (see Appendix D). Representative examples include the Stanton, Philadelphia (figs. 7-7 to 7-9), and Loew's Midland, Kansas City, Missouri (fig. 7-10). From reading these ledgers of commissions, one would not guess that America was in the grips of the Great Depression. Rather, it exemplifies the delay often felt by the finishing trades in times of economic downturns. This occurs, in part,

7-7 *Street View*, **7-8** *Proscenium arch*, and **7-9** *Interior*, Stanton Theatre, Philadelphia, PA, ca. 1929.

because money for interior decoration is allocated at the time an original general contract for the building is drawn up. After the economy rebounds, a firm is often three to five years behind in the resumption of normal business and therefore the last to feel economic improvement.

An American invention, the movie palace, was a high point in the history of American decorative arts. A completely controlled artificial environment created for the masses, the movie theater was, in reality, a palace for the people. Eager moviegoers swarmed to these places not only to see a film but also to experience vicariously the grandeur of times past—to primp in a French boudoir, lounge in a Moorish sultan's hall, or witness the spectacle of a wedding procession for a Maharaja's daughter (fig. 7-11). The creators of these environments were fully aware of the power they wielded. Lamb was a preeminent practitioner of this genre. In an issue of *Motion Picture News* dated June 29, 1928, he wrote the following:

> I noticed the indications of an impending change in the temperament and moods of the American public with regard to the design and decoration of such public institutions as motion picture theatres. I noted a lessening in the response of the average patron to the charm of architectural backgrounds patterned after the works of the Adam brothers. There was an underlying demand for something more gay, more flashy, a development for which there is much precedent in the history of architecture. For this reason, I began to favor in my designs an entirely different style, leaning towards the periods of Louis XVI and the very rich productions in the Italian Baroque style.
>
> During the course of the years in which I have specialized in the planning and building of motion picture theatres, architecture has become so important that the interiors of the theatres now are really educational for all those who are interested in this art, in decorative painting, modeling, etc. It is most essential today for the architect to follow a style to the most minute detail.
>
> With thousands and thousands of young people intensely interested in the arts, the theatre architect is assured of a wide and discriminating public for his productions. . . .

In answer to Lamb's endorsement, the Rambusch firm took out an advertisement in *Architectural Forum* (fig. 7-12), expressing its appreciation for his "continued confidence." As a nod to Lamb's work, the firm also

7-10 Leif Neandross, designer; *Partial view of theatre*, Loew's Midland Theatre, Kansas City, MO, 1927. **7-11** *Mural of Wedding Procession of Maharaja's Daughter*, sketch for Loew's State Theatre (Thomas W. Lamb, architect), Syracuse, NY, 1921. **7-12** *Advertisement* in *Architectural Forum*, September 1930.

included an interior image of the Loew's Theatre at 175th Street, Manhattan, which Lamb had designed.

In the same year, Rambusch completed design work on the Hollywood Theatre, also in Manhattan. The Grand Foyer (fig. 7-13), articulated by double-height Corinthian columns, was sumptuously decorated with layered patterns and gold-leaf encrustations that were illuminated by a dramatic chandelier. Above the proscenium arch (fig. 7-14), the firm was responsible for trompe-l'œil painting made to look like stretched silk damask in the shallow dome. Such theaters represented the pinnacle of movie-palace extravagance.

Another facet of this pinnacle was the work of John Eberson, who created the "atmospheric theater." This type of movie palace initially simulated the outdoors in the mode of an architectural fantasy (fig. 7-15), some of which contained mural references to the Roman campagna. Over time, however, several of Eberson's designs responded to changes in taste, especially influences of Art Deco and the industrial sleekness of Art Moderne (fig. 7-16 shows Rambusch-patented Downlites, incidentally, in the decorative scheme; figs. 7-17 to 7-19 show other Eberson theaters from the late 1930s). Rambusch executed countless commissions for the range of his work, including the Silver Spring Theatre, as well as designs by other architects who were masters of their trade. One might ask, what exactly was the relationship between the architect and the interior designer in these vast and complicated enterprises? In the same interview printed in *Motion Picture News*, Lamb mentioned only one name:

> I want to take this opportunity to thank Mr. Harold W. Rambusch for his excellent handling of my ideas in the theatres illustrated herein. The decorative scheme is the most essential part of the house after the architectural background has been set and the quality of this decoration, though inspired by the architect, is largely left for the decorator to complete.

The initial decision about the particular historic style of the interior was often a joint one between architect, designer, and client. Once determined, the mode of expression, selection and arrangements of colors, and the details of execution were all in the hands of the interior decorator. The decorator's knowledge of color, tonality, and nuance, along with their experience and understanding of the change that takes place between a small color rendering and actual placement of color on

the vast walls, were all brought to bear during the actual implementation of a commission. As Lamb asserted: "Without qualification, it is [the interior decorator] who establishes the final tone and atmosphere of the room."

Rambusch not only set the color and tone in a particular room. The company also managed lighting, which created the ambiance of a controlled environment—or series of environments—which influenced the patron, even unconsciously. A mannered progression often unfolded from the vestibule (where only a hint was given of what was to come) to the richness of the lobbies, and then, eventually, to the grandeur and opulence of the auditorium.

However, the areas of control, and the role of the decorator, vis-à-vis the architect, were to change within the space of a decade. By this time in America, generally the architect was an academically schooled individual. Consequently, architects were taking over more intellectual, as well as actual, control of the building process and leaving fewer matters to the sole discretion of experienced, competent craftsmen. This trend, which began in the late 1920s, would eventually widen into a split, separating those who conceived the decorating scheme and those who only executed it under supervision. Two

of America's greatest movie houses, both of which were decorated by the Rambusch Decorating Company, exemplify this change in dynamic.

S. L. "Roxy" Rothafel was the acknowledged impresario of movie palaces. He was determined in 1927 to make the theater that was being erected on the northeast corner of 50th Street and 7th Avenue, and slated to bear his name, the apotheosis of its genre. Having worked frequently and successfully with Rambusch, he was puzzled when the firm did not enter the widely advertised competition. Deluged by sketches made on speculation by firms across the country, Roxy called and personally invited Rambusch to enter a bid. Harold Rambusch refused and told Roxy that that the competition was not the way to go about it. He prophesied that the final result would only end in confusion. Months elapsed and a second call from the board still could not persuade Rambusch. Finally, with opening day alarmingly close, another frantic call was issued: would Mr. Rambusch please come immediately to meet with the assembled board? Harold entered the room. The massive mahogany table was piled high with competition entries and the walls were covered with sketches. Roxy pleaded with Harold for an opinion. Harold responded that a selection of judgment was impossible; there were simply too many choices. What was now needed was a manager to orchestrate the entire project by setting the scheme in motion and getting the work done on time. Harold then left the room. The next day, the Rambusch Decorating Company received the contract to design, supervise, and manage the entire project.

The sketch for the interior (fig. 7-20) was prepared by Rambusch's chief designer, Leif Neandross. It was accepted and the work began at a frantic pace. Several of the firms who had submitted proposals were engaged as subcontractors for certain aspects of the work. Every part of the interior was within the jurisdiction of Rambusch. For example, carpet samples made for the domestic

7-13 *Grand Foyer* and **7-14** Leif Neandross, designer; *Proscenium arch: detail*, Hollywood Theatre (Mayer & Schneider [M&S] Circuit; Harrison G. Wiseman, architect), Manhattan, 1930.

7-15 *Partial view of theater*, Pitkin Theatre (Loew's circuit; John Eberson, interior architect), Brooklyn, ca. 1929. **7-16** *Interior: showing ceiling Downlites in decorative scheme* and **7-17** *Partial view of the stage*, Silver Spring Theatre (John Eberson, architect), Silver Spring, MD, 1938. **7-18** *Partial view of theater*, Auburn Schine Theatre (John Eberson, architect), Auburn, NY, 1939. **7-19** *View of the screen*, Beverly Theatre (John Eberson, architect), Washington, DC, 1938.

SILVER SPRING SHOPPING CENTER
SILVER SPRING, MARYLAND
ALEXA REALTY CO., OWNE
JOHN EBERSON, ARCHITECT
MOHLER CONSTRUCTION CO., BUIL
SEPT. 16, 1938 No. 11

market were woefully inadequate in their decorative impact. Harold casually tore an ad from the back of a magazine showing a paisley design on a cravat. He had this enlarged sixty times. The resulting carpet, woven by Mohawk Industries, was for many years the company's most popular commercial item. And, after its debut in the Roxy Theatre, this particular carpet pattern appeared in movie theaters around the country for several years. As previously advocated by Lamb, who served as a consultant on the Roxy, the interior decorator controlled the interior space and created the atmosphere that engaged the moviegoer and set the tone for the entire entertainment experience.

A few years later in another great theater, the dynamics were very different. Despite the Depression, work on Rockefeller Center continued. In addition to actually providing jobs, the project was a harbinger of better times to come and had a profound psychological effect on the city and the nation. It was a living act of faith in the intrinsic strength of the American capitalist economy. The large complex that comprised the buildings of Rockefeller Center was designed by a consortium of architectural firms: Reinhard & Hofmeister; Corbett, Harrison & MacMurray; and Hood and Fouilhoux. Rambusch was awarded many commissions to work on both the exterior and interior of numerous buildings in this brilliantly conceived city-within-a-city. For more than a decade, the firm was retained to maintain all the artwork at Rockefeller Center. In the late fifties, management decided that, in the future, in-house maintenance personnel would assume this responsibility. Lack of knowledge, skill, and inexperience all combined to produce some uncomfortable results. In the years after this decision, Rambusch was called upon to restore its own work at Rockefeller Center because it had not been well cared for.

An entry in the Rambusch ledger for September 9, 1932, reads: "Rockefeller Center Theatre #10." (The name "Radio City" did not appear until several months later). Wallace K. Harrison determined all the interior decoration and set the colors to be used in the 6,000-seat theater. Harrison's aim was to create a new kind of

atmosphere, one that would make a bold, modern statement. He decided on a scheme of silver and blue for the lobby. Following the terms of the contract, Rambusch covered the vast lobby ceiling with oxidated-aluminum leaf to give the effect of silver. A few days before the theater was scheduled to open, Roxy—who was in charge of the house—came in and vehemently objected to the effect. In fact, he rejected outright the decorative treatment of the space. Knowing Rambusch's long association with Roxy, the architects called Harold in the hope that he might influence Roxy's opinion. However, Harold agreed with Roxy—the effect of silver on audiences was chilling, and not conducive to the warm and friendly atmosphere he wanted in a theater. Two days later, Rambusch received a contract to put gold leaf over the silver tone on the lobby ceiling (fig. 7-21). Within a forty-eight-hour period it was finished for opening day: Christmas, 1932. In the words of Lamb: "Gold is the acme of wealth, warmth, and coziness."

Clearly, the role of the interior decorator was in a state of change. The age of specialization had begun

7-20 Leif Neandross designer, *Partial view of theater*, sketch, Roxy Theatre (Walter W. Ahlschlager, architect), Manhattan, 1927.
7-21 *Lobby, showing gold leaf on ceiling*, Radio City Music Hall, (Edward Durell Stone & Donald Deskey, architects), Manhattan, 1932.

to grow in America, and, with it, a separation between those making theoretical decisions or selections and those with the actual experience that comes with execution. More and more decision-making power, especially regarding interior design and decoration, was being assumed by architects.

Treatment of the vast, scalloped ceilings in the Radio City auditorium exemplifies the importance of a craftsman's knowledge of both materials and their actual practical application. A dynamic and changeable effect was desired to vary the mood of the streamlined space. Because of their many years of experience and experimentation, Rambusch had learned that certain colored lights could selectively pick up the same color on an applied surface and thereby give the effect of a single hue. In order to achieve this effect, the ceiling of the Music Hall was hand-sponged with three different colors. On close inspection, the result was a mottled effect with some of the prepared white plaster base still visible. When red lights, hidden in coves, were shown on the horizontal surface, the ceiling appeared to be red. The same effect was possible with blue or yellow lights. Each light picked up its companion color on the ceiling. Thus, the ceiling could be orchestrated and modulated, just as a mighty Wurlitzer organ could do with sound.

After the Depression, theater construction slowed. Consider a cluster of theaters in Titusville, Pennsylvania (fig. 7-22); Huntington Station, New York (fig. 7-23); and Charleston, West Virginia (fig. 7-24; the latter of which cost $3,491). Each offered an inventive decorative scheme to the client. But none, however, would ever match the grandeur, expense, or decorative ingenuity of the heyday of the American movie palace. In the post–World War II sprawl of suburbia, "shoe-box" movie theaters were tucked into many shopping malls. Although some of these theaters were somewhat elaborately decorated, most were painted a single color or covered with a washable wall covering. An attempt at "decoration" might be made with a gaudy lighting fixture or a lone chandelier placed in the truncated lobby. In the case of the Tennessee Theatre (fig. 7-25), Nashville, Rambusch offered a metal mural to fill a limited, subdued space in the 1950s. By this time, functionalism and economy were the watch words and they only continued to be more so in subsequent decades.

One exception of the general trend to economize in the fifties and sixties—by using in-house maintenance personnel to freshen up or paint out original decoration—were the aims of flamboyant impresario, Billy Rose. It is

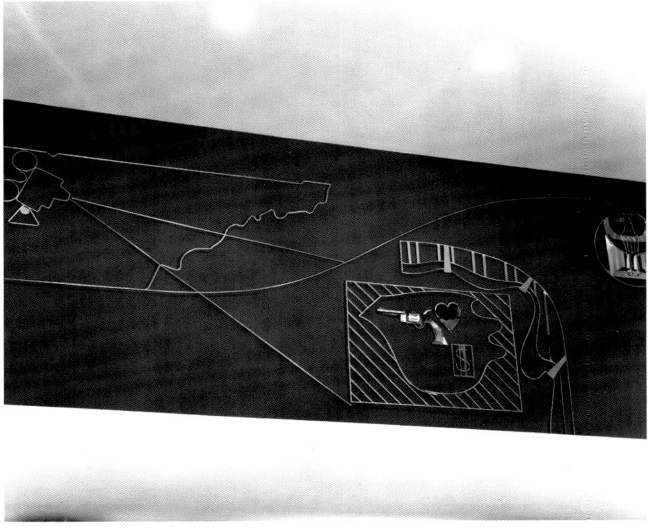

7-22 *View of the house*, Penn Theatre (Warner Brothers' circuit; Victor A. Rigaumont, architect), Titusville, PA, 1939. **7-23** *Wall decoration and lighting*, Huntington Station Theatre, Huntington Station, NY, ca. 1940. **7-24** *Proscenium arch*, Virginia Theatre, Charleston, WV, 1944. **7-25** *Lobby mural*, Tennessee Theatre, Nashville, TN, 1950.

possible that he became acquainted with the Rambusch Decorating Company when Rose was manager of the Hippodrome, in Manhattan, where the firm was completing contracts. In any case, he developed his own empire and in 1959, invited the company to execute the decorative scheme of theater set designer Oliver Messel, shown on a sixteen-by-twenty-by-ten-inch paper model rendered in watercolors. This was intended for the old National Theatre that was then renamed the Billy Rose Theatre in Manhattan. Rose was also the last in the line of Rambusch clients for whom the firm designed and executed elaborate interior schemes in houses or apartments of movie barons. His spacious, double townhouse on East 93rd Street was also lavishly decorated, painted, glazed, and gilded by the firm's craftspeople. These projects included murals and trompe-l'œil borders along with many other types of work.

As the heart of America's great cities were stricken by urban blight, great metropolitan movie palaces were left to languish. Some movie houses were divided into several smaller theaters. The Brooklyn Paramount was converted into a college basketball court. In 1963, Rambusch even turned one—Loew's Woodside—into a church (fig. 7-26). Many theaters were demolished to make way for parking lots. The Loew's theater in Columbus, Ohio,

7-26 *Sanctuary*, Saint Sebastian Church (formerly on the Loew's circuit), Woodside, Queens, 1963.

designed by Thomas Lamb and built in 1928, had an interior designed and executed by Rambusch that seemed destined for demolition in 1969. However, one citizen, Mrs. Kenneth (Mary) Bishop, refused to accept this death sentence and spearheaded a drive to save and restore the grand house as the Ohio Theatre. Individual efforts such as hers were immeasurably helped by the Main Street Project that was sponsored by the National Trust for Historic Preservation. Revitalization of urban downtown areas proved then, as it does now, to be both historically and economically beneficial.

At the Ohio Theatre, Rambusch in the early 1980s was commissioned to restore work it had executed half a century before. Peeling polychromed and gilded walls and ceilings were restored and stabilized. Ornate plaster work was painstakingly cleaned and, where necessary, regilded (fig. 7-27). A search over the course of many months unearthed a purveyor of red damask that was identical to the disintegrating original. Old photographs, together with Rambusch files, facilitated an exact duplication of elaborate draperies with gadroons and decorative fabric tapes. Old lighting fixtures were removed, cleaned, and rewired. These elements were featured as part of a sophisticated new lighting system required for the multi-purpose theater, which is today part of the Columbus Association for the Performing Arts Center.

For other shining examples of the company's restoration work, turn to Manhattan. Two Schubert properties opened in 1917: the Plymouth Theatre and the Broadhurst Theatre. By 1985, both were returned to their former glory, sparkling with lighting fixtures of Austrian crystal and polished brass, that had been newly designed and fabricated in the Rambusch workshops at 40 West 13th Street. The firm has thus restored many types of buildings where it completed original designs decades before. Theaters old and new have increasingly required the attention of Rambusch. In the 1970s decorative, festive lighting and, occasionally, an elaborate metal sculpture were the primary decorative elements. In the 1980s there was a revived interest in painted decoration and special effects. The restoration in 1983 of the Carolina Theatre (fig. 7-28) in Greensboro, North Carolina, utilized these same techniques that had been disdained for so long. The walls of this classically proportioned theater were painted to imitate ashlar travertine. The majestic, free-standing columns that frame the proscenium arch were marbleized. Other surfaces were painted and glazed. Reminiscent of those painted and delicately gilded so long ago by Frode Rambusch at the Jefferson Theatre (see fig. 7-6), its lithesome figures took the theater into the twenty-first century, where new generations can enjoy it.

7-27 *Plaster restoration and regilding*, Ohio Theatre (Loew's with United Artists' circuit; Thomas W. Lamb, architect; Anne Dornin, designer, 1928), Columbus, OH, lighting and decoration restored by Rambusch, 1978–1983. **7-28** *Proscenium arch*, Carolina Theatre (James M. Workman, architect, 1927), Greensboro, NC, Rambusch restoration, 1983.

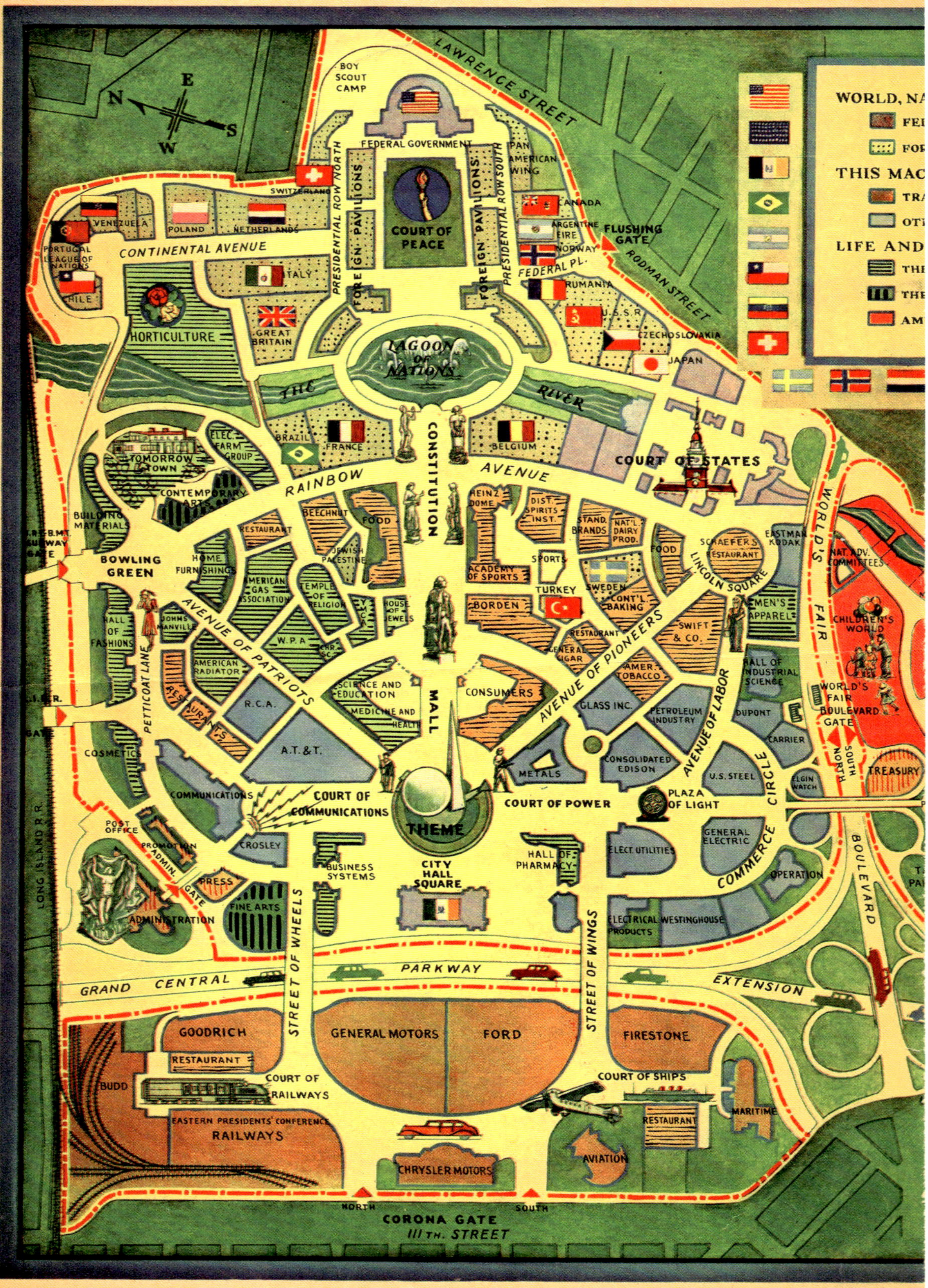

THE THEME: The World's

THE PLAN OF THE FA

CHAPTER VIII

New York World's Fair, 1939

The genesis of the international exhibition was the Great Exposition held in London in 1851. Prince Albert energetically promoted the event. Its purpose was to provide an opportunity for the display of inventions and objects that demonstrated advancements in all areas of human endeavor. A nexus for artists, craftsmen, manufacturers, viewers, and consumers, the exhibition was a place to learn, admire, and exchange information on an unprecedented scale.

After the exposition in London, other nations began to hold international exhibitions as well. In 1912, a convention relating to international exhibitions was held in Berlin that resulted in the signing of an accord and, eventually, the organization of an international regulatory agency, the Bureau International des Expositions (BIE), which was committed to education, innovation, and cooperation. The first international exhibition in America was held in Manhattan in 1853. Its London-inspired Crystal Palace was erected on the west side of Fifth Avenue, between 42nd and 43rd Streets. Shortly after the success of that fair, in 1876, Philadelphia became the site of the Centennial Exhibition. Perhaps the most highly publicized exposition in fair history was the World's Columbian Exposition in Chicago of 1893. Its program stated succinctly that the purpose of its events was to "set forth the display made by the Congress of Nations, of human achievement in material form, so as to more effectually illustrate the progress of mankind in all departments of civilized life." A few decades later in 1933, Chicago again was the site of a major exposition: the Century of Progress, marking the city's centennial anniversary. Architect, theater and set designer, and illustrator Joseph Urban (1872–1933), for whom Rambusch had worked in New York, was the color coordinator for this entire fair. In addition, ledgers list billing for two painting and decorating commissions—one for the New York State exhibition (Eugene Schoen, technical advisor), and the other, for the Time and Fortune Building (Nicolai and Faro, architects). This latter building, made to look like a row of books on a shelf, was painted with bold repeat stencils. It enclosed a vast seventy-by-seventy-by-twenty-foot reading room that featured the longest magazine rack in the world. Unlike at other exhibitions, fairgoers, at no charge, could peruse periodicals from around the globe.

Enthusiasm in 1939 was all pervasive for the New York World's Fair in Flushing Meadows-Corona Park, Queens (fig. 8-1). It marked the 150th anniversary of the inauguration of George Washington in New York City, the nation's first capital. Technological advances in almost every sphere of human activity were part of educational displays and exhibitions. Enthusiasm, talent, and money made this fair a success. New York architect Ralph Thomas Walker (1889–1973) was a significant figure in its organization. As chairman of the Design Board, he was particularly concerned with the relationship between numerous artists who were invited to participate and the craftsmen who would execute the designs. Walker consulted Harold Rambusch and the latter's recommendations became the formula for awarding this type of work. The first fee was for the study, development, and presentation of a sketch of the proposed project. After the Board approved this general idea for the design, a second allowance was given for labor, materials, delivery, and installation. To ensure the quality of the work, a third fee

8-1 *Plan*, New York World's Fair, Flushing Meadows-Corona Park, Queens, 1939.

8-2 Hildreth Meière, designer; Rambusch Decorating Company, fabricator and installer; *Mural over entrance* and **8-3** Hildreth Meière, designer; Rambusch Decorating Company, fabricator and installer; *Joseph Bisso placing the Torch of Medicine in the hands of Hippocrates*, metal mural for building entrance, Medicine and Public Health, Science and Education Building, New York World's Fair, 1939.
8-4 Albert Kahn, architect; Norman Bel Geddes, designer; *General Motors Building*, model, 1939.

was allocated for supervision. With this structure, the architect was able to retain control of the project from start to finish.

The scope and variety of projects at the fair were ideal for the Rambusch company. The firm's wide experience and the adaptability of its skilled personnel allowed for a variety of creative, customized solutions to the challenges of design and fabrication that arose. Work hierarchies and the levels of responsibility were complex and varied with each commission. On some projects Rambusch worked directly for an architect. For example, the exterior decorative painting of the Switzerland Building was a commission from architects William Edmund Lescaze (1896–1969) and John E. Weber. In another instance, the client was the Board of Design of the fair. Rambusch designed and executed the mural map in the Board of Governors' Room and also painted the World's Fair stations of the Long Island Railroad as well as those of the IRT and BMT subway lines. Yet another type of business relationship existed where Rambusch, the Board of Design, and the individual artist worked together. Rambusch executed Lyonel Feininger's mural on the façade of the Marine Transportation Building. On the Medicine and Public Health, Science and Education Building, artist Hildreth Meière designed a multi-piece metal mural (figs. 8-2 and 8-3), which was fabricated and installed by Rambusch under the supervision of the artist and the Board of Design.

Four projects among the dozens executed by Rambusch at this international exposition were particularly challenging. The first involved Albert Kahn's General Motors Building (fig. 8-4), where the auditorium was designed to hold people waiting to pass through the "World of Tomorrow" exhibition in electric cars. As a diversion and for instruction, three large maps were needed to show the highways of 1903, 1939, and 1969 in America. Roads of 1939 were to be visible individually or in conjunction with those of 1903 or 1969. The initial proposed design by Norman Bel Geddes (1893–1958) required miles of neon tubing and was considered too costly. Rambusch came up with a solution that achieved the desired effect at a fraction of the cost: ten percent of the original Geddes estimate, to be exact.

The design utilized blue light and special metallic paint. The roads of 1939 were fabricated in polished

8-5 Albert Kahn, architect; *General view of Ford Motor Building*, model, **8-6** Walter Dorwin Teague, designer; Rambusch Decorating Company, fabricator; *Highways of 1969*, exhibition panel, and **8-7** Walter Dorwin Teague, designer; Rambusch Decorating Company, fabricator; *Highways of 1903, 1939, and 1969*, exhibition panels, Ford Motor Building, New York World's Fair, 1939.

aluminum, and those dating from 1903 were illuminated by a red light, which were keyed to the red painted lines of the 1903 roads and those of 1939. When the light changed to green, the roads of 1939 and 1969 could then be compared. Thus, the different colored lights conveyed different levels of information on the map. Designer Leif Neandross and engineer Sven Bruun worked with Harold Rambusch to develop this ingenious solution.

The second and third challenging commissions occurred at the Ford Motor Car exhibition (fig. 8-5). Another set of maps were required for general viewing, also representing the same three time periods as those in the General Motors Building exhibition. But because of space constraints, a single, flat map would not do. The solution devised by Rambusch for designer Walter Dorwin Teague (1883–1960) was the construction of ten, twenty-foot-high triangular shafts which turned in unison, every minute. All the units of side C, representing 1969, produced a complete map (fig. 8-6). Sides A and B represented the earlier points in time (fig. 8-7). Clearance between the stationary shafts and the movable trylons was a mere one-eighth inch. Specifications guaranteed that the trylons would work silently without stopping for two years. In the event of malfunction, prompt service was guaranteed by Rambusch day and night.

A model of an automobile engine at the Ford building was equally challenging. It was eight times larger than an engine's actual size and it measured forty-five by twenty-five feet (fig. 8-8), and was constructed to demonstrate the engine's operation. Six roundel displays were also part of this commission at ground level. These addressed the techniques of the refining and manufacture of such materials as rubber, steel, and oil that were needed to make an automobile engine. The panels were to be illuminated progressively. The project was a natural undertaking for Rambusch because it involved design in a range of disciplines that included painting, woodwork, and lighting. The model also had to be guaranteed to operate flawlessly for two years. Rambusch rented extra workshop space just to make and assemble this giant example of a mechanical wonder.

The fourth challenging commission involved the Medicine and Public Health, Science and Education Building Complex (fig. 8-9), which was the largest building at the fair. It commanded a site that was located between the Theme Plaza, where the iconic Trylon and Persiphere stood, and Constitution Mall. Meière's metal mural (see figs. 8-2 and 8-3) was located at the entrance

1903

1939

1969

8-8 Walter Dorwin Teague, designer; Rambusch Decorating Company, fabricator; *Model of an automobile engine*, Ford Motor Building, New York World's Fair, 1939.

8-9 Mayers, Murray and Phillip, architects; *Medicine and Public Health, Science and Education Building*, model, New York World's Fair, 1939.

8-10 Hildreth Meière, designer; Rambusch Decorating Company, fabricator and installer; *Dragon of Ignorance*, scale model, photograph from 2009, and 8-11 Hildreth Meière, designer; Rambusch Decorating Company, fabricator and installer; *Modern Medicine*, mural, Medicine and Public Health, Science and Education Building, New York World's Fair, 1939. 8-12 John M. Sitton, designer; *Genius of Progress*, metal mural with red enamel, Business Systems and Insurance Building (Gugler, Slee and Bryson, architects), New York World's Fair, 1939.

that faced the intersection of the Avenue of Patriots and Hamilton Place. Diverse exhibitions in the building seemed to defy categorization until the designer settled on a unifying theme of research and development. Meière created a design portraying humankind as a child, aided by a doctor and nurse, behind whom stood Hippocrates holding a torch symbolizing the light of research and development. Its rays were intended to blind the Dragon of Ignorance (fig. 8-10), which was positioned at the left of the composition, retreating into the darkness. These figures, five times the size of the human figure, were cut and worked in stain-finished aluminum and the dragon was accentuated with polished brass. In other locations on the building, the Rambusch firm executed many murals. These included another Meière design for "Modern Medicine" (fig. 8-11), and such diverse murals as "Man, Between Past, Present, and Future," "Primitive Man and Civilized Man," "The Picnic," "Comte de Rochambeau," "Tadeusz Kosciuszko," which were all commissioned by Mayers, Murray and Phillip, the architects of the complex.

Many other exhibitions utilized the skill and inventiveness of Rambusch art-metal craftsmen. John M. Sitton designed a 300-foot, metal-with-red-enamel mural for the Business Systems and Insurance Building. Entitled "Genius of Progress," (fig. 8-12), it was paired with a companion, 200-foot metal mural, with over-life-size, faceted, sheet-metal figures of Benjamin Franklin, Louis Pasteur, and Joseph Lister. These figures were attached to the façade with three-inch steel pins that allowed for the play of light and shadow. The group was further enlivened by red-enameled metal ribbons, or pennants, weaving in and out of the figures. At another location, the Consolidated Edison Pavilion, Rambusch metal craftsman Louis Hansen designed and executed a repoussé copper relief of Mercury's head. The sample (fig. 8-13) remains at the Rambusch studio today. Many years before the fair, in 1923, Frode had met Hansen in Copenhagen and had invited him to come work at Rambusch. He even helped Hansen obtain proper entry permits for doing so.

In exuberant, dramatic form, and at thirty-foot high, one can also turn to the Distilled Spirits Exhibition Building (figs. 8-14 and 8-15) in the food zone of the fairgrounds. The mural portrayed abstracted images of wheat and corn framed by large clusters of grapes, the latter of which was the basis of the wine industry. The overall building was as sleek and streamlined as the General Motors Buildings and others. The façade

CHASE & SANBORN COFFEE
DISTILLERS

RESTAURANT
NORTH

of the Johns-Manville Building was ornamented by a single fourteen-foot figure made of repoussé aluminum, sprayed with the so-called "miracle mineral" of the period: asbestos. Fourteen-gauge aluminum was the base metal of figures made for the AT&T Building. And yet another project executed by Rambusch metal craftsmen was a colossal hand that was nine feet in height. It was made of aluminum for the Botany Worsted Mills Exhibition.

Elsewhere at this fair were painted murals by independent artists, such as Martha Axley. She designed a winding, marine industrial landscape on the Electrical Products Building (fig. 8-16) that Rambusch executed. In the Chapel of the Good Shepherd at the Vatican Pavilion, Rambusch was commissioned to create candlesticks and a crucifix. In the area of lighting, approximately 500 Downlites were utilized in various fair buildings. Rambusch's advances with this particular fixture gained recognition on a large scale. The Russian Building used nearly 250 of them. By the autumn of 1939, further recognition was manifested by that building's organizers' decision to ship all of these lights back to Russia, presumably because the technology of the light was of interest to them.

Although painting and decorating were then (and still are) traditionally seasonal trades, tradespeople worked year-round on this exciting project. Many kinds of unusual effects were employed in the Heineken Dutch Town and Merrie England (figs. 8-17 and 8-18). A base of gray paint covered the area initially. Then, the area was stenciled with simulated brick coursing. At both pavilions, a heavy coating of a reddish-brown-colored mixture was then spackled thickly onto the delineated "bricks." When the stencil was removed, the gray base layer was perceived as mortar. Some of the simulated bricks were painted black to achieve a convincing weathered effect.

During preparations for the this world exposition, Rambusch fielded as many as 300 workers on projects that ranged from design and shop work to on-site installations. Einar Nielson was in charge of all the firm's work at the fairgrounds. Not to be overlooked was the normal flow of other work simultaneously moving through the design rooms and workshops. This was a challenging period: one of intense, prodigious effort, which was all completed in less than two years between January 1938 and August 1939.

The World's Fair of 1939 was perhaps the last great, truly cooperative venture in the United States wherein architects, artists, decorators, designers, and craftsmen

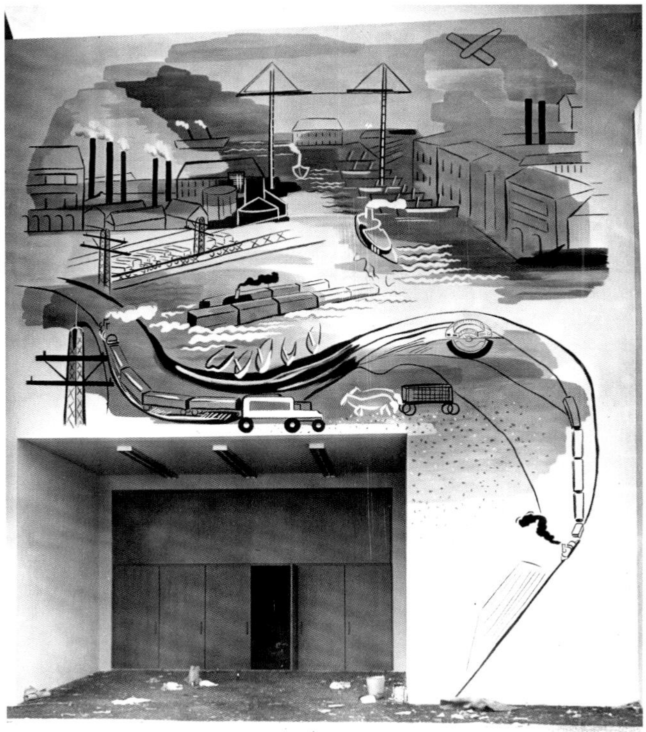

8-13 Louis Hansen, metalsmith; *Study for Mercury, The Spirit of Communication*, copper, Consolidated Edison Pavilion, New York World's Fair, 1939. **8-14** and **8-15** Witold Gordon, designer; Rambusch Decorating Company, fabricator; *Distilled Spirits Exhibition*, Distillers Building (Morris Sanders, architect), New York World's Fair, 1939. **8-16** Martha Axley, designer; Rambusch Decorating Company, fabricator; *Mural*, Electrical Products Building, New York World's Fair, 1939.

worked with parity. After World War II, not only did the character—and even the purpose—of fairs begin to change, in part due to the explosion in instant world communications, but also because the practice of architecture and the relationship between architects and the allied crafts changed as well.

The increasingly strident proponents of the International Style dismissed on aesthetic grounds the value of decoration and hand craft. Naturally, there was a lessening of work that resulted in the atrophy, and eventual demise, of many larger craft workshops. Trained experienced craftsmen—veterans of the stringent apprentice system—were equal in competence to the builder or architect who also had passed through a period of apprenticeship or the atelier system related to the Ecole des Beaux Arts in Paris. All too soon, after World War II, specialty craftsmen—including gilders, carvers, plasterers, upholsterers, painter-decorators, and all manner of finishers, who had trained to aid architects in completing interiors—had vanished. Recognizing the lacunae left by the demise of independent interior decorative arts and craft workshops, many large architectural firms started their own interior design departments. Scenic artists today also employ many of the skills that former artisans had exercised.

The new edge of commercialism in American architectural practice, and with it the attendant and seemingly all-pervasive bidding process, further altered the role of the architect and the architect's relationship to the trades. Extending further into the actual finishing of the building, which had been the purview of the specialized interior decorator, the architect began issuing specifications and accepting bids with increasing frequency. This change would eventually cast the architect into the role of comparative shopper for his or her client. But in the 1930s, the exhilarating experience of the New York World's Fair, the successful joint effort, and the camaraderie of architect, artist, and craftsman was still vivid.

"World's Fairs? I love them!" exclaimed Hildreth Meière who designed eleven decorative themes for the

World's Fair of 1939. In an interview published in *American Artist* in September 1941, she continued: "Fantastic, ephemeral, with all the glamour and beauty of fireworks which burst for a brilliant moment and then quickly fade, they dramatize the things we know of life but never quite believe." Adding some solicitous and cautionary comments about craftsmen, she noted:

> It is very important for us to pay more attention to craftsmanship in this country. Architects have a tremendous responsibility towards craftsmen. Marble workers, metal workers, wood carvers, all craftsmen connected with the decoration of buildings, are getting scarce. Who is going to do this work when all the old craftsmen are gone? Everything possible should be done to preserve the spirit of artistry.

These words were not heeded, alas, and sadly, exactly the opposite came to pass.

8-17 *Heineken Dutch Town, on the Zuiderzee*, The Loop, and
8-18 *Merrie England*, New York World's Fair, 1939.

RAMBUSC

CHAPTER IX

War Effort

On the face of it, it would seem that a firm engaged for a half century in the fanciful decoration of theaters, ballrooms, and private residences as well as symbolic-laden painting of church interiors and the design and fabrication of altar furnishings would not be in a good position to aid the United States in its World War II defense efforts. However, in 1941 Michael McCarthy, the firm's treasurer for twenty years, negotiated a joint industry-wide agreement between labor (represented by a Mr. Ackeley) and management that painters and decorating contractors nationwide would avoid all strikes for the duration of the war. This action paved the way to settle whatever disagreements might arise. The adoption of such an unprecedented agreement became well known when it was publicized on the nation's newsreels, and it set the standard for many other similar union-employer agreements.

The firm's history of individual creation of objects not subject to mass production ultimately became its strength. A letter dated April 24, 1942, from the US War Department Office of the Chief of Engineers designated the firm as "qualified" to carry out work for that Department. The head of Warner Brothers Theatres assured the War Department that the firm worked "well under pressure as far as getting things done on time was concerned." Their experience of painting hundreds of theater interiors would soon be put to other uses outdoors. Rambusch transformed domestic airfields, storage depots, and factories into pretend orchards, meadows, and hillsides. Rambusch's chief designer Leif Neandross had served in a camouflage unit in the Panama Canal Zone during World War I. He knew that in-house experiments at the Rambusch company could best determine the results of outdoor painting on various surfaces. Four different colors would appear as representations of four different natural elements when dry.

Equipped with this information, individual color sketches were made in the studio from scale drawings of the area to be camouflaged, provided by the Army Corps of Engineers. Homer Schiff Saint-Gaudens, son of American sculptor Augustus Saint-Gaudens, was the colonel in charge of the Camouflage Section in the Second Army. After the sketches were approved, the Rambusch team would travel to the actual site and set up a mobile shop in a massive truck (fig. 9-1). Full-sized layouts, with a scale of one foot equal to twenty feet (similar to the process of sizing a cartoon for a stained-glass window or a mural), were laid on the ground to be interpreted by on-site artists, stained-glass experts, or muralists from the studio. To facilitate the daily layout, as described in a letter by William "Bud" Haley (fig. 9-2), the area to be painted was prepared with ten lengths of white clothesline placed twenty feet apart. Red ribbons were tied at twenty-foot intervals on these clothes lines, thus providing a grid against which the patterns of orchards, furrowed fields, and the like could be outlined. Workers made outlines with whitewash dribbled from a three-gallon watering can. The effect of orchards was created with mere brush marks made at fifteen-foot intervals for "tree trunks," around each of which a fifteen-foot circle with a scalloped edge was delineated. Initially, the trees were painted three-quarters green and one-quarter black to account for shadows. However, from the air this effect was unconvincing because, in reality, more shadow would be evident with each leaf casting its own

9-1 William Haley, artist; *Paint truck and scale grids, in ca. 1943*, watercolor, ca. 1970.

Re Camouflage
Martin Field
Baltimore Md
1941
Eng.

28 MT. AIRY ROAD, CROTON-ON-HUDSON, N.Y.
February, 4, 1969.

Dear Viggo:

The "camouflage" sketch is now finished and I will get it in the mail today. Before telling you of the memories of this work at the Martin plant I would like to say that the one thing above others in the few things that I sell these days, is that the buyer sees them first. Then he, the prospective purchaser, is not commited to work which really may NOT come up to his expectations. This releaves me of any anxiety. It is my wish that YOU approach this sale in the same manner.

Now to explain the way OF the work we did there in Baltimore. This may be "old hat" to you, but here it is;

We marked a grid in the runway with clothes-lines 10 feet apart on which were tied red cloth 10 feet apart to make the squares. These squares were the full-size of the scale drawings on the blue-print. I remember that at one time one of those prints was blown away- this was not good for security reasons, which accounts for the B.P.s in the background being anchored with a paint pail. The garden sprinkling-can with the battered and stopped-up spout for delineating the lines was the work of a real genious. The man in the background is at the can of water which has this diluted paint.

The red banners were strung along a run-way where there was work in progress. There seemed to be a continual blaze of some sort of smoky material which, I presume was a supplement to the wind-sock seen in the distance.

I see that an Army Engineer named Campbell is doing something along the Hudson River.

Best wishes, Viggo, and hope that we don't have to do more camouflage.

Reed Haley

shadow. The proportions of trees to shadow were then flipped: trees were painted one-quarter green and three-quarter black to create a more natural result. Paint was supplied from pressurized tanks holding between two and thirty gallons, one for each color. The tanks were kept in the mobile shop and paint was fed through a hose attached to a truck. In this way, a 200- to 400-foot-wide strip could be painted at one time.

On one commission at Martin Field, in Baltimore, Maryland, Rambusch was the lowest bidder with a bid of 2.5 cents per square foot, with the entire job constituting three million square feet. The officer in charge demanded a guarantee that the paint would not fade. But the cheapest bituminous paint was specified by the US Army Corps of Engineers. When a call to headquarters confirmed that this material would indeed eventually fade, no guarantee was required. Soon, military and civilian airfields, arsenals, ordinance depots, chemical plants, airplane assembly factories—many such buildings in excess of 100-million square feet, from Maryland to Nebraska—all became protected by the coloration of Rambusch's painted "decoration."

Oddly enough, work at the World's Fair of 1939, that ephemeral place of amusement, prepared the Rambusch Company for another wartime project. The army was having great difficulty teaching untrained technicians how to use an anti-aircraft searchlight. A simulated training situation had to be created. It had to recreate closely the actual experience so that operators would be fully prepared when manipulating the real sixty-inch-beam searchlight. Victor G. Anderson, a Rambusch employee and former optical engineer, became a product engineer at the Sperry Gyroscope Company, and he was assigned the problem. He wrote specifications for a teaching tool. His solution (figs. 9-3 and 9-4) involved making a unit that combined engineering, design, fabrication, and assembly of a prototype with the possibility of eventual mass production.

Rambusch took on this challenge with an open contract. The prototype was made of wood, paint, metal, and plastic, and all the hand-machined axels and special clutches, gears, and switches were connected with chains, belts, and miles of electric wiring to animate the unit. Joaquin Santos, who a few years earlier had been a draftsman in the office of Bertram Goodhue, masterminded the solution. Axel Larsen, master metal craftsman, came out of retirement to make the gears by hand. S. J. O'Brien provided the complex wiring of circuits and transmitters. Securing material for this

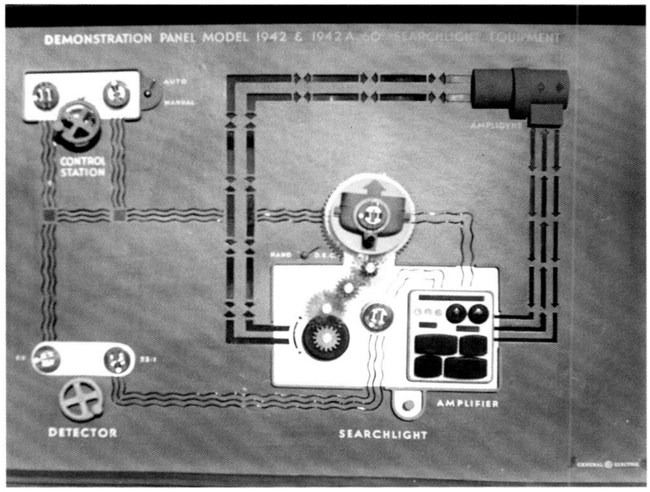

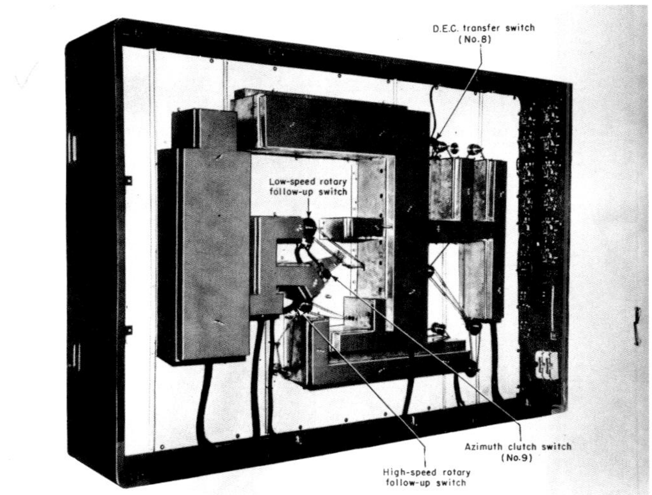

9-2 *Letter*, from William "Bud" Haley to Viggo F. E. Rambusch recalling camouflage painting projects during World War II, February 4, 1969. **9-3** Victor G. Anderson, designer; Joaquin Santos, Axel Larsen, S. J. O'Brien, fabricators; *Instructional panel (front) for operators of sixty-inch anti-aircraft searchlights* and **9-4** *Instructional panel (back) for operators of sixty-inch, anti-aircraft searchlights*, for Sperry Gyroscope Company, ca. 1943.

9-5 *"Echo Box" for radar-detection systems*, ca. 1944. **9-6** *US Postal Service "Forever" Stamp, commemorating the USS* Missouri, 2019; original radar antenna, built ca. 1944. **9-7** *Advertisement, describing the Black-out Ventilator*, ca. 1941.

top-priority project was not a problem, so it was completed in six months. Although approximately 100 units were made, the design was not mass produced.

Another tool for communication was the "Echo Box" (fig. 9-5), which was constructed of sheet copper, hand cut, and silver soldered accurately to within a tiny fraction of an inch. Its real purpose initially was a mystery as were many elements fabricated in the Rambusch workshops during the war. In actuality, the box was the seminal unit of a complex experimental radar system. It, as well as other small parts made by Rambusch, were assembled by the Sperry Gyroscope Company within two of their own large parabolic reflectors. These reflectors were nicknamed "Mickey Mouse Ears." The result was the prototype of a radar receiver. Several dozens of these large handmade, composite units were assembled and tested. When perfected, they were mass produced. One of the original generations with a Rambusch-fabricated Echo Box at its center was mounted on the USS *Missouri* (fig. 9-6). It was on her decks that the Japanese surrender was signed, thus ending the war. The radar antenna on this ship also was one of sixteen units produced by Rambusch because of their knowledge of the art and science of optics, easily transferrable to the needs of radar detection.

The most frequently produced item that was conceived, designed, and patented by Rambusch was the Black-out Ventilator (fig. 9-7). The problem was to find a solution that would ventilate the holds of Merchant Marine freighters and tankers without allowing light to escape from the inside. In the patented Rambusch design, this goal was achieved by placing two spiral passages inside a unit that fit into a porthole opening. Spiral channels allowed for air flow upward and downward. The unit could be rotated to catch fresh air for the inside of the ship. The blackout effect was achieved because at no point were the metal surfaces parallel in the air passage and a progressive zigzag of baffles eliminated rays of light. The initial patent was further improved and exceeded all government standards of performance. More than 10,000 units, often made on twenty-four-hour notice, were installed on American ships. Rambusch, as a lighting-fixture firm, which had been producing light in many facets of its business, now had learned how to eliminate it.

Some war materials fabricated by Rambusch were shipped abroad. For example, the sixty-inch-beam, anti-aircraft searchlight sent out parallel beams of light. But because of British climate conditions, there was a

BLACK-OUT FOR A BRIGHTER FUTURE

RAMBUSCH

2 WEST 45th STREET, NEW YORK 19, N. Y.

PIONEERS

in developing efficient airport (porthole) Black-out Ventilators. The first ventilator to meet United States Maritime Commission test requirements for air flow and black-out.

STILL GOING STRONG

Rambusch Patented Blackout Ventilators are constantly being approved by, specified by, and used by the U. S. Navy, U. S. Maritime Commission, War Shipping Administration, and Army Transport Service, on numerous specific contracts.

Materials, construction and finish conform with the latest U. S. Maritime Commission specifications.

We draw attention to the following statement by Mr. John W. Markert, Chief, Heating and Ventilating Branch, U. S. Maritime Commission, which appeared in an article in the March 1944 issue of "Heating and Ventilating" —

"It must not be forgotten that poor workmanship and irresponsibility cannot be tolerated with this type of equipment for SHIPS and LIVES depend on it. A law is no good without the means for enforcing it, and a specification is worthless unless the material furnished is in accordance with it."

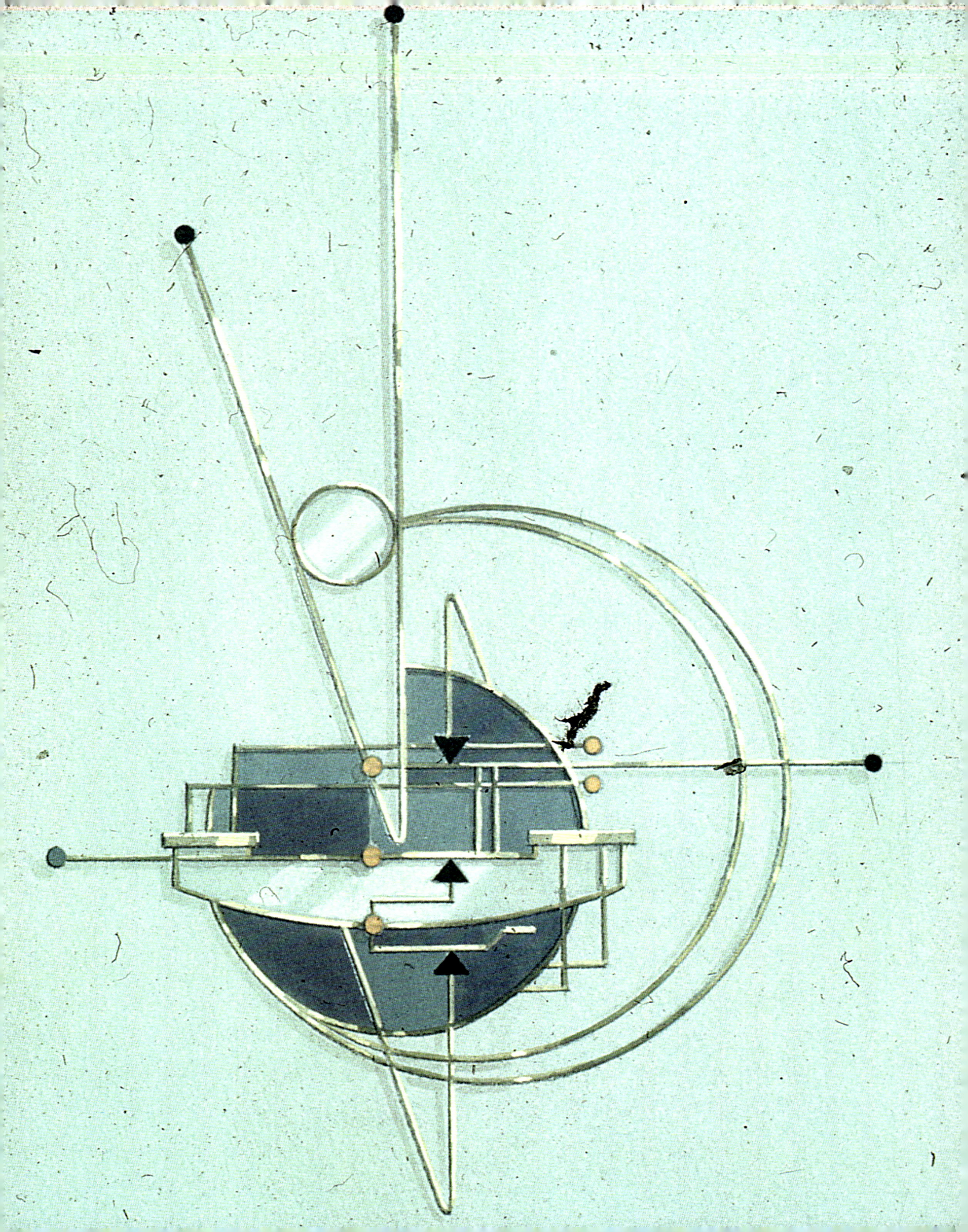

crucial need for wider illumination. Engineer Victor Anderson conceived of a solution at his Sperry laboratory and Rambusch again was his fabricator. The special light was a five-by-five-inch metal grid on which were mounted, at twelve-inch intervals, twenty-five Fresnel lenses. These kinds of lenses previously had been known for their ability to collect light and redirect it in a horizontal beam, making them useful in lighthouses. The grid on the Anderson/Rambusch light was attached to the face of a sixty-inch-beam light, allowing the light to fracture when passed through the battery of lenses. Parallel beams were spread out, thereby creating a more widely illuminated area. One single beam could now floodlight the low sky, even in cloudy conditions.

Rambusch collaborated with Anderson yet again on another war-related project. Because President Reginald Gillmor of Sperry Gyroscope Company constantly received visitors from the Pentagon, he wanted an impressive space constructed in which to greet them, exhibit their latest technologies, discuss contracts, and perform experiments. This space was dubbed the President's Demonstration Room and, alternately, the Fundamentals Room (figs. 9-8 and 9-9). Anderson designed this space, the centerpiece of which was a sixty-inch-diameter, rotating aluminum globe with the world's continents shown in relief (fig. 9-10). Made by Rambusch, it was specially treated to glow when bathed in ultraviolet light. Except for the moving, glowing globe, the room

9-8 Victor G. Anderson, designer and engineer; *Design for Wall Decoration*, **9-9** *Interior view*, and **9-10** *Interior view: detail of Gyro Compass Globe, indicating North*, President's Demonstration Room, Sperry Gyroscope Company, ca. 1943.

9-11 *Ceramic candlesticks*, ca. 1943. **9-12** *Batik banners: detail*, Chapel, United States Coast Guard Academy, New London, CT, ca. 1945.

was dark. When he worked at Rambusch, Anderson designed Shovelites located in the ceiling to provide wall illumination. When a dimmer was pressed, these lights would gradually brighten and fill the room with gentle illumination from what appeared to be an invisible source. Gillmor's stage was then set to go about the work of inspection and negotiations with his guests. Visitors never tired of this preliminary show.

Traditional areas of Rambusch endeavors—the creation, design, and decoration of spaces for worship—were also adapted to wartime needs. Such projects included adaptation of furnishings traditionally made of now-scarce material such as metal. Light fixtures were made of plastic and Masonite (see figs. 4-14 and 4-15) and candlesticks (fig. 9-11) were made of glazed ceramic. Large chapels, such as that of the US Coast Guard Academy, New London, Connecticut, were completed during this war period (fig. 9-12). Rambusch continued to design chapels that could be easily transformed to suit different denominational needs. The project for Bangor Naval Base, Bremerton, Washington, from 1983, is one such commission.

Korean Veterans Memorial

Vietnam War Memorial

For small temporary chapels on land or at sea, Rambusch used the medieval form of the triptych. The three-panel hinged format was light, durable, and easy to transport. These triptychs were beautifully painted, enameled, gessoed, and gilded—devotional aides that could be placed on any horizontal surface to provide a focus for liturgical celebration as well as private prayer. Several of these were made in the Rambusch shop on 48th Street. When a ship arrived in port, it picked up a triptych for use. The idea and funding for this project came from wealthy patrons connected with the USO. Many artists responded, including Hildreth Meière and others. (Rambusch has donated to the Archives of American Art of the Smithsonian Institution a complete set of color postcards that portray the work of various artists who participated in this program).

All Rambusch skills and capacities were redirected to the production of items both practical and decorative for the United States war effort. These same processes were involved in non-war work: the presentation of a problem, design of a solution, and fabrication of a product. In recognition of the firm's contributions, the Army Corps of Engineers awarded the firm an "E-for-Effort" brass-and-enamel, lapel pin. All employees received lapel buttons for their involvement in this cause. One is still proudly kept in the firm's safe.

In still later years, the company created two memorial panels remembering New York Life Insurance Company veterans of the Korean War and Vietnam War, approximately seven by seven feet in size and cast in bonded bronze. The models for this project (fig. 9-13) portray the designers' reliance on classical ideals to convey honor and remembrance. In these wars, as in others, including World War II, these soldiers made the ultimate sacrifice.

9-13 Tom Glisson, designer and artist; Dominic Facci, sculptor; *Two scale models of war memorials for New York Life Insurance Company veterans*, clay, ca. 1990.

FRANCE
CHRISTIANITY

CIVIC EDUCATION
MEN'S RESTROOM

CHAPTER X

State Capitols and Other Public Spaces

The noble public interiors of dignified courthouses and distinguished state capitols are the American, democratic versions of the palaces of Europe. Beginning in 1920, with a commission for painting, decorating, and lighting in the Virginia State Capitol, which had been designed by Thomas Jefferson, Rambusch has provided similar services in thirty-four of America's state capitol buildings. Rambusch painters and decorators, stained-glass artisans, and lighting experts move carefully, with easy confidence in the heady atmospheres of these spaces. Stage upon stage of scaffolding is an integral part of decorating them.

In the 1930s, and subsequent decades, the firm completed various works in this realm in the Midwest and West. Designed by Bertram Goodhue, the Nebraska Capitol is a prime example of Rambusch's collaboration with artist Hildreth Meière (fig. 10-1) beyond the New York World's Fair of 1939. From 1931 to 1932, the firm executed her designs. It also gilded the 400-foot-long frieze in that capitol's House of Representatives. Ledgers indicated a total bill of $7,887 for this job. In 1936, the company completed work on the Ohio State Office Building, now known as the Thomas J. Moyer Judicial Center (figs. 10-2 and 10-3). From 1958 to 1974 Rambusch in that state's capitol provided a range of services: it set color schemes for public areas; lit the House, Senate, and Rotunda; and restored and moved enormous murals. A five-phase lighting program was devised for the Illinois Capitol from 1978 to 1980 (figs. 10-4 and 10-5). And, at the Colorado State Capitol, in 1984, when the lead-glass skylight was leaking, it was taken down, piece by piece, and repaired in the firm's stained-glass studio. Sturdy bronze lighting fixtures—some weighing a half ton—from the capitol's chambers and halls were cleaned, rewired to modern standards, and reinstalled.

An apogee of custom, handmade work coming out of the Rambusch workshops was a commission for the New York State Capitol, Albany. It took 600 craftsperson hours to complete five yellow-brass chandeliers that measured six feet nine in size, with an additional hanging stem of six feet (fig. 10-6). All of the fixture's cast elements, including decorative leaves that measured three and five-eighths inches square, went through ten steps of preparation. Attaching these leaves in the final stage of assembly demanded an extra hour of highly demanding precision handwork. Each of the related two-armed wall sconces have 101 parts that were made by hand. Period photographs and extensive historical research helped determine the final designs, carried out under the supervision of capitol architect Albert C. Brevetti.

Besides state capitols, public spaces in many other government buildings were decorated by Rambusch. In the early 1930s, Cass Gilbert designed a thirty-story skyscraper for the US Courthouse at Foley Square, Manhattan. Elevator lobbies of each floor have identical, ornate, and deeply coffered plaster ceilings (fig. 10-7). Institutional green paint once masked the crisp classical details of their lovely rosette motifs. Rambusch's task was to remove layers of paint and prepare six different color schemes to differentiate each floor's lobby. The firm also painted the area behind the columned portico of the vast main lobby and installed new lighting.

10-1 Hildreth Meière, designer; *House Chamber: gilded frieze*, Nebraska State Capitol (Bertram Goodhue, architect), Lincoln, NE, 1931–1932. **10-2** *Grand Concourse*, Thomas J. Moyer Judicial Center (Harry Hake, architect), Columbus, OH, 1936, photograph from 2017.

10-3 *Supreme Court*, Thomas J. Moyer Judicial Center (Harry Hake, architect), Columbus, OH, 1936, photograph from 2018.

10-4 *Rotunda: dome* and **10-5** *Chandeliers*, Illinois State Capitol, (Cochrane and Piquenard, architects, 1867), Springfield, IL, stained-glass and lighting restoration, 1978. **10-6** *Reproduction chandelier*, yellow brass, New York State Capital, Albany, NY, ca. 1985. **10-7** *Elevator lobby: painted and gilded rosettes, with related decoration*, US Courthouse at Foley Square (Cass Gilbert, architect 1926–1936), Manhattan, decoration and lighting renovation and restoration, ca. 1975. **10-8** *Advertisement, listing examples of painted decoration*, 1932.

Six principal courtrooms were cleaned and decorated. The then-presiding judge of the Court of Appeals of the Second Circuit commissioned the company to create a new circular, stained-glass window—with the symbol of the scales of justice at its center—for the courtroom originally occupied by Justice Learned Hand.

The lobby of one of America's most celebrated buildings came to Rambusch because the firm was the lowest bidder. A period advertisement proudly proclaims this commission at the top of a list of then-recent work (fig. 10-8). The company had not previously worked for the firm of Shreve, Lamb & Harmon when they were awarded the decoration and lighting contracts for the lobby of the Empire State Building in 1931. The architects prepared the design. In the vestibule, ceiling lights were hidden behind smoked glass. The lobby was illuminated by indirect cove lighting. The ceiling was decorated with gold, platinum, and aluminum leaf in an arrangement of circles and stars. Nervous about finances, the architects asked Rambusch to review their prices. But the firm maintained its bid. The work proceeded and the job actually came in under budget. Ledger accounts read:

Empire State 1931	
January	$3040.00
February	$1227.00
March	$1850.00
April	$8600.00
May	$13.86
August	$1000.00
September	$95.00

On June 3, 1931, the firm received a letter from Andrew J. Eken, Vice President, Starrett Brothers and Eken, the builders on the project. "We were more favorably impressed by the manner in which your work on the Empire State Building was conducted than we have been with the operations of any decorators in a very long time . . . you do not evade responsibility as so many firms do in your line of work."

Rambusch was then invited to design and execute a scheme for the sales area of the enclosed observation deck at the top of the building. A mirror image of the panoramic view was created by Alfred Tulk on canvas in the company's studios. It was a tricky process, but the whole mural was installed in just two days (fig. 10-9). When completed, this allowed a viewer to turn around and identify buildings in the metropolitan landscape. New York was not the only site for large commissions. That same year the firm did extensive painting and decorating work in the library of the Oriental Institute, University of Chicago (fig. 10-10) at a cost of $13,450. Also in this period, Rambusch was so proud of Leif Neandross's work for the National Title Guarantee Company in Brooklyn, it showed his work off in a full-page advertisement in 1930 (fig. 10-11).

The firm always maintained its ability to produce stenciled or free-hand decorative painted interiors and murals even when painted decoration was out of fashion. This type of work came back into vogue by the turn of the twentieth century. The pie-shaped pieces of ceiling between the spines of the octagon dome in the lobby of architect Cesar Pelli's World Financial Center, Battery Park City, Manhattan, are stenciled with squares arranged in patterns and painted in subtle tones of gold, pink, and blue (fig. 10-12). The design was computer generated.

Built for the bulk of the population, nineteenth-century American banks and churches were designed as the grandest, most elaborately decorated, and imposing public structures that were routinely visited. For many immigrants, parting with cash was anathema. Banks, in particular, needed to project an image of absolute security and longevity in order to become the custodians of their potential customers' hard-earned money. Within the first decade of its existence, Rambusch decorated several banks. An advertisement of 1906 in *Sweet's Indexed Catalogue of Building Construction*, listed the Seaboard National Bank and Corn Exchange Bank, both in Manhattan, and the Williamsburg Trust Company, in Brooklyn, as completed commissions. Over the

10-9 Alfred Tulk, designer; *Panorama, Observation Deck*, mural, Empire State Building, Manhattan (Shreve, Lamb & Harmon, architects), 1931. **10-10** *Library*, Oriental Institute, University of Chicago (Mayers, Murray and Phillip, architects), Chicago, IL, 1931.

10-11 Leif Neandross, designer; *Advertisement, depicting an example of a painted ceiling,* 1930.

10-12 Kenneth Verosko, artist; *Finished dome*, painted stenciling, World Financial Center (Cesar Pelli, architect), Manhattan, 1985.

years, Rambusch has worked in countless such financial institutions around the country. On Wall Street alone, more than one dozen Rambusch commissions were executed in lobbies or banking rooms of the great exchanges and banks.

A few financial institutions deserve special mention. In Cleveland, the Union Bank of Commerce has an unusual floor plan with entrances facing two downtown thoroughfares. The interior consists of two rectangular banking rooms set at forty-five-degree angles to one another. Lighting for these twin spaces was designed and fabricated by Rambusch. The architect Peter van Dijk set the color scheme. This project won the Ohio State American Institute of Architects Award for Restoration in 1978. In Manhattan, the majestic Bowery Savings Bank, designed in 1894 by McKim, Mead & White, at one point in its history drew its customers from nearby Chinatown. (The building is now a restaurant and event space and no longer serves as a financial institution.) When the directors of the bank in ca. 1986 engaged Swanke Hayden Connell Architects, this firm in turn commissioned Rambusch to restore the interior. Supervised by architect John Peter Barrie, the job involved the creation of a relighting program that provided task and decorative architectural lighting as well as the use of the entire repertoire of the company's decorating skills. Painted decorations included gilding, glazing, and marbling eighteen forty-foot columns. The dark cavernous space was illuminated at night and provided an element of safety and pleasure to passersby. This interior received a Lumen Award.

At Hershey, Pennsylvania, the site of the famous chocolate factory, an exceptional school for orphans was founded in 1905 by Milton S. and Catherine S. Hershey. In 1970, the school engaged architects Clifford and Melissa Coleman, who, in turn, commissioned Rambusch to create a memorial to the founders in the grand rotunda (fig. 10-13) of a new auditorium and theater. It was to serve as a gathering place for tourists as well as theatergoers. Rambusch designer Leif Neandross, then in his sixtieth year with the firm, created a place of tribute. The 100-foot-diameter room had a marble floor, and Neadross designed a twelve-foot diameter Florentine design at its center. The circular pattern was distinguished by twelve pietra dura scenes made of semi-precious stones, including lapis lazuli, onyx, agate, and malachite. Each section of the design depicted an event in the lives of the founders. Nine crystal chandeliers, large bronze grills, and a pair of bold bronze stair railings leading to the balcony completed the festive and functional rotunda. Continuing attendance still proves that it is as attractive a place to visit as the nearby chocolate factory.

In the theater itself, Rambusch created the largest "flying" mosaic since Louis Comfort Tiffany's example in the Mexico City Opera House in 1911. The art work is suspended above the stage and can be lowered as a backdrop for Sunday worship.

Sometimes only Rambusch's design and fabrication skills in lighting were required. Fixtures by the firm have illuminated many airport concourses. The designers of the renovated terminal for Trans World Airlines, LaGuardia Airport, wanted special urns to provide indirect lighting. The firm produced them in 1980. These groups of lights appear as if they are suspended in midair (fig. 10-14). Closer examination reveals that one corner of each of the four shallow, scooped, square units was affixed to a corresponding corner edge of a column. This system was employed on several columns in the terminal. These fixtures washed the ceiling with light. At Lambert Airfield, St. Louis, Missouri, architect Minoru Yamasaki wanted only invisible light sources for his design. Rambusch complied and lit the broad concourses from hidden sources below the shallow vaults that extended from the top of the ticket counters (fig. 10-15).

10-13 Leif Neandross, designer; *Grand Rotunda, depicting floor medallion*, mosaic intarsia, perspective sketch, Milton Hershey School, Founders Hall (Clifford and Melissa Coleman, architects), Hershey, PA, 1970. **10-14** *Light fixtures*, Trans World Airlines Terminal (Robert C. Mock, architect), LaGuardia Airport, Queens, 1980.

10-15 *Ticket-area lighting*, Lambert Airfield (Hellmuth, Yamasaki & Leinweber, architects; Roberts & Schaefer, dome consultants), St. Louis, MO, 1956. **10-16** Claude Engle, lighting consultant; *Experimental mock-up of lighting fixtures*, for the National Gallery of Art (I. M. Pei, architect), Washington, DC, ca. 1978.

Architect I. M. Pei specified a flawless bathing of light to fall on an immense interior wall of Tennessee marble, the dominant feature of his atrium of the East Building of the National Gallery of Art, Washington, DC (see fig. 4-22). The evenly illuminated 360-foot-long, sixty-foot-high wall was to serve as the background, or screen, for the ever-moving mobile by Alexander Calder. It was almost impossible to illuminate such a large expanse without slight shadows or waves of uneven illumination. Rambusch spent four years from, start to finish, on the special units under the supervision of lighting consultant, Claude Engle. Ongoing testing and adjustments were made using the exterior seven-story wall of the firm's building in Manhattan's Greenwich Village for a mock-up, which Pei inspected in person (fig. 10-16). When the specially made units were installed in Washington in 1978, they achieved a flawless effect. What had seemed impossible just took a bit longer than expected.

Lighting another concourse was essentially an artistic rescue. The Greybar Arcade leading to Grand Central Terminal from Lexington Avenue contained six vaults. Originally, the ceilings of each were painted with murals showing different forms of transportation. Over time, the beauty and color of the murals had become difficult to see because of accumulated dirt. An expedient solution was to paint them out, which had indeed occurred with five of the vaults. For the last one however, an alert from an observant commuter brought a reprieve. Because Rambusch had been completing a lighting program on the Grand Concourse, nearby company representatives offered to clean and preserve the last remaining transportation mural for the same price as the maintenance company was charging to paint over it. Work was executed between midnight and 5:00 a.m. each night until it was completed.

Grand spaces can also have grand problems. The Kennedy Center in Washington, DC, presented an unusual situation. When architect Edward Durell Stone was on a whirlwind tour of Europe, he either ordered—or accepted as donations—tons of crystal for the long central lobby and many theaters in the performing arts center. When Stone returned to the States, the project was in a muddle. What had been bought? What had been donated by various nations or manufacturers? What wiring was included? When would the shipments arrive? Rambusch was hired to sort out and manage all the decorative lighting for the complex. As a gesture of thanks, the firm was given the commission to design and fabricate the fixtures for the Eisenhower Theater, the Kennedy Center's venue for theater and dance.

In Boston, two large projects occupied the firm for many years. Over time, Rambusch worked on the Hatch Memorial Band Shell time and again. In the late sixties, in the case of the Boston Pops Orchestra, conductor Arthur Fiedler wanted special illumination for the band shell, which is located on the edge of the Charles River. He wanted lighting that would evoke the musical experience for the listener, even if the person was deaf. The firm worked out a series of colored lights and painted washes that Fiedler himself could modulate (fig. 10-17).

With Mary Baker Eddy's Mother Church, First Church of Christ, Scientist, in Boston, Rambusch's commission was similarly intricate. By the early twentieth century, the congregation had outgrown its original gathering space. The resulting Mother Church Extension was built and is where the church gathers today, especially for its national meetings. The large classically domed space holds some thousands of members. Over time, church staff had struggled to brighten the expanded space and, in 1965, Rambusch was hired to help. The firm's family of fixtures fit right in, as they were specially designed to integrate lighting into large architectural spaces by making use of

10-17 *Lighting*, Hatch Memorial Band Shell, Boston, MA, 1940–1968.

10-18 Stanley Peterson, lighting designer; *Mother Church, First Church of Christ, Scientist* (Franklin I. Welch, 1894; Charles Brigham, 1904–1906; and Solon Spencer Beman, 1904–1906; architects), Boston, MA, 1965. **10-19** Read Viemeister, *Key, First Flight*, tile mural, Dayton, OH, 1975.

elements such as coffers, cornices, rosettes, and the like. Certain units provided light for the congregation to be able to read bulletins and hymns, others provided accent light for areas where members addressed the community, and still others provided architectural light to reveal the beauty of the interior overall (fig. 10-18). All were integrated and built into the structure inconspicuously. The complete system was engineered by Rambusch lighting engineer Stanley Peterson and assembled in the firm's fixture shop. Dimmers controlled an incandescent system easily adjusted for all events, changing with ease to meet the needs of each phase of a worship service or planned gathering.

The firm's experience with grandly scaled sites was also evident with its work in the 1920s at the Lincoln Memorial. The lack of correct lighting on the monumental statue of Lincoln gave Daniel Chester French a jolt of surprise. He was shocked and dismayed when his sculpture was installed because the initial lighting made Lincoln's face look like a death mask. Edward Rambusch,

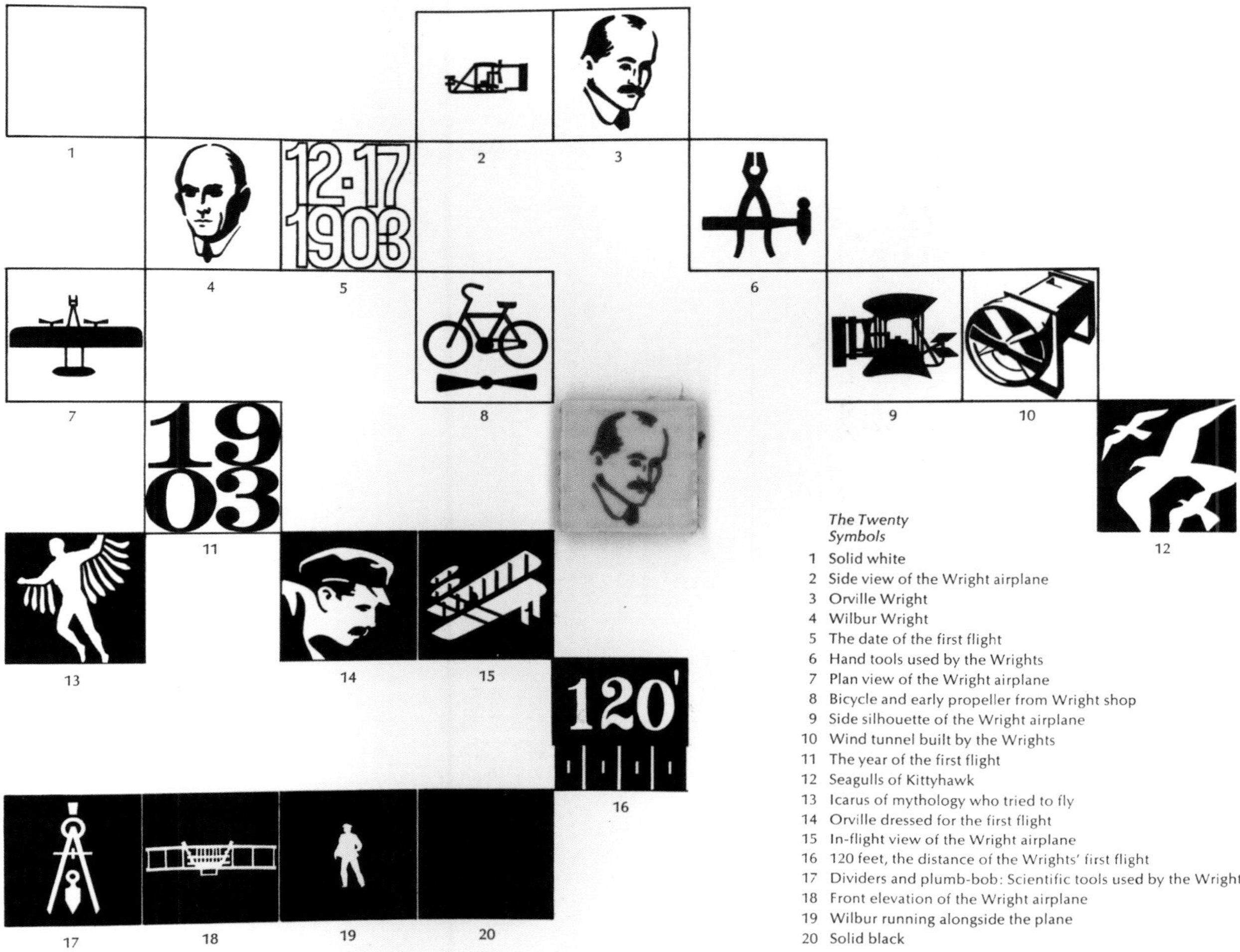

The Twenty Symbols

1 Solid white
2 Side view of the Wright airplane
3 Orville Wright
4 Wilbur Wright
5 The date of the first flight
6 Hand tools used by the Wrights
7 Plan view of the Wright airplane
8 Bicycle and early propeller from Wright shop
9 Side silhouette of the Wright airplane
10 Wind tunnel built by the Wrights
11 The year of the first flight
12 Seagulls of Kittyhawk
13 Icarus of mythology who tried to fly
14 Orville dressed for the first flight
15 In-flight view of the Wright airplane
16 120 feet, the distance of the Wrights' first flight
17 Dividers and plumb-bob: Scientific tools used by the Wrights
18 Front elevation of the Wright airplane
19 Wilbur running alongside the plane
20 Solid black

conversant with the technology of using down lights, produced a solution. The benign pensive expression of our martyred president is now well known.

In the tradition of the atmospheric theatres, Michael Dukar, Rambusch's chief designer, conceived "Little Old New York" for the Trans-Lux Corporation in 1972, which created the multi-media New York Experience for visitors and tourists. At the McGraw-Hill Building, he transformed a problem lobby two stories below 6th Avenue into a re-created platform of the old 6th Avenue el. Then the visitor descended via a long escalator, to the "streets" of New York, circa 1876. Views of the East River, the Brooklyn Bridge, Jefferson Courthouse in Greenwich Village, and gas-lit shops and stalls offered diversions while awaiting entrance to the show. One of the stage props in the vestibule was the original vegetable cart of Louis Balducci of the now-famous food market. Although the sensory-packed presentation closed in 1989, many still remember its exuberant evocation of a city known for its intensity and excitement.

Using technology was an integral part of a distinctive Rambusch commission. The Wright Brothers and Kitty Hawk are synonymous in most people's minds, but less well known is that the work and experimentation preliminary to their historic flight was done in their bicycle shop in Dayton, Ohio. In 1975, as part of a downtown urban renewal project, plans were developed for the Aviation Hall of Fame. Behind a clear glass curtain wall, the lobby became the focal point of the new urban center. A mural bold enough to be seen from afar, but detailed enough for close-up inspection, and rugged enough for the constant wear-and-tear of audiences going into the auditorium, were the criteria on which the design program was to be based.

Read Viemeister, founder of V. Designs, Yellow Springs, Ohio, contacted Rambusch. He wanted to use the image of the historic flight in a novel way aided by a computer. The famous photograph of the Wright Brothers' flight at Kitty Hawk was enlarged and analyzed using the Ben Day process, a printing and

photoengraving technique for producing areas of gray or color with dots. Each dot represented a tesserae in the completed, 1,134-square-foot mural, which weighed 3,000 pounds. In the mural design, each dot was to be replaced by a one-by-one-inch tile. Viemeister designed twenty tiles that Rambusch reproduced, ranging tonally from dark to light (fig. 10-19). Tile one was completely white and tile twenty was completely dark brown. The other eighteen had symbols ranging from five- to ninety-five-percent coverage of dark brown with appropriate symbols related to Kitty Hawk: profiles of Orville and Wilbur, length of flight, a propeller, and so on. Thousands of these tesserae were created and then silk-screened in Italy. Each was precisely placed in locations designated by computer analysis of an enlargement of the famous photograph, in order to create a twenty-by-sixty-foot ceramic mural. This mural was later moved by Rambusch to the National Museum of the US Air Force at Wright-Patterson Air Force Base, outside Dayton.

Lighting and painted decoration all enhance public spaces, but often some instructional and decorative messages are required. Rambusch has made clocks and dozens of maps in every conceivable material: glass (carved, colored, leaded), wood (inlayed, carved, painted, gilded), mosaic, tile, cork, and metals (iron, bronze, aluminum, and brass in forged, cast, brazed, and welded modes). Some of these maps have been made to the design specifications of an architect or artist. One such instance is a map made of scrap metal for Moore McCormack Steamship Lines that was fabricated according to Hildreth Meière's design. Others have been original Rambusch designs. All have told a story, such as the map of 1965 for the Atlantic Coast Line Railroad (fig. 10-20).

Perhaps the most public of all Rambusch commissions was the gilding of the Gothic spire above the pyramidal gold Ludovici ceramic-tile roof and the four corner turrets of the New York Life Insurance Company at Madison Square, Manhattan (fig. 10-21). It can be seen from miles around. Twenty-two-carat, double-gold leaf was placed on the seven-story, fifty-five-foot-high lacy termini of the skyscraper that is an integral part of the illuminated fairyland of the nocturnal skyline of Manhattan.

10-20 *Map for the Southern Railroad*, bronze screen, with carved and gilded maple and walnut, Jacksonville, FL, 1965. **10-21** *Gilded spire (above pyramidal roof) and turrets,* New York Life Insurance Company Building (Cass Gilbert, architect, 1925–1928), gilding 1968.

St:Marc

CHAPTER XI

Restoration

Preservation pioneers in the United States, upon recognizing the importance of our architectural heritage and American-made objects, began to rescue, conserve, and restore them. The very first such group was the Mount Vernon Ladies' Association, founded in 1853. Restoration as we know it today, however, came about largely as a result of the national preparations for the Bicentennial. In contrast to the celebration of 1876 with its singular focus in Philadelphia, the emphasis in 1976 was to be on local history and discovery. Considerable activity at the local level led to the realization of the significance of older structures in urban and rural neighborhoods. The adjective "Victorian" was no longer pejorative. In some instances, in fact, there was a 180-degree swing and anything older than a certain age was perceived as good and worthy of being saved and restored.

Laws were enacted that had an impact. The National Historic Preservation Act of 1966 and the Federal Historic Preservation Tax Incentives program of 1976 stimulated, in both theoretical and monetary terms, the preservation and restoration of the nation's building stock. Emphasis moved from tearing down to keeping and maintaining. Hidden interiors and actual structures of buildings were subjected to scientific inspection and close examination. Paint samples were taken from walls and subjected to microscopic examination to determine the various layers, types, and colors of paint that were used in a particular room from its earliest construction to the present. In great public interiors where redecoration necessitated erecting costly scaffolding, it was often found that only two or three layers of paint had been applied to the ceilings and clerestory walls over a period of 100 years or so. Another technique especially useful in discovering large-scale decorative schemes was, and still is, the painstaking manual removal of paint, layer by layer.

In one sense, Rambusch has always been in the interior restoration business though the firm did not use that term or, in its early years, discuss the philosophical ramifications now hotly debated by preservationists. For example, in 1910, Rambusch worked in the original Waldorf-Astoria Hotel "freshening up" original designs dating back to the 1890s. Frequently when a church was redecorated, the old, and often original, stencil or free-hand decoration was retained, cleaned, and in-painted where necessary. This treatment was the case at two different junctures, in 1954 and 1989, at Saint Peter Cathedral, Erie, Pennsylvania (fig. 11-1).

Another example was the redecoration and restoration that were both part of a commission awarded to Rambusch by Central Synagogue in the mid-1960s. As the oldest New York State congregation that worshipped without interruption on its original site, this house of worship was built to the design of architect Henry Fernbach in 1870. Fernbach was a member of Temple Emanu-El, where he had collaborated two years earlier with Leopold Eidlitz on its design. Both temples were a striking, exuberant mixture of Moorish- and Gothic-inspired forms of decoration. After nearly a century Central Synagogue's original interior was dark and dirty. To the congregation it seemed dated and old fashioned. In an effort to attract new, younger members to the temple, the building committee decided to redecorate. Rambusch was engaged to

11-1 *Decorative program of transept*, Saint Peter Cathedral (Patrick Charles Keely, architect, 1874–1893), Erie, PA, decorated 1911; cleaned and refurbished 1954 and 1989.

11-2 Edward Bierstadt, photographer, *Library and parlor*, Glenview (also known as the John Bond Trevor House; now the Hudson River Museum), Yonkers, NY (Charles W. Clinton, architect, 1876–1877), artotype from Henry Whittemore, *Homes on the Hudson: Historical, Illustrative, Descriptive* (New York, n.d. [ca. 1880?]). **11-3** *Discovery of original Eastlake decoration from 1880,* and **11-4** *Eastlake design, visible after removal of eight coats of paint*, Glenview (also known as the John Bond Trevor House; now the Hudson River Museum), Yonkers, NY (Charles W. Clinton, architect, 1876–1877), 1978.

create a new, simplified decorative scheme but one sympathetic to the style of the architecture. The firm made studies and sketches that were accepted. But, when the old scheme had to be primed over in preparation for the new, the congregation had a change of heart. Work was halted. Rambusch was given a new contract to replicate the original decorative program of the 1870s.

Of several extensive restoration commissions by Rambusch, three representative examples show the range of conditions found by the painter-decorator. The first was at Glenview, which had been built in 1876 for financier John Bond Trevor in Yonkers, New York. Architect Charles W. Clinton had chosen the then-fashionable Eastlake style for the interior (fig. 11-2). The property, now the home of the Hudson River Museum, overlooks the majestic Hudson River. By 1978, everything in the decorative program was gone—entirely painted out—compared to its original form. Restoration of the mansion was part of local Bicentennial celebrations. Three principal rooms on the ground floor were selected for restoration. Underneath the sheen of institutional green, Allan Stewart, master decorator

at Rambusch, discovered elaborate stenciled patterns, boarders, ceilings, and cornices hitherto invisible (figs. 11-3 and 11-4). New sets of stencils were drawn to duplicate the original patterns of 1876 (fig. 11-5). In the drawing room, paint removal revealed a gold-leaf background on which originally had been painted, freehand, a bird with exotic and colorful plumage. Using the faded and marred original scheme as a guide, the rooms were painstakingly restored. Rambusch craftsman Allan Stewart cut stencils (fig. 11-6) and he and painter-decorator Victor Melin applied paint matching the original historic colors with the stencils in place (fig. 11-7). Each color required a different stencil. The final step was to in-paint small areas freehand (fig. 11-8). In each room, a portion of the wall and ceiling was left as it appeared before restoration, or, in other words, when the previous paint layers had been manually removed. The result: visitors can compare the original Eastlake design, a ghostly basis for subsequent documentation, with the final gloriously restored decoration (fig. 11-9).

At the Ballantine House (figs. 11-10 and 11-11), the second type of late-twentieth-century restoration project faced by Rambusch, the original painting was untouched but covered with a half-century's accumulation of dirt and soot. Designed by architect George Edward Harney for beer-baron John H. Ballantine, the house was completed in 1885 and today is part of the Newark Museum of Art in New Jersey. Its original interiors by D. S. Hess Company were an eclectic mélange, exhibiting the bourgeois passion for collecting. The house is exceptional because its archives contain a complete set of original photographs, letters, plans, specifications, and bills. One letter instructed the architect to incorporate in the new building construction materials from the two row houses that had been demolished on the site. Most important, overall, the information from these many sources was critical to the meticulous restoration of the house to its original appearance.

Unlike the Trevor Mansion, most of the rooms in the Ballantine House had never been repainted. The decision was made to return it to its original state of 1885 by refreshing the existing decorative scheme. In addition to careful cleaning and in-painting, this necessitated putting new Dutch metal (a malleable form of brass that simulates gold leaf) on the ceiling of the study. The greatest challenge was cleaning and restoring the dining room where, above the oak wainscoting, its walls were covered with Lincrusta-Walton, a wall covering

11-5 Allan Stewart, painter-decorator; *Reworking design drawings for the creation of pounce layouts* and **11-6** Allan Stewart, painter-decorator; *Cutting stencils*, Glenview (also known as the John Bond Trevor House; now the Hudson River Museum), Yonkers, NY (Charles W. Clinton, architect, 1876–1877), 1978.

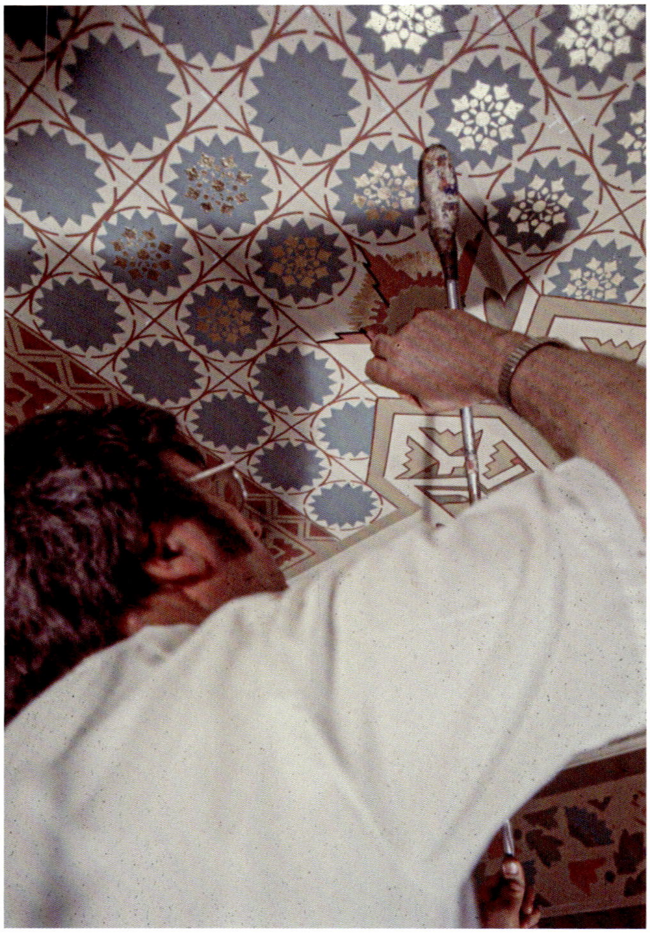

11-7 Victor Melin, painter-decorator; *Stencil painting,*
11-8 Allan Stewart, painter-decorator; *Freehand in-painting*, and
11-9 *Dining room, completed ceiling and wall decoration*, Glenview (also known as the John Bond Trevor House; now the Hudson River Museum), Yonkers, NY (Charles W. Clinton, architect, 1876–1877), 1978.

"'In every house where it is practicable there should be a room specially devoted to quiet and retirement . . . for the purposes of study, writing or reading.' *Beautiful Homes*, 1878

'. . . treat the library with reverence. Here the masters of thought make rendezvous . . . here History brings you the past and Science pours out her Secrets. . . .There are great and stately libraries where the curiosities collected by the varicus generations of the family, and still preserved, are stored—the old chests, bits of armor, weapons . . . heirlooms, and interesting objects of one sort and another . . . this library, in all its quiet and grave dress, may be found the pleasantest room in the house.' *Art Decoration Applied to Furniture*, 1877

"Woodwork: Cherry.
Floors: Herringbone pattern oak and cherry parquet.
Ceiling: Plaster beams and gilded plaster ceiling panels.
Walls: Soft old red painted plaster with gilded plaster ornament.
Window: Stained glass. Original cost, $460.00 Window depicts the Ballantine name—Bael meaning fire and Antin meaning worshiper.

"Room retains its 1885 decoration.

"Furnished with numerous comfortable chairs, the Library features the Morris chair (on the right) ordered for Mr. Ballantine by his wife in 1885. The lace curtains in the Library and the other public rooms date from the 1890 period."*

*Quoted from Philip H. Curtis, *Newark Museum Quarterly*, vol. 27, no. 4 (Fall 1976; second printing 1985), pp. 27 and 29, above and right.

"'The first impression . . . which the Dining-room should make . . . is that of solid comfort. There is to be no airy trifling either with colors or fabrics. . . . the mistress of the house will do well . . . to have her table linen white and sufficient, her silver plenty, her glass lustrous and engraved, her china [*sic*] attractive to the eye, since cheerfulness and beauty here have great power over cheerfulness and beauty elsewhere, the dining-room being in some measure the laboratory of the house.' *Art Decoration Applied to Furniture*, 1877

"Woodwork: Mahogany.
Floors: Oak and cherry parquet.
Ceiling: Mahogany beams. Molded papier-mâché panels 'illuminated with antique metal colors.'
Walls: 'Metal colored papier-mâché antique leather paper,' known as 'Japanese Leather paper.'
Windows: Stained glass with floral and foliate forms. Original cost, $154.00."[4]

11-10 *Library* and **11-11** *Dining Room*, Ballantine House (now the Newark Museum of Art), Newark, NJ, 1885.

impregnated with solidified linseed oil. When Dutch metal is glazed, it gives the effect of tooled, Moroccan leather—a popular decoration in late-nineteenth-century mansions of the very wealthy. Because the museum possessed most of the original furniture and draperies, they were able to duplicate the rooms exactly as they appeared in archival photographs. The Ballantine House now represents an extraordinarily accurate restoration, a true period piece.

A third extensive restoration project, representative of the company's preservation efforts, took place in 1980 on the West coast, in Sacramento, at the Crocker Art Museum. Judge Edwin Bryant Crocker, one of three millionaire brothers, commissioned architect Seth Babson in 1870 to design a mansion that eventually took three years to complete. The original interiors, including an art gallery, were late-Renaissance revival in style. After Crocker's death, the house was donated to the municipality of Sacramento. Although there had not been drastic changes made to the interior since the finishes were applied in 1873, neglect and overuse had taken their toll. Rambusch master painters and decorators, ranging from two to eight men at a time, took five months to restore nine rooms, including three areas shown here (figs. 11-12 to 11-14). These spaces presented a venerable textbook of every conceivable type of painted decoration technique. As many as forty-nine colors were used in a single room.

From a technical point of view, the most challenging aspect of the restoration was painting a particular space to appear as if silk damask had been stretched on the walls. This desired effect was achieved to perfection by master-decorator Ronald Millard, who in the early 1950s had completed a formal three-year apprenticeship in Rambusch studios. Only when a person touched it could one be convinced that it was really painted. Close examination reveals that this effect was achieved with a base coat that is actually three tones of blue, with an almost imperceptible delineation between the edge of each area. A stencil and fleur-de-lis overlay give the effect of the luxurious material. In addition to painting, Rambusch was required to complete other related restoration work. Plaster moldings that had broken or fallen had to be replaced. Casts were made from existing pieces and from these forms new moldings were created which, when gilded, could not be differentiated from the original. The project overall received a national award for preservation and restoration from the American Institute of Architects.

11-12 Ronald Millard, *Gallery: detail of wall decoration*, **11-13** Ronald Millard, *Gallery: detail of ceiling*, and **11-14** Ronald Millard, *Gallery: detail of column*, Crocker Art Museum (Seth Babson, architect, 1870), Sacramento, CA, 1980.

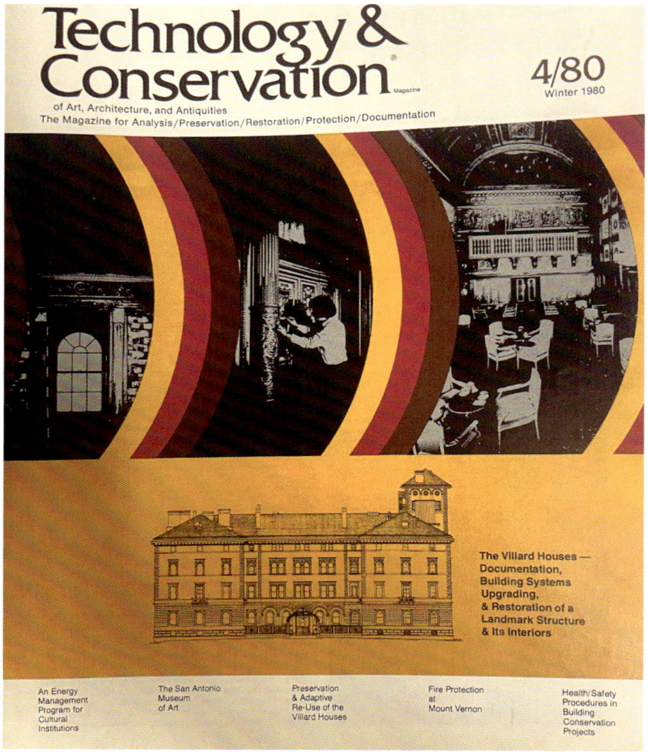

Technology & Conservation Magazine
4/80
Winter 1980
of Art, Architecture, and Antiquities
The Magazine for Analysis/Preservation/Restoration/Protection/Documentation
The Villard Houses — Documentation, Building Systems Upgrading, & Restoration of a Landmark Structure & Its Interiors
An Energy Management Program for Cultural Institutions
The San Antonio Museum of Art
Preservation & Adaptive Re-Use of the Villard Houses
Fire Protection at Mount Vernon
Health/Safety Procedures in Building Conservation Projects

11-15 Cover of *Technology and Conservation*, issue relating to Villard Houses documentation and restoration, April 1980. **11-16** Ronald Millard, *Painting decorative detail* and **11-17** Stefan Scheidling, *Repair of exterior lighting bracket*, Villard Houses, later the Helmsley Palace Hotel and now the Lotte Plaza Hotel (Joseph Morrill Wells of McKim, Mead & White, architects), Manhattan, 1975.

Sometimes Rambusch had to dismantle an entire room in order to preserve it. The Board of Directors Room of the Metropolitan Life Insurance Company was built as part of quarters that were constructed in 1893 in Manhattan. Before the building was demolished in 1958, the room, which had taken on symbolic meaning to the company, was dismantled by Rambusch and put into storage. A space with the exact same dimensions was included in the plans for the new building. After cleaning the wainscoting and the elaborately carved Santo Domingo mahogany woodwork—which included broken-arch pediments over the fireplace and mantle—Rambusch reinstalled the entire room in the new headquarters. The mantle had been fashioned after one at the Chateau de Villeroy in France. Above the wainscoting, craftsmen reconditioned and rehung the red and green, tooled Moroccan leather that had originally been on the walls. They also reinstalled the plaster ceiling. Its sixteen deeply coffered squares, each with pendant rosette, were enriched with classical details. On this embellished plaster surface, 3,000 leaves of gold were laid down. The result was both subtle and opulent. This commission was a dress rehearsal for the infinitely larger, and more complex, Villard Houses commission in the mid-1970s.

There, Henry Villard had hired the architectural firm of McKim, Mead & White to create a U-shaped, brownstone palazzo inspired by the Palazzo della Cancelleria in Rome. Completed in 1882, it appeared to be a single dwelling. Yet, Joseph Morrill Wells from the triumvarate firm had designed six individual dwellings for the building, which stands behind Saint Patrick's Cathedral. America's leading artists and artisans embellished the original interiors: Augustus Saint-Gaudens, John La Farge, and Louis Comfort Tiffany among them. Evocative and sophisticated, their spaces combined modern expression with Renaissance antecedents. Long after other private Madison Avenue residences had been replaced by new office buildings, the Villard Houses remain intact, their interiors transformed into office space. When Harry Helmsley announced a plan for a new hotel on the site, it was clear that the plan was not respectful of the McKim, Mead & White building. Public outcry forced the owner and the architect, Emery Roth and Son, to rethink the new design for the real-estate magnate.

A revised, acceptable program made the courtyard, and the Villard Houses that embrace it, into the entrance of the hotel. Guest rooms were to be located in back, in

a new tower. Harry and his wife Leona lavished great care and attention on the restoration of the interiors that were to become the hallmark of their signature hotel (see fig. 6-16). Rambusch was commissioned to inventory and remove all artwork, fixtures, hardware, lighting fixtures, glass, and anything else that might be stolen or damaged by the blasting and drilling that was necessary for erecting the fifty-five-story tower. This work was celebrated in an issue of *Technology and Conservation* (figs. 11-15 and 11-16).

The skills of every Rambusch workshop were called into play in the restoration of the rooms in the south wing, also known as the Whitelaw Reid portion of the building. In the paint shop—and also sometimes on site—painters restored murals, glazed, gilded, burnished, and painted trompe l'oeil and other special effects. In the stained-glass shop, artists removed, cleaned, and recamed the semi-opaque, rock-crystal-like leaded windows fabricated by Louis Comfort Tiffany. In the art metal shop, craftspeople removed bronze capitals in the Madison Room and cleaned, chased, regilded, glazed, and returned them to the top of their marble columns. They also restored brass decoration on wood doors. A most unusual feature was the Arabesque pattern that enriched the pair of oak doors leading into the original library. The pattern was created by the massing of thousands of faceted, brass pin heads. Over the years, many of these had fallen out, leaving gaps in the pattern. Hundreds of these tiny brass pins were made by hand, given facets, and then used to fill in the spaces in order to produce the density of the original design. Finally, in the lighting workshop, Stefan Scheidling and other workers were instrumental in restoring eight-foot-high, exterior bracket, Strozzi lanterns. (fig. 11-17). The lights were removed, restructured, cleaned, rewired to code, and then reinstalled with hidden uplights to increase general illumination.

Some specific tasks highlight the detailed complexity of this project. A decorative device consisting of adages celebrating hospitality were discovered underneath several layers of paint. Similarly used in ecclesiastical interiors of the period, these didactic attributes seemed a part of the American character. The sayings were lettered in gold leaf and glazed as a frieze in what was the dining room that then became the bar.

Most ornate was the original Music Room designed in 1886 by Wells. Except for the walls above the high wainscoting that were covered with silk brocade, virtually every surface was textured, carved, and covered with gold leaf. To restore this surface, Rambusch had to first prepare the subsurface for the application of gold leaf with French sizing. At the moment when the precise consistency of the sizing was ready (which varied according to the weather), sheets of gold leaf were applied. Single leaves measuring three- and-five-eighths of an inch square of beaten gold were applied sheet by sheet. Certain scrolls or pendants were highlighted. In these areas the surface was covered with a gesso mixture before application of the gold leaf. After this area had set, it was rubbed with an agate-burnishing tool. Restoration-architect James Rhodes supervised this project.

In such work, the levels of accuracy in restoration depend in part upon available information. Sometimes paint samples can be obtained by scientific microscopic analysis. Matching new to old colors and often using old recipes for paint composition can result in an exact match. Other times documentation available is in the form of photographs or written descriptions, as was the case with Ballantine House. With these, too, an accurate restoration or recreation can be accomplished. In the 1980s, restoration did not always simply consist of refurbishing or replacing the old. It involved an increasingly complex set of decisions to be made by the client and was, in part, dictated by the origins and the desired use of the particular building.

Take, for example, the case of Richard Upjohn's Gothic-inspired Trinity Church on Wall Street, Manhattan. Because the church was completed in 1846, the accretion of several layers of decorative treatments and painting since then had completely changed the character of the interior. In 1975, two decisions were made: to restore the original interior and also to redesign the chancel to accommodate new forms of liturgical celebration. However, it was mandatory that the design program retain, in situ, the marble reredos screen that originally had been donated by John Jacob Astor. It needed to remain against the rear sanctuary wall. Rambusch worked on this project for eight years. Close examination of the walls revealed the original paint color, and ultimately, the firm was able to meet the new goals for this faith community. Furthermore, it supplied a new lighting system that accentuated the strength and beauty of the church's architecture.

It is also important to mention that old decoration and design does not necessarily equal good decoration and design. A church in Victoria, British Columbia, provides a useful case study in the philosophy of restoration. The Gothic-revival Saint Andrew's Cathedral, built in 1890, was embellished on the interior by local craftsmen working with Gothic-inspired stencils around the sanctuary windows and in the side chapels. The overall effect was an elaborate, but undistinguished, provincial Gothic interior. Locally made furnishings also were Gothic inspired, with one or two possibly having been purchased from a Montreal stock church-furnishing house. In 1964, in keeping with the trend towards decorative simplification, the newly installed bishop closed the church for two weeks. When the doors were reopened, parishioners returned to a church that had been stripped. Gone were the familiar altar and furnishings. All the walls were whitewashed. The only hint of a Gothic reference were wooden arches in the clerestory that were saved by their inaccessibility. The congregation was stunned and outraged.

Twenty years later, in 1983, a newly organized parish committee was charged with the task of replanning the sanctuary and reviewing the general condition of the church's interior. The committee sought and engaged Rambusch. Jointly, they discussed a decorative scheme for the interior. Although the original decoration could easily have been replicated, the congregation was not interested in such a move. After much study, they commissioned a new decorative scheme that evoked the spirit of the Gothic, but was not a slavish imitation of the ornamentation that had been applied three-quarters of a century earlier. Instead, an original

source, the Book of Kells, provided design inspiration. Purists among restoration professionals might challenge this approach. However, the dynamics of a worshipping congregation were at work here, insisting on a space that acknowledged its history without being subservient to it. The congregation prevailed.

Two later commissions further exemplified the range in the art of restoration at Rambusch. York and Sawyer designed the New York Academy of Medicine in Manhattan in 1925. Cain, Farrell & Bell, restoration architects, commissioned Rambusch to refurbish the organization's auditorium (fig. 11-18). Enough of the original decoration was still visible and provided irrefutable evidence for a path forward. Rambusch decorators, led by master-decorator Howard Zucker, stenciled, glazed, stripped, and laid copper and gold leaf in this beautifully proportioned room. Fabric was stretched on the walls just as Frode Rambusch originally had done a century before in another location, at the Cincinnati Opera House. Original light fixtures were cleaned, rewired, rehung, and supplemented by with hidden indirect lighting units that set the room aglow in its elegance.

11-18 *Auditorium*, New York Academy of Medicine (Cain, Farrell & Bell, restoration architects), Manhattan, ca. 1995.

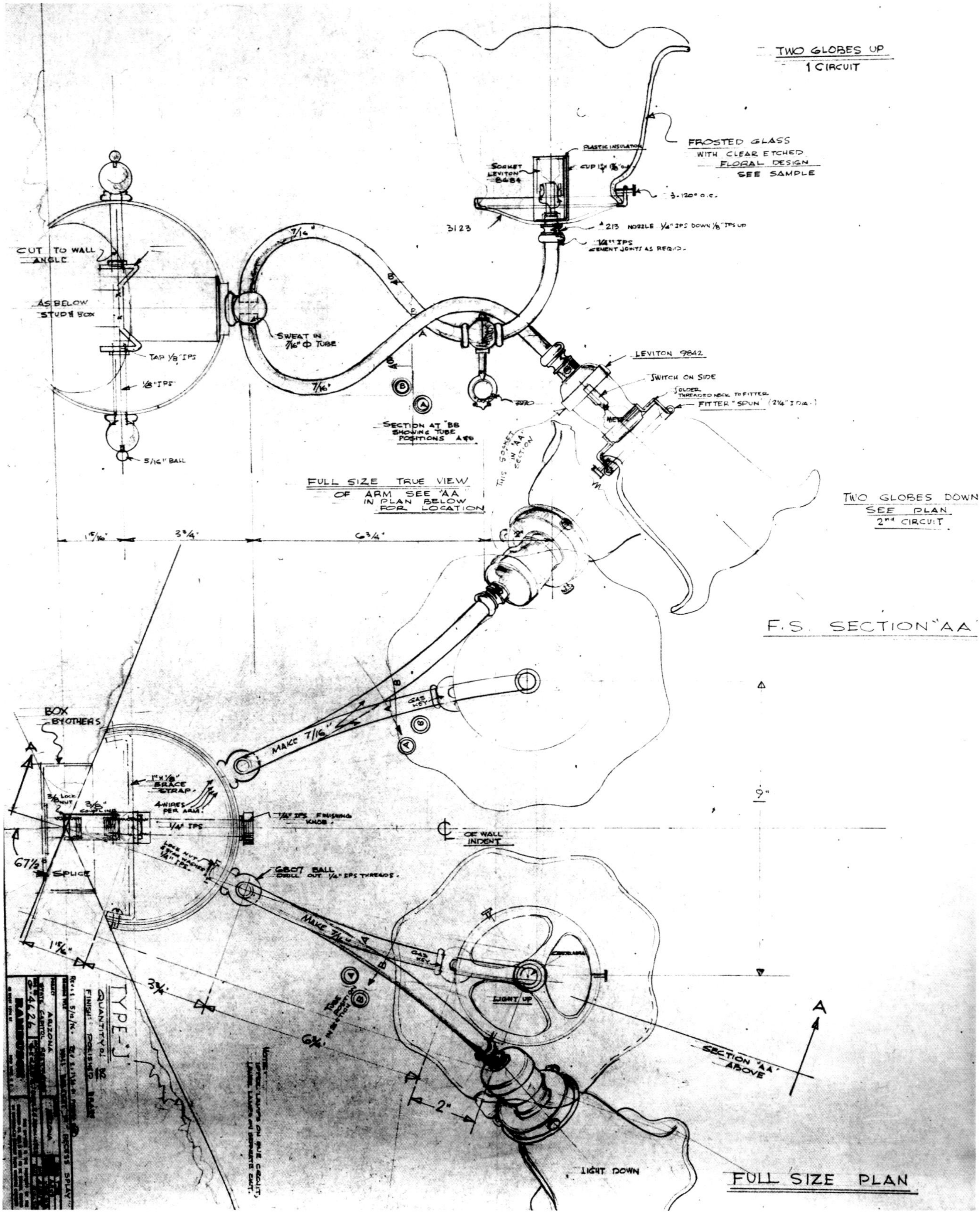
TWO GLOBES UP
1 CIRCUIT
FROSTED GLASS
WITH CLEAR ETCHED
FLORAL DESIGN
SEE SAMPLE
LEVITON 9842
SWITCH ON SIDE
SWEAT IN
7/16" Φ TUBE
CUT TO WALL
ANGLE
AS BELOW
STUD BOX
5/16" BALL
SECTION AT "BB
SHOWING TUBE
POSITIONS A & B
FULL SIZE TRUE VIEW
OF ARM SEE "AA"
IN PLAN BELOW
FOR LOCATION
TWO GLOBES DOWN
SEE PLAN
2nd CIRCUIT
F.S. SECTION "AA"
BOX
BY OTHERS
CENTER OF WALL
INDENT
SPLICE
SECTION "AA"
ABOVE
LIGHT UP
LIGHT DOWN
TYPE-J
FULL SIZE PLAN

Edward P. Meany (1854–1938), legal counsel to American Telephone and Telegraph Company, commissioned New York–architect Percy Griffin to design for him a suburban mansion in Convent Station, New Jersey. Alnwick Hall, completed in 1904, was true to its fifteenth-century Northumberland manorial prototype. Its interiors were decorated in a medley of historic styles. Of Tudor design, the twenty-four-by-sixty-foot Great Hall was the setting for Rosaline Meany's famous musical entertainments, where a thirty-piece orchestra performed. Among the notable performers were Efrem Zimbalist and Alma Gluck. Delmonico's Restaurant catered such functions. An Adamesque drawing room had a delicately painted, illusory ceiling with trellises of roses and vines. Another room was decorated with carved oak, linen-fold wainscoting. The house was also an up-to-date physical plant, with a piping vent in each room for modern vacuums.

Intervening years have seen Alnwick Hall used in a variety of ways—as a Lutheran church, and now as an office building. In the possession of the Chatham Trust Company, it is dubbed The Abbey, and has been restored and refurbished for adaptive reuse as a small branch bank and commercial office space. The four most significant rooms on the main floor were restored by Rambusch. The floral ceiling and other original surfaces, were cleaned and painted. Other areas, where nothing of the original was intact, were treated in a manner suitable to the architectural style of the room. Tarnished silver-plated sconces and also gold-plated sconces (with Wedgewood medallions) were all cleaned, replated, rewired, and installed. The house, now an increasingly rare example of its genre, has taken on a new life.

From freshening up the decoration of the Waldorf-Astoria in the early 1900s to an exacting duplication of a documented interior at Ballantine House to creating new interiors in the manner and spirit of the old, Rambusch's involvement in restoration is evident. Since the late 1970s, accuracy has been the watchword. Rambusch designers, to ensure precision, turned with increasing frequency to period photographs, written descriptions, and old trade catalogs before putting pencil to paper.

Turn-of-the-twentieth-century illumination technology accounted for the design of another large commission. As electricity began to be used, many still considered it a novelty that would not endure. Those who were more conservative continued to cling to gas. In an effort to appease both of these sectors, manufacturers produced a composite fixture that could emit light from either gas or electricity. Sconces and units of this type were used in James Riely Gordon's Arizona Territorial Capitol, Phoenix, built in 1900. In 1975, when the building, by then a museum, was being restored, architect Gerald Doyle discovered one of the discarded original fixtures in the cellar. Using it as a pattern and model (fig. 11-19), Rambusch designed and fabricated an entire family of replicated fixtures—approximately 100 in all. They now provide illumination for this fully restored building.

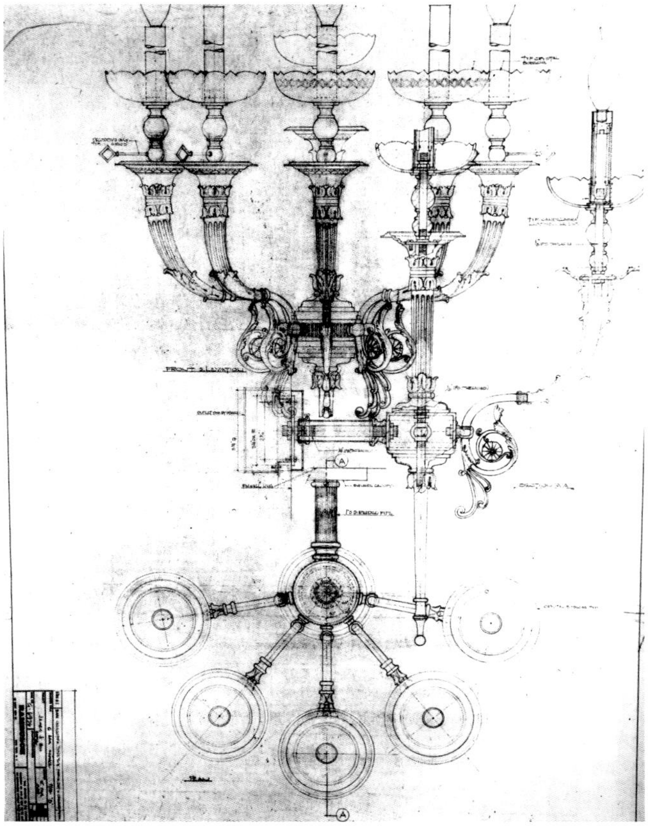

When Amtrak hired Skidmore, Owings & Merrill to upgrade some of its stations, architect S. Lee Carlson called the Rambusch firm. The high-ceilinged main waiting room of Newark Station, designed in 1932 by McKim, Mead & White, is flooded with light from clerestory windows during the day. But by the early 2000s, at night, it was gloomy. Two of the original four spherical lighting fixtures banded by signs of the Zodiac and cast in nickel silver were found in the subbasement of the station. Taken to Rambusch workshops, they were cleaned, rewired, and used as models to make the other

11-19 David Burliuk, renderer; *Sconce*, scale drawing, Arizona Territorial Capitol (Gerald Doyle, restoration architect), Phoenix, AZ, 1980. **11-20** Bohdan Hamersky, renderer; *Sconce*, scale drawing, James J. Hill House, St. Paul, MN, 1985.

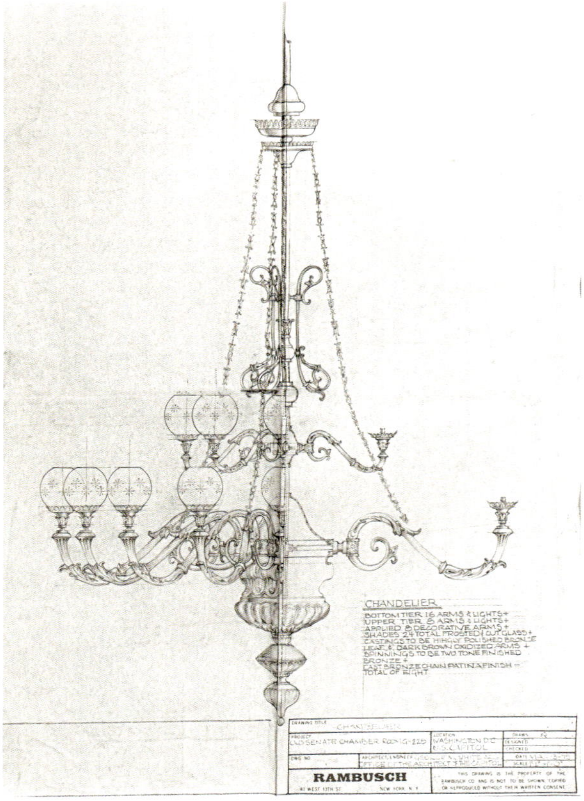

two fixtures that were needed. In the freshly painted, refurbished station, one cannot discern the old, refurbished fixtures from the new.

Not only public spaces call for Rambusch lighting-restoration skills. Millionaire railroad-baron James J. Hill had built a mansion for himself in the Summit Avenue neighborhood, St. Paul, Minnesota, in the same year that his Great Northern Railroad crossed the Rocky Mountains into the Pacific Northwest. This residence, now a National Historic Landmark, was constructed in 1891, and it incorporated the latest technology in heating and illumination. The interior of the house unfolds from a 100-foot entrance hall. By the end of 1985, Rambusch reinstalled more than 100 light fixtures, chandeliers, brackets, and other elements made of silver, gold-plated bronze, and embellished with crystal. They were redrawn, reconstructed, rewired, or replicated by the firm (fig. 11-20)—often from mere fragments.

A final case in point is the restoration of the original Senate Chamber, a Bicentennial project. Robert Cornelius of Philadelphia in 1837 made the original twenty-four-light, whale-oil chandelier that lit the chamber. Modified to burn gas in 1847, it eventually was removed. To determine the design of the original, Rambusch designers turned to period sources. An engraving of 1847 by Thomas Doney depicting the space during the Clay-Webster debates was a good beginning. Examination of other sources continued to add necessary details. But it was understanding the technology of the whale-oil lamp that was essential to determine the final design. Rambusch handmade an eleven-foot-high brass replica so accurate that whale oil, stored in the central reservoir, could flow by gravity through the hollow arm and be drawn by capillary action up the wick to a flame. Although the resulting fixture (figs. 11-21 and 11-22) was wired for electricity, all the engineering for its original function was in the twentieth-century replica that the company designed. Even with the restoration of the stained-glass dome at the Chicago Public Library (fig. 11-23), Rambusch expanded upon their experience in treating the historic fabric of buildings with great care. Time and again, the firm has proven its commitment to top-level restoration in a variety of circumstances.

11-21 Jan Rieger, renderer; *Whale-oil lighting fixtures in Old Senate Chamber*, US Capitol, Washington, DC, 1976. **11-22** *Whale-oil chandelier recreated for Old Senate Chamber*, brass, US Capitol, Washington, DC, restoration, 1975. **11-23** *Dome restoration*, Chicago Public Library, Chicago, IL, ca. 1980.

POSTERITY·OF·THOSE·WHO·ARE·YET·VNBORN
BOOKS·ARE·THE·LEGACIES·THAT·A·GREAT·GENIVS

CHAPTER XII

International Commissions

Rambusch has worked outside the borders of the United States for decades. From this continent to others, the company has tackled restoration projects of many building types. In the public sector, one can look to their work at the Legislative Assembly of the British Columbia (fig. 12-1) and other projects that will be discussed in this chapter. Regarding ecclesiastical buildings, the firm became involved in restoration efforts within the first decade of its incorporation. Frode decorated the Cathedral of Prince Edward's Island, Canada, and Saint Patrick's Church, Halifax, Nova Scotia, before 1908. How were these international contracts made? Most likely it was through the firms for which Frode had previously worked, including Arnold & Locke. In the tradition of itinerant painter-decorators, churches decorated by this Brooklyn-based firm can be documented from as far away as Montreal.

In 1917, in Halifax, Nova Scotia, an unexpected and tragic event occurred that would increase Rambusch activity dramatically in Canada. On December 6, two ships loaded with munitions exploded in the harbor, devastating the town. Saint Patrick's Church, which had been built between 1883 and 1885, was significantly affected by the explosion. After emergency measures were taken, its rector called Rambusch and invited the firm to reconstruct the church's ruined interior. The rector of the Church of Saint George, Halifax, wrote in the *Parish Magazine* in 1919: "I can truly say that the oftener I see it [Saint Patrick's] the better I think it, under certain lights it has been a very artistic effect. The decoration is classic and in keeping with the architecture of the church." Other commissions then followed. Because of the amount of time it would take to do this work, foreman Otto Jansson moved to Halifax and lived there for three years with his family. At the suggestion of Canadian Bill Moriarity, the Rambusch Company of Canada was established in October 1918, and he later served on its board. This measure also facilitated crossing the border with designs. The Candian office remained in Halifax until 1971, after which it was moved to Toronto.

Most of the early commissions awarded to the Canadian office were ecclesiastical. From cathedrals in Saskatoon, Winnipeg, to local parish churches, the range is varied. At the Romanesque Saint Mary's of the Lake Cathedral, North Bay, Ontario, one can compare views before and after a comprehensive interior and lighting renovation by Rambusch in 1927. Beforehand, bands of single point sources of light marked the nave ceiling; the arch over the main altar; and the treatment of the altar, apse, and nave columns (fig. 12-2). For the renovation, Leif Neandross came up with a more streamlined approach for lighting and he redesigned other interior elements (fig. 12-3). Some years later, in 1937, the firm decorated a chapel in 1937 for the Sisters of Saint Martha, Antigonish, Nova Scotia. Compare another two views, this time, of the Holy Angels' Church, St. Thomas, Ontario (figs. 12-4 and 12-5). In ca. 1945, both of the angel statues flanking the altar arch, midway up the wall, were taken down and one of them was placed in a niche in back of the altar. At the same time, two additional angels were painted lower on the wall framing the apse. Non-metal lanterns with plastic cylinders and Masonite angels, which had been developed during the war (see fig. 4-14), also replaced earlier light fixtures.

12-1 *Restoration and engineered lighting, Legislative Chamber*, Legislative Assembly of British Columbia, Parliament Buildings (Francis M. Rattenbury, architect; Alan Hodgson, restoration architect), Victoria, British Columbia, 1892-98; restored 1973-84.

During the twentieth century, the Canadian branch of the company developed a small, but strong, presence receiving commissions for secular and ecclesiastical painting, decorating, and lighting work all across Canada. Ledgers indicate a painting-decorating contract for $4,240 at the Granite Club, Toronto, in the 1920s, as just one example of many regarding secular work. A sampling of later commissions include the Glenbow Art Museum, Calgary, Alberta (1972); the work with Hodgson at the Parliament buildings in Victoria, British Columbia (1974), noted at the beginning of this chapter; and crystal chandeliers for the twin Jubilee Auditoria, Calgary and Edmonton, Alberta (1984). The records of these and other projects by the Rambusch Company of Canada are in the Library and Archives Canada in Ottawa.

It was not only north of the border that the New-York-based American firm was invited to complete commissions. In the 1930s and 1940s, work was executed in places as distant as South Africa, the Bahamas, El Salvador, and Cuba. Banco Popular was a large commission in 1939 from architect Chauncey W. Riley in San Juan, Puerto Rico. Although no visual documentation exists, the manner in which the decoration was executed can be deduced from a ledger entry. A bill for $10,000 reads "Stippler." This term refers to a method of texturing walls by hand with a special brush, a technique that had been used frequently in the earliest church decoration by Rambusch in the 1890s to 1910s. But subsequently for a couple of decades, it fell into disfavor in the United States because it was time consuming and expensive.

In the realm of theaters, Rambusch designed and decorated over fifty movie houses for the Loew's circuit before deciding to build one in Johannesburg, South Africa. The interior scheme was designed by Rambusch and presented as a tinted rendering. A Rambusch employee recalls that a prototype of the scheme was executed in the United States—probably the Pitkin Theatre, Brooklyn (see fig. 7-15), which was decorated in 1929 for $20,000. With the sketch as a guide and his own experience and talent for organization, foreman and master-decorator Otto Jansson was dispatched to Johannesburg. In architect Thomas Lamb's job book, it appears as "X1009" completed in February 1931. In Rambusch's ledger, this theater is cited as being finished in June 1932 for $11,000. If the Pitkin was the prototype, one might assume that the difference in price from that of its Brooklyn precursor was the result of lower wages paid to local South African workers selected and trained on the job by Jansson. A few months later, an additional bill was submitted to the company for "all windows in front of the house painted with aluminum bronze." Elsewhere, in Durban, South Africa, still later another bill for a theater was sent to H. Moskowitz in Manhattan. The Nazareth Chapel in Capetown, South Africa, was transformed by Rambusch Decoration for $1,227.

As late as the mid-1940s, John and Drew Eberson's popular concept of atmospheric theaters was exported south of the border with Rambusch again serving as fabricator. In the Panama Canal Zone, in 1949, the firm decorated a theater in Balboa according to the Ebersons's design for $7,981. Roman Catholic, Lutheran,

and Union churches were also decorated by the firm in the same zone. The latter was interdenominational and served American canal workers and their families and was supported by the National Council of Churches. Again ledgers show the pattern that after Rambusch was commissioned to do one job in a particular town, very soon after it was commissioned, to do more work in the same area.

Out of necessity, and with some reluctance, in late 1923 Rambusch began to look on other shores for craftsmen and fabricators, especially for wood carving, mosaic, and marble work. Italy offered willing and skilled craftsmen anxious to carry out jobs. Simple economics made executing work abroad attractive. However, unwilling to relinquish control of designs—and even more important, the quality of execution—Rambusch made a business arrangement with Florentine architect,

12-2 *Sanctuary: nave, before renovation*, Saint Mary's of the Lake (now known as the Pro-Cathedral of the Assumption), North Bay, Ontario, Canada, built ca. 1905, this view ca. 1927. **12-3** Leif Neandross, designer; *Sanctuary: nave, after renovation*, Saint Mary's of the Lake (now known as the Pro-Cathedral of the Assumption), North Bay, Ontario, Canada, after 1927. **12-4** *Sanctuary, before renovation* and **12-5** *Sanctuary, after renovation*, Holy Angels' Church (Henry Langley, architect, 1871–1872), St. Thomas, Ontario, Canada, photographs from 1945 and 1950, respectively.

Mario Liccioli. He was quite capable and conscientious, and maintained a small Rambusch office at Via Strozzi #4. Liccioli personally supervised hundreds of commissions executed in Italy from the mid-1920s until his death in 1954. Many larger Florentine studios had salesmen moving through the ecclesiastical market in the United States. But by dealing directly with craftsmen, Rambusch eliminated the cost of the middleman and was confident of the quality of the finished product.

The exterior mosaic mural on the General Motors Building in Caracas, Venezuela, was designed by Rambusch in New York, executed in Italy, then shipped directly to Caracas. In 1946, the Hegeman-Harris Company received a bill for the blue-and-white mosaic panels that decorated the building's distinctive façade. This multi-national effort provided a good background for quite a large undertaking that would occur in the next decade.

When he fell ill, Luis Cardinal Concha archbishop of Bogotá, Colombia, became a patient at the Mayo Clinic in Rochester, Minnesota. He stayed in Saint Mary's Hospital, part of the Mayo complex, where Rambusch had designed and decorated its chapel. The Cardinal knew of the firm's work but now had the opportunity to see it first hand. After being discharged from the hospital, Cardinal Concha made a trip to the Rambusch studios in Manhattan. He immediately awarded a commission for the Metropolitan Cathedral of Medellín, which would ultimately involve artists and craftsmen on three continents and take a decade to complete.

The cathedral was an empty shell. Originally built to a design that resulted from a competition conducted by the Colombian Embassy in Paris, its architect had never visited the site. The resulting building, which had taken ten years to complete at that point, seemed alien and lifeless in its surroundings. A special law in Colombia at the time prevented Rambusch from becoming directly involved in the implementation of the job. The law required that an employer had to be responsible for lifetime economic support of a worker if that worker became ill or injured on the job while employed by the company. Rambusch could not possibly assume such a risk and another plan had to be developed. The entire interior and all its appointments were designed in Manhattan, executed in Italy, and shipped to Colombia, where they were installed by local laborers employed by the diocese. When advice or assistance was needed, supervisory personnel from Rambusch were employed by the diocese on a per diem basis.

12-6 Joaquin Santos, designer; *Scale model of wood carving for baldachin*, Metropolitan Cathedral of Medellín, Colombia, 1953.
12-7 Peter White, designer; *Rendering of the seal of the United States*, graphite and watercolor, for US Embassy (Edward Durell Stone, architect), New Delhi, India, 1959.

Joaquin Santos was the designer for this challenging and complex commission. One of the many furnishings was a baldachin. After a model was created (fig. 12-6), its fabrication occupied an entire village of wood carvers in the northern Italian Alps. The only place in the vicinity large enough to hold a mock-up of all the pieces for the sixty-foot endeavor was a local armory, which Rambusch rented to assemble the baldachin and to make sure it was completed as designed. It was then disassembled and put on a ship bound for Colombia. The ambassador of Colombia expedited transportation of this costly object. From start to finish, the project took ten years to complete. In 1953, a monstrance was created with twelve pounds of pure gold and 100 one-karat diamonds that cost $49,300; it was designed and fabricated at Rambusch for the diocese.

Also in Colombia in 1953, near Bogotá, Rambusch was commissioned to create an elaborate tabernacle. Located in the center of an ancient lake high in the mountains and more than 10,000 feet above sea level, was the venerated Sanctuary of Montserrate. Many local people who visited at that time made the last few hundred yards of their approach on their knees. The firm's completed tabernacle was integral to this shrine.

Further into the late 1950s and into the 1970s, commissions from patrons in international settings continued to come to Rambusch. These included designs for a pair of stained-glass windows for the Sacred Heart Chapel, Tokyo, and the monumental US shield (fig. 12-7), the only decoration that was hung on Edward Durell Stone's grillwork facade of the American Embassy, New Delhi. For this coat of arms, Rambusch produced shop drawings that were used for fabrication of the final, diaphanous, fifteen-foot-diameter bronze shield in India. In Puerto Rico, decorative painting and stained glass were also installed in the executive mansion and the

12-8 Homer Hill and Ronald Millard, artists; *Trompe l'oeil mural*, Bacardi Rum Company, Cataño, Puerto Rico, 1972. **12-9** Richard Julian Zimmerman, renderer; *Rotunda: cross section*, watercolor on paper, Legislative Assembly of British Columbia, Parliament Buildings (Francis M. Rattenbury, architect, 1892-98; Alan Hodgson, restoration architect), Victoria, British Columbia, 1973-84.

office of the governor. Two murals painted on canvas in the Rambusch workshops, designed by Homer Hill and executed by Ronald Millard, were rolled up and taken to the island for installation at the Bacardi Rum Factory (fig. 12-8). The marble steps and objects on them were all painted in a trompe l'oeil effect. They offered an instructive, fanciful telling of the story of distilling rum. So convincing were they that a railing had to be installed to keep visitors from touching the wall.

Later, in the 1970s, in Italy a project was developing regarding John Neumann (1811–1860), a Bohemian by birth, a Redemptorist by choice, and a Bishop by Papal decree. He had spent most of his adult life on the East Coast during the early and mid-nineteenth century. Neumann was responsible for the erection of the Cathedral Basilica of Saints Peter and Paul, Philadelphia, begun in 1846 by Napolean LeBrun (1821–1901). In honor of the celebration marking Neumann's canonization in 1978, a monumental painting of the new saint was to be unfurled from the balcony of Saint Peter's Basilica in Rome. Traditionally, the production of such a likeness, in former times a tapestry but now a painted canvas, was the artistic domain of Italian artists. John Cardinal Krol, Bishop of Philadelphia, decided to break with that tradition. He wanted the likeness of Neumann to be made in America. He also wanted the saint to be portrayed as the Bishop of Philadelphia with LeBrun's impressive cathedral in the background, not as a priest floating on clouds. Rambusch, having worked at the cathedral for three generations, was awarded the commission. Artist Leandro Velasco designed and painted a sixteen-foot-high-by-eight-foot-wide, full-length portrait of Neumann, which, when finished, fluttered from the famous balcony of Saint Peter's.

Across the world in Jerusalem, a city where the dense layering of religious traditions is edifying, Christians in past centuries had marked small simple crosses for each episode of Jesus's path to Calvary. In 1961, it was decided that each episode, or station as they are more colloquially known, on the Via Cruces should also have a pictorial commemoration. Rambusch invited artist Alsa Mandel to design and model the cast-bronze second station for James Perry, O.F.M., and architect Brother Cajetan J. B. Baumann, O.F.M.

In 1978, the Rambusch Decorating Company assisted architect Alan Hodgson in the renovation of the Legislative Chamber for the Assembly of British Columbia in Victoria, Canada. The main focus was to design and renovate lighting fixtures for the illumination of

ABC MDEGHI JKLT

chamber proceedings on live television (see fig. 12-1). Rambusch also developed a spectacular color scheme for the Rotunda (fig. 12-9) Furthermore, the firm repaired, replaced, painted, and fired broken stained-glass elements from the building's principal windows. This project contributed to the Rambusch Company of Canada being asked to design, engineer, and supply lighting fixtures and equipment for the national parliament buildings in Ottawa. There, the firm completed work in the Memorial Chamber within the Peace Tower, House of Commons, Senate, and main committee rooms. Their scope also included recreating gasoliers for the East Block appropriate to the original date of the building.

A few years later, in 1984, in Puerto Rico, a humorous twist occurred related to a consulting commission involving an ancient convent in old San Juan. After World War II, the government acquired the complex and converted it into a luxury hotel called El Convento. The former (and now deconsecrated) chapel became the dining room. The Puerto Rican government, anxious to profit from legalized gambling, had decided to make the dining room into a first-class casino. Rambusch was commissioned to change the décor—especially the lighting so that the space would function attractively and efficiently as a gambling hall. The main window in the chapel-with-casino was to be filled with a stained-glass window designed by Leandro Velasco depicting the Goddess of Chance, Fortuna. The project never came to fruition because the space was deemed too small to become profitable.

Rambusch lighting fixtures were always in demand elsewhere on the international scene in the late twentieth century. Scottish-architect Sir Basil Spence came to Rambusch to review the lighting solution the firm had designed for the new Coventry Cathedral after World War II. The drawings were approved for installation. At the last moment, however, fixtures manufactured in England were substituted that ultimately utilized the Rambusch lighting program. The firm's expertise with lighting fixtures also was the avenue that led to a series of impressive foreign designs and fabrication commissions, beginning in the late 1970s and continuing into the next decade. The US Army Corps of Engineers had a series of contracts with the Saudi Arabian government to provide infrastructure for their new and rapidly developing country. The Corps, along with the international architectural firm,

Leo A. Daly, were responsible for planning and designing entire communities and cities, including roads, airports, sewer systems, mosques, public spaces, and ministry buildings, in addition to royal apartments and reception facilities. Leo A. Daly, Jr., over the course of thirty years, had developed a fruitful professional relationship with the Rambusch firm, and they produced many sacred and secular projects together. Their collaboration blossomed with the projects in Saudi Arabia

Daly and his son Leo III recommended Rambusch to the Corps' own interior designer, Thomas Zumwalt. They knew that the firm would be competent and reliable in the design, fabrication, and implementation of their concepts for a series of dazzling, large-format crystal chandeliers and sconces. Rambusch employee Peter White designed one set per year, from 1979 to 1982, for each of four locations: the Saudi Arabian National Guard Headquarters, Riyadh (fig. 12-10); the V.I.P. Facilities, Ras al Mishab; the Naval Reception Facility, Jeddah; and the Naval Headquarters, Riyadh. One of these chandeliers was a half dome of polished and chrome-plated steel, seventeen feet in diameter. Along the armatures, at one-inch intervals, were strung crystal garlands.

12-10 Peter White, designer; *Chandeliers and sconces*, National Guard Headquarters (Leo A. Daly, architects), Riyadh, Saudi Arabia, 1985.
12-11 *Royal Reception Lounge,* (embroidered bullion of Royal Coat of Arms not visible), Jedda Airport, Saudi Arabia, 1983.

This massive fixture was installed on a mirrored ceiling that created the illusion of an entire ball of crystal. Other design details and motifs evoked the cultural history of Saudi Arabia, such as the symbols of crossed swords and palm trees. Cast in bronze and hand chased, these ornaments were juxtaposed to the crystal. At the Royal Reception Lounge, Jedda Airport, Saudi Arabia, Rambusch again designed a very large half sphere out of crystal and mounted it on a ceiling mirror to create the effect of a complete crystal ball (fig. 12-11).

These large Saudi commissions had two parts: design and fabrication on the one hand and installation supervision on the other. Several teams of Rambusch craftsmen went to Saudi Arabia to help install these massive lighting fixtures. It was like working at the Tower of Babel, with crews from all over the world. Koreans, Filipinos, and Vietnamese lived in compounds, doing this work in lieu of accepting national military duty in their home countries. Rambusch maintained a business relationship with an established large Saudi family firm. For generations I. E. Ahmed and Mohammed Saleh Kaki have been an integral part of the commerce of their growing country and their country's expanding economy.

For a small family company, one that has never actively sought work outside the North American continent, the record shows a surprisingly wide geographical spectrum and diversity of commissions. Indeed, after its first 100 years, in 2018, the fourth generation of the Rambusch family was commissioned to create the *Mater Ecclesiae* (fig. 12-12) for the Vatican Gardens, in Vatican City. The company's wide-ranging work in interior decoration and design, art metal, lighting, and stained glass in diverse private and public spaces constitutes a century-long commitment to art and craft that continues to this day.

12-12 *Mater Ecclesiae*, Vatican Gardens, Vatican City, 2018.

E-1 *Blessed Stanley Rother Oratory,* Cathedral of Our Lady of Perpetual Help, Oklahoma City, OK; cathedral, 1923–24; Rother Oratory, 2019.

EPILOGUE

Charles D. Linn, FAIA
Editor, *Rambusch: The Next Generation*

The title of this book, *Rambusch: The First 100 Years, 1898–1998*, hints that the story of the Rambusch Decorating Company did not end in 1998. Far from it. As of 2024, the date of this volume's publication, Rambusch has celebrated 125 years in business, and then some. Edwin Peter and Martin Viggo Rambusch, the twin great grandsons of Frode Rambusch, still guide the firm with the enthusiastic vision and energy of their forefathers. They are the sons of this book's author Catha Jackson Grace and Emeritus Chairman of the Board Viggo Bech Rambusch.

Assuming the helm of a company that has an abundant artistic legacy—and a reputation for stellar engineering, project management, and quality workmanship—is not easy. But both Edwin and Martin grew up steeped in the culture of Rambusch, surrounded by artists, artisans, and designers. As boys they donned hardhats and worked on jobs each summer. They spent days in the firm's library exploring rare art and architecture books and listened to both of their parents and others tell innumerable stories around the dinner table. They traveled to Europe to visit workshops and meet clients here and abroad. Both spent their years preparing to join the Rambusch firm.

Edwin earned an undergraduate degree in art history with a minor in economics at Bates College, and an M.F.A. in Lighting Design from the Parsons School of Design (now a part of the New School). Martin earned his undergraduate degree in fine art at Tulane University and received an M.S. in Historic Preservation from the Columbia Graduate School of Architecture, Planning and Preservation. After their undergraduate studies, each completed intensive, specialized internships in every one of the firm's studios, and once they had earned their graduate degrees, they returned to the firm as employee-owners. In 1998, Edwin took the helm of the Lighting Division and today is company president. Martin took over the Crafts, Liturgical Arts, and Stained-Glass Division at that time and is now chairman of the board. Today, Rambusch continues with four craft studios of historic lineage. The Artwork and Liturgical Environments Studio, and the Stained Glass and Mosaics Studio, operate under direction of Martin and the Custom Lighting Studio and Engineered Lighting Studio are directed by Edwin. Often a project will engage more than one entity.

Work from each of the studios is shown here in seven remarkable projects. These represent only a few of the hundreds of completed projects under the direction of Edwin and Martin over the course of the last twenty-five years. No matter what the project is, work coming out of the four Rambusch studios is always done based on sketches and models designed by the firm. Martin and Edwin continue the firm's tradition of never devoting itself to a single artistic style, but rather directing solutions to meet specific project and client needs and executing these projects with the finest workmanship.

During the last five decades Viggo Bech, Martin, and Edwin have been more attuned to actively engaging their clients in the process of design than studio masters have traditionally been in the past. They often approach projects using what they call informally the "thread of design." This is a process in which the firm helps its clients, or their communities, discuss every aspect of their project in a process that gives them ownership in its outcome. It is accomplished through a series of goal-setting and project-learning sessions that take place throughout the process of conceptualizing, evaluating preliminary designs, evaluating work in progress a project. Using the thread of design, Rambusch helps its clients achieve clarity through the refinement of forms, details, and materials. The process also helps manage expectations, budgets, and schedules. Rambusch has done work for virtually every type of client community and religious denomination. Hundreds of Catholic, Episcopalian (and many other Protestant churches), as well as many Mormon temples, synagogues, and mosques have all utilized work by the firm.

The Artwork and Liturgical Environments Studio is a design studio in every sense of the word. Some projects that it produces are religious and rich in iconography, and others are purely aesthetic and secular. Liturgical environments are, by definition, religious and designed by this studio to enhance the celebration of the liturgy to make it more inspirational and participatory. These are where all of the elements that Rambusch has designed come together in a single place, whether they are stained glass windows or mosaics, new or reconfigured furnishings, such as ambos, altars, and cathedra, or custom designs for marble flooring. One example is the Cathedral of Our Lady of Perpetual Help in Oklahoma City, Oklahoma. The Cathedral was established as a parish church in 1919 and the cathedral finished in 1924. For the church's rededication in 2019, a full interior design and renovation was undertaken, including the creation of a new Blessed Stanley Rother Oratory that memorializes the Roman Catholic priest from Oklahoma who was murdered in Guatemala in 1981. Rambusch was approached to design and shape a new liturgical environment, including the altar, cathedra, ambo, reredos, and the Oratory, itself.

With this project, a special opportunity arose. Wisely, many dioceses had saved objects of value from churches in their jurisdictions that were destined for demolition. Secured in protected warehouses, these objects awaited selection and placement in new locations. Rambusch obtained from one of these warehouses a beautiful marble reredos from a closed church in Baltimore. The company then reworked it to become the Cathedral's new altar of repose and inspired new furnishings that revitalized the Cathedral's interior. The design of this entire worship space yielded a rare occasion for the existing furnishings to have continuity with the use of a family of design elements, such as using four types of rare, richly colored marbles. These were carried from the reredos throughout the remaining sanctuary pieces, including the stone table supporting the reliquary in the Oratory. Sealed within the altar in the sanctuary are first-class relics of Blessed Stanley Rother and four other Saints. The Oratory itself is located in the southern transept of the Cathedral, giving an intimate setting for veneration and prayer in the presence of Rother's relic. Rambusch designed the portrait of Blessed Stanley on the Oratory's rear wall and the polished brass and crystal tabernacle that holds the relic itself (fig. E-1). During the project, Rambusch additionally planned and installed a multi-scene lighting system for its own engineered and decorative LED fixtures. Finally, Rambusch was selected to design the banner, twenty-four feet by sixteen feet, displayed at the Beatification Mass for Rother.

The most remarkable project done by the Stained Glass and Mosaics Studio in recent years are the mosaics inside the Trinity Dome of the Great Upper Church of the Basilica of the National Shrine of the Immaculate Conception (fig. E-2). Since 1931, Rambusch has been involved in many projects at the National Shrine. After Rambusch's successful completion of mosaics in two other domes at the Basilica—the sixty-foot Redemption Dome and Incarnation Dome—in 2013, the Board of Directors, the Friends of the Basilica group, and other donors, were ready to plan for a mosaic for the interior of the great eighty-eight-foot diameter Trinity Dome. This central and largest of the shrine's five domes is located over the crossing and had been unadorned since the Basilica's completion in 1959. The Shrine conducted an international competition, inviting twenty firms to submit proposals. It selected those of three firms, all of which were compensated, but without the commitment for the winner to proceed. Rambusch won this competition and ultimately was allowed to move forward with the project. Once completed, the mosaic dome by Rambusch was—and still is—considered a masterpiece and crowning jewel of the National Shrine.

The design process included studies for the Trinity Dome that were developed for more than a year by Rambusch's design team—including Leandro Velasco, who provided the initial sketches that served as the departure point. As concepts and designs evolved, they were presented to the Basilica's iconography committee. Rambusch worked with the group to address a multitude of questions, such as how the Trinity and Our Lady were to be represented. It was determined that Mary would be shown as the Immaculate Conception facing the Trinity, which included God the Father and the Son (fig. E-3).

The final design had room for twenty-two figures, including two archangels who flank the Trinity and two

E-2 Leandro Velasco, designer; *Trinity dome*, Great Upper Church, Basilica of the National Shrine of the Immaculate Conception, Washington, DC, 2016–18.

E-3 Leandro Velasco, designer; *Viggo Bech Rambusch, reviewing finished mosaics of God the Father and the Son [left to right], with design represented in reverse on paper,* at workshop in Spilimbergo, Italy, for the Great Upper Church, Basilica of the National Shrine of the Immaculate Conception, Washington, DC, 2016.

E-4 and **E-5** Viggo Bech Rambusch, concept designer; Joseph A. Oddi, delineator; Joseph Petrovics, sculptor; Bedi-Makky Art Foundry, fabricator; *FDNY Memorial Wall of 09.11.01* and *Detail of Twin Towers*, bronze bas- relief, FDNY Ten House, Ground Zero, Manhattan, 2006.

choir angels who flank Our Lady. Eighteen saints who were significant to the Americas and to the Basilica were chosen by the committee. The work progressed for two years as the Reverend Monsignor Walter R. Rossi, Martin Rambusch, and Rambusch artists supervised and refined the work while it was being fabricated and installed at the Basilica. The figures of the Saints are sixteen-feet high, and those of God the Father and Our Lady are thirty-two feet high. In the tradition of Saint Mark's Basilica in Venice, the dome's sky is composed of 22-karat gold tesserae.

An example of a project that is secular in nature, yet one that also honors heroic figures, is the FDNY Memorial Wall for the Fire Department of the City of New York (figs. E-4 and E-5). Rambusch managed the entire project, producing the conceptual design and scale models used in its development. Completed in 2006, this permanent monument honors the 343 firefighters on the FDNY's active-duty roll who were killed during the terrorist attack and subsequent collapse of the World Trade Center buildings on September 11, 2001. It is located on the west wall of the Engine 10, Ladder 10 fire station, also known as "Ten House," on the corner of Greenwich Street and Liberty Street. Only the latter street separates Ten House from the World Trade Center Plaza. Due to its location, the firehouse was heavily damaged and its staff decimated by the tragedy.

According to the FDNY, the purpose of the classical-realist composition was to depict every group of people, type of vehicle, and apparatus that responded to the crisis that day. The monument is a six-foot-high, fifty-six-foot-long bas-relief. Consisting of fourteen panels put together in three sections, it was cast from a total of 8,000 pounds of bronze and is one of the largest bas-reliefs made of that material in the United States. This project was the collaborative effort of a dedicated team that raised funds and created the sensitive sculpture, which fuses emotion and design. The lower part of the memorial lists all the active members of the FDNY by rank alphabetically who fell that day, and it includes a timeline of the events and recovery efforts. Rambusch illustrator Joseph Oddi and sculptor Joseph Petrovics created and refined the depiction. The firm also orchestrated the casting work and the installation. The Custom Lighting Studio additionally created inconspicuous, weatherproof, wall-washing luminaires to graze the front surface of the sculpture. These nine, four-foot-long, hand-made picture lights enhance the warmth of the burnished bronze, reveal the sculpted metal, and highlight its focal points. A custom-made, programmable dimming system allows the cherished memorial to be bathed in light around the clock.

The Engineered Lighting Studio and Custom Lighting Studio are separate yet closely related. Both began with the design and manufacturing of light shields for churches. A separate business for engineered lighting at Rambusch slowly began emerging during the 1920s and 1930s. An engineered luminaire is one whose performance is determined by applying the physics of light to a fixture's design in order to achieve a desired result, such as an even wash of light over a room's horizontal or vertical surfaces. Whether the luminaire has a beautiful appearance—and some Rambusch fixtures are works of art and in museum collections (see figs. 4-17 and 4-21)—is often not as important is its ability to be manufactured. By the time Harold and Viggo F. E. Rambusch's cousin Edward Rambusch had invented the Downlite, and patented it in 1939, the company's ambitions to continue innovating in this new field of engineered lighting were fully established. Many of Rambusch's later inventions in lighting are documented in this book.

Today, innovation remains a key part of the culture of the more recently established Engineered Lighting Studio, as each successive generation of light sources demands its own technical makeover. For example, its new Mark V LED Downlites only bear the slightest familial resemblance to Edward's Downlite. Now circuitry for "driving" the LEDs and sophisticated dimming systems are part of the fixture. Rambusch has developed a proprietary LED cooling system it calls "Flite," which permits a high volume of LED-sourced light to be generated, even in a fixture with a small profile, while its capacity for expelling excess heat protects the expected long lamp life of the LEDs. As electronic dimming computers, Bluetooth communications, and color control systems become ever more complex, the firm continues to adapt its products to them. Many of the innovations of the Engineering Studio are incorporated, unseen, into work done by the Custom Lighting Studio.

Because the design of high-end residential, commercial, and religious spaces always requires luminaires that are either one-of-a-kind or limited production items, Rambusch's Custom Lighting Studio thrives. Some may be based on the suggestions of an interior or lighting designer. Some are for a single project or replications of existing fixtures that have gone missing with no pictorial references to use as a starting point. Others might involve pieces of old fixtures handed to Rambusch in a box, and

E-6 *Illumination study for period rooms*, J. Paul Getty Museum, Los Angeles, CA, 1998.

E-7 *Detail, European period room: as if it were lit by candles centuries ago*, J. Paul Getty Museum, Los Angeles, CA, 1998.

E-8 Frédéric Auguste Bartholdi, designer; *Original Statue of Liberty torch and flame, after phases of flame redesign by others*, repoussé copper and glass, exhibition centerpiece at Statue of Liberty Museum, Liberty Island, Upper New York Bay, original fabrication, 1876; included in monument, 1881–86; restored and installed by Rambusch Decorating Company, 2018.

E-9 Frédéric Auguste Bartholdi, designer; J. Supor & Son, riggers (at left); *Disassembly of original Statue of Liberty torch and flame, before restoration and exhibition installation*, repoussé copper and glass, Statue of Liberty Museum, Liberty Island, Upper New York Bay, 2018.

it creates what the rest of it might have looked like based on its designers' knowledge of historical fixtures.

Both the Custom Lighting and Engineered Lighting Studios will always remain true to the firm's roots as a craft shop where much of the work—casting, polishing, brazing, painting, and wiring—is still done by artisans, many of whom are long-term employees. Its ability to continually evolve its lighting offerings is possible because these artisans pass metal fabrication traditions from one generation to the next.

In some circumstances, lighting designers turn to the Rambusch Engineered Lighting Studio to develop a solution to a problem for which no off-the-shelf fixture exists. While designing the lighting for fourteen rooms of period European furniture designed by architect Thierry Despont for the decorative arts wing of the J. Paul Getty Museum in 1998, the late Howard Brandston asked the company to create a new downlight. His task was to lull visitors back in time by presenting environments lit as they might have been centuries ago. Brandston wanted light to come through tiny ceiling apertures rather than from track lights often used in museums that hang, he once complained, "from period ceilings like so many bats."

A trick of the eye was needed to make ambient illumination appear to be coming from candles, while doing what only modern illumination can do: enrich the visual experience by bringing focus to specific objects, emphasizing their finishes and three-dimensional shapes. Working with him on a full-scale mockup, Rambusch produced an illumination study (fig. E-6) to illustrate the light emanating from a novel, multifunctional, recessed museum fixture. The resulting luminaire's reflector design is fully adjustable: it can wash walls with light, accent specific pieces of art, and provide downlighting, all from one unseen fixture tucked above the ceiling. The resulting rooms are jewel boxes filled with filigreed eighteenth- and nineteenth-century French furniture, tapestries, painted silks, and *objets d'art* (fig. E-7). Fewer luminaires were needed than was typical for museum displays, and with dimmers extending lamp life and helping create the look of candlelight, maintenance and savings in power costs were substantial.

The restoration, relocation, and relighting of the original torch and flame of the Statue of Liberty is an example of a project where the work of the Custom and Engineered Lighting Studios overlapped. In 2018, Rambusch was selected by Phelps Construction to lead a team of artisans to move this artifact to the new eponymous museum that was scheduled to open the following year. The original flame had been modified several times (fig. E-8). Shortly after the Statue had been completed, holes were punched into the its copper sheathing in a failed attempt to make it function as a lighthouse. Later, the sheathing was redesigned further. Rectangular openings were cut into the copper, which created a grid into which amber panes of glass were placed. These leaked badly for decades, causing damage to the torch, flame, and arm below. In 1984, Frédéric Auguste Bartholdi's original gold-leafed flame design was recreated at the top of the Statue and the first flame relocated to a museum in the Statue's pedestal. Now, with the construction of the Statue of Liberty Museum, it had yet another home and life.

Under the direction of Rambusch, the 3,000-pound torch and flame were moved 470 feet using a special, hydraulically-stabilized vehicle (fig. E-9). It was then cleaned, conserved, and reassembled on site based on recommendations established by a conservation survey ordered by the firm. Rambusch's work on the "lamp beside the golden door" (to quote Emma Lazarus) concluded with the creation of new lighting inside the flame that makes its old amber glass glow. This new LED illumination system inside the flame can be programmed for color, density and light intensity. The use of LED technology was made possible in the tight space through the use of Rambusch's proprietary fixture cooling system.

Undoubtedly the Utah State Capitol in Salt Lake City is the largest restoration and re-creation project the Custom Lighting Studio has undertaken, with more than 1400 individual luminaires handled over the course of the five-year project. At the outset, it was clear that an innovate approach would be required for the process of choosing a contractor for the restoration. At the request of David H. Hart, then Architect of the Capitol, legislation was passed to allow the selection process to consider hands-on experience and merit rather than price alone. After the extensive qualification process Rambusch was chosen to restore and replicate all of the historical light fixtures within this grand Beaux-Arts building.

Contracts specified a complete inventory, assessment, removal, disassembly, restoration, and reinstallation of the Capitol's 450 existing fixtures, including the chandelier that had pride of place in the Rotunda (figs. E-10 and

E-10 *Rotunda chandelier: removal for restoration process*, Utah State Capitol (Richard Kletting, architect, 1912–15; Robert N. Pett, architect and David H. Hart, Architect of the Capitol, later restoration); Salt Lake City, UT, ca. 2003.

E-11 *Rotunda chandelier: historical assembly study*; Utah State Capitol (Richard Kletting, architect, 1912–15; Robert N. Pett, architect and David H. Hart, Architect of the Capitol, later restoration); Salt Lake City, UT, 2004.

E-11). All of the fixtures were documented, disassembled, packed and sent to Rambusch workshops. The company then created a hierarchical family of new fixtures to replace those lost over the years. Forty-six kinds of luminaires were created by "harvesting" elements from existing heirloom fixtures, and then skillfully blending them into new complementary designs. To achieve this, molds were made of original components and used to make new bronze castings.

The resulting inventory of new parts assured the continuity of design throughout the interior, while reducing cost. A separate medallion featuring a beehive, Utah's state symbol, was incorporated into multiple pendant fixtures. Various finishes included multiple layers of hand-rubbed, burnt-umber glaze. More than 1400 individual luminaires were handled over the course of the project.

The Milken Center for Advancing the American Dream, located across Pennsylvania Avenue from the US Treasury Building in Washington, DC, is a project that tested the capabilities of both lighting studios at Rambusch. The Milken Center, which is scheduled for completion in 2025, was founded by philanthropist Michael Milken and dedicated to the proposition that all people who have a dream and the drive to achieve it should have the opportunity to make it come true. The Center's new home comprises several historic buildings that are being modernized to provide museum space and an auditorium, a banquet hall, and private offices for the Milken Foundation. Two of the buildings once housed the Riggs National Bank and the American Security & Trust Company. They blend with each so seamlessly they are often thought to be the same building.

During the extensive reconstruction and repurposing of these buildings for the Center, the Milken family expressed a desire to preserve and reuse as many of the existing rooms and their architectural features as possible. The lead architect and the lighting design firm Available Light selected Rambusch for the careful restoration and replication of the historic fixtures. The firms worked together to refurbish existing luminaires and develop and refine new decorative fixtures for the museum. After several adjustments and the installation of a full-size mockup to validate scale, proportion and illumination, the fixture designs moved into fabrication.

The resulting chandeliers are made of yellow brass and have layers of decorative details, starting with a variety of unique cast acanthus leaves, hand-formed arms and decorative twisted rope. The chandeliers are topped off with mouth-blown, opal-white glass shades. Hidden within the chandeliers are two additional illumination elements. Within the body ring of the fixtures are engineered LED downlights for task lighting, while small uplights hidden in the chandelier crown add sparkle to the brass chain and the ceiling canopy. Companion wall sconces share details and mouth-blown glass shades with the chandeliers.

Three generations of Rambusches have done work in the complex of buildings where the Milken project is located. In the late 1950s Rambusch provided recessed downlights for the banking hall of the American Security & Trust Company. Then in the 1980s, Viggo Bech Rambusch created two bronze torchieres for the new entrance of the same building (see fig. 3-8), which allowed easy access to the US Treasury Building, across the street.

The thought that three generations of the Rambusch family have worked in the buildings that make up the Milken Center, and that other buildings exist where all four generations have worked such as Saint Raymond's Church in the Bronx (see fig. 1-15), is a satisfying way to sum up *Rambusch: The First 100 Years, 1898-1998*. The Rambusch Decorating Company is a remarkable family business, in itself a tradition, and indeed one that has its own culture. It has prospered in good times and endured in bad, through ingenuity and a willingness to meet diverse challenges. The family has accepted change, adopted new technologies and artistic styles, and had an openness to taking on whatever artistic or technical challenge that might come along. It has survived wars, economic depression and recession, and, in 2020-2021, something few who are not epidemiologists had ever heard of before: a pandemic.

That Frode's childhood sketches from more than 160 years ago were collected and preserved, as have been the countless drawings, letters, and photographs produced by the Rambusch company since then shows that the family has always understood it was doing something significant, and that it was essential to maintain and preserve the documents that record it. These are tangible markers that have, above all, indicated a spirit of optimism and faith in the future. The successes that Edwin and Martin Rambusch have enjoyed in running the company over the past quarter century are a fine indication that they have inherited their forefathers' joy in bringing beautiful art, environments, and light into the lives of people, and that their company will be around for many years to come.

ACKNOWLEDGMENTS

I am indebted to several friends and colleagues for their contributions and guidance along the way in preparing this book. First, my thanks go to Geraldine M. Rohling and Charles D. Linn, for their fine Introduction and Epilogue, respectively. This book is richer for their astute observations and perspectives. Barbara S. Christen has edited the text for clarity and flow of ideas throughout. I deeply appreciate her keen eye, tenacity, and knowledge of architectural history and design that she brought to bear. She also exhibited care and precision in checking the accuracy of sites and references. Because of her involvement, the documentation of *Rambusch: The First 100 Years, 1898–1998* is more complete.

Regarding early drafts and technical issues, I am grateful to Lori Buti for putting my original manuscript into digital form. Dayle Keller exhibited consummate skill in reworking the text, questioning exactitude, imposing order, and much more. Mati Gavasheli, graduate of the Rhode Island School of Design (RISD), brought talent and enthusiasm to the beginning graphic design possibilities for this book. His father, David Gavasheli, provided invaluable assistance in scanning many items from the Rambusch Decorating Company archives that are included here. Company photographer Kevin Simonson provided much-needed skill and and support in providing photographs. For any omissions or errors that I have overlooked, I take full responsibility.

I also want to express my gratitude to Charles A. Birnbaum, President and CEO of The Cultural Landscape Foundation, for his guidance in navigating the publishing realm and helping us find Oro Editions. Stacee Gravelle Lawrence at Cydonia Editions provided timely and helpful advice in this process.

Previous generations of the Rambusch family, especially Viggo F. E. Rambusch, company president from 1961 to 1963, had the foresight to preserve thousands of Rambusch drawings and records. These and later materials, covering the years between 1910 and 1984, have been deposited at the Department of Drawings & Archives of Avery Architectural & Fine Arts Library, Columbia University. My children and their families have given unfailing support and inspiration for which I am so thankful. Lastly, to my dear husband and lifelong partner Viggo, I am profoundly grateful for your encouragements over the course of seeing this project to fruition. You have enlivened the narrative with enumerable details about the history of the Rambusch Decorating Company and your continuing good judgment and humor at every juncture have been a precious gift.

Catha Jackson Grace
New York, NY

APPENDIX A

Interior Decoration firms, Manhattan: 1880s–1890s and Previous Rambusch Affiliations

Except for the listing of Arnold & Locke, in Brooklyn, which was a separate city until 1898, the information below comes from the New York City Directories. (I am indebted to Mosette Broderick, who supplied many of these addresses). The directories indicate the following locations of interior decoration firms:

1884
Tiffany Studios
333–341 Fourth Avenue
(Stained-glass and interior design)

William Baumgarten & Co.
369 Fifth Avenue
(Aubusson-style tapestries and design)

Herter Brothers
894 Broadway
(Cabinet making and other furniture, interior design, and upholstery)

Herts Brothers
298 Fifth Avenue
(Furniture and interior decoration)

L. Marcotte and Company
[no address]
(Cabinet making and interior design)

Pottier & Stymus
375–377 Lexington Avenue
(Furniture and interior design)

George A. Schastey
1683 Broadway
(Furniture, architectural woodwork, interior decoration, curtains, and upholstery)

Arnold & Locke Studio*
250 Fulton Street, Brooklyn
(Painting and decorating)

1893
Rambusch & Pettit
120 Court Street, Brooklyn, New York

1894–1896
Rambusch & Pettit
1193 Broadway

This location was next door to the elaborate Fifth Avenue Theatre, which had been designed by Francis H. Kimball.

1897–1898
Gibson Art Glass and Decorating Company*
142 East 33rd Street
Frode Rambusch, chief designer

* These entries were supplied by the author.

APPENDIX B

Letter of Incorporation

Articles of Incorporation, December 1898.

Fol.1 State of New York, :
:ss:
City and County of New York. :

WE, THE UNDERSIGNED, all being persons of full age, and at least two-thirds being citizens of the United States, and all being residents of the State of New York, desiring to form a Stock Corporation, pursuant to the provisions of the Business Corporations Law of the State of New York, do hereby make, sign, acknowledge and file this certificate for that purpose as follows:

F I R S T : The name of the proposed corporation is the "RAMBUSCH GLASS and DECORATING COMPANY."

2
92

S E C O N D : The purposes for which said corporation is to be formed are the manufacture and sale of stained glass, the execution, manufacture and sale of ecclesiastical and domestic decorationsfor churches, houses and other buildings, and of sculpture, relief and mosaic work.

T H I R D : The amount of the capital stock is Twenty-five Hundred Dollars, all of which shall be

3 Common Stock.

F O U R T H : The number of shares of which the capital stock shall consist is Fifty (50) of the par

210-92-1

value of Fifty Dollars each, and the amount of capital with which said corporation will begin business is Twenty-five Hundred Dollars.

F I F T H : Its principal business office is to be located in the Borough of Manhattan, City of New York, in the County and State of New York.

4 S I X T H : Its duration is to be fifty years.

S E V E N T H : The number of its Directors is to be three.

E I G H T H : The names and Post-office addresses of the Directors for the first year are as follows:--

N A M E .	POST-OFFICE ADDRESS.
Frode C. W. Rambusch,	No. 401 St. Nicholas Ave.,N. Y. C.
William F. Hencken,	No. 22 West 82nd Street, N. Y. C.
George D. Hencken,	No. 22 West 82nd Street, N. Y. C.

5 N I N T H : The names and Post-office addresses of the Subscribers and a statement of the number of shares of stock which each agrees to take in the corporation, are as follows:

N A M E S .	POST-OFFICE ADDRESSES.	NO. OF SHARES.
Frode C.W.Rambusch,	No. 401 St.Nicholas Ave.N.Y.C.	ONE.
William F.Hencken,	" 22 W. 82nd St.N.Y.C.	FORTY-EIGHT.
George D. Hencken,	" 22 W.82nd St.N.Y.C.	ONE.

6 IN WITNESS WHEREOF we have made, signed, acknowledged and filed this certificate in duplicate.

Dated December, 17th, 1898.

Frode C W Rambusch
William F. Hencken
George D. Hencken

STATE OF NEW YORK. :
: ss.
CITY AND COUNTY OF NEW YORK. :

On this seventeenth day of December, 1898, before me personally came FRODE C. W. RAMBUSCH, WILLIAM F. HENCKEN and GEORGE D. HENCKEN, all of whom are to me personally known and known to me to be the persons described in and who made and signed the foregoing certificate, and they severally and duly acknowledged to me that they had made, signed and executed the same for the uses and purposes therein set forth.

Chas. Ruxton

KINGS CO.
Certificate filed in New York.

210-92-3

F. Rickeman, the first Rambusch apprentice, detail from studio interior of Rambusch & Pettit, Interior Decorators, 1193 Broadway, near 28th Street, Manhattan, ca. 1895.

APPENDIX C

Impressions of an Early Employee

The following letter from ca. 1950 offers impressions of an apprentice's lot at the end of the nineteenth century.

* * *

433 W. 49th Street Los Angeles 37, CA

Dear Mr. Michael McCarthy:

When on my most happy visit to you and the Rambuschs [sic], where you and all the heads of departments, etc., of so great a firm so kindly received me in a way so far above my highest expectations, even from all the employees I met, you said it might be well to send you a sketchy description of how I met dear Mr. Frode Rambusch and what happened as well as I can remember during the firm's infancy, you might say. Well here goes, and I hope I will not bore you by making too much of a story, a thing I might easily do knowing my inclinations and limitations.

Well, I first met Mr. Frode Rambusch, my dear old boss and real friend in Mystic, Connecticut, my New England home. He had come there to finish some figure subjects he had painted in New York and to superintend the decorative work on Capt. Spicer's Mansion—it could rightly be called a palace. I could say, as in architecture and decoration and furnishing, it equaled many palaces I have seen in the old world. Capt. Spicer was a retired sea captain of the old Civil War and pirate chasing days—one of the few millionaires of those early days. My dear old dad was his overseer, florist, and gardener on his large estate.

Mr. Rambusch at the time was doing the work for a firm called "Tidden & Arnold," later called "Arnold & Locke." My father and Mr. Rambusch became fast friends for years. They had many happy evenings at our home where he often brought his sweet pretty wife and later his curly haired boy, Harold to see us. We were so proud for many years of the decoration Mr. Rambusch did in our parlor (for an Xmas present) as the living room was called in those days. We were the envy of our neighbors.

I was about 15 years old I think at that time, and I used to go and watch Mr. Rambusch work. He liked me and I worshipped him, not only for his ability as an artist, but for his kindly nature to me, only a punk kid. One day while watching him work on a ceiling, I happened to step back and knock over a paint pail and I got hell from the painter foreman. Mr. Rambusch told him to sit on a tack or something to that effect and told me that when I was old enough—18 years—and after he had started a firm of his own, I could come to New York and be his apprentice. I went there and earned the large salary of $5.00 per week, so with the help from home financially, I got on finely and Mr. R. insisted I go to the evening classes at the National Academy—those days on 14th Street—and to Pratt Institute, Brooklyn, later.

Mr. Rambusch lived in Hastings for awhile. He sent me to paper a room there. It looked like a crossword puzzle when you could get over the first shock. He thought I felt hurt when he said "I can't let you hang paper again." I never have since, thank God.

Our studio at that time was at 1193 Broadway, corner of 26th Street I believe [sic]. Sometimes the pickings were rather slim in the decorative line, so I had to paint storefronts, roofs, etc. Dogs worried me a lot, mostly when doing storefronts. They had a funny way of showing their opinion of my work. It displeased me a lot.

I liked roofs better except on cold days. Once when slopping red lead on a Mr. James roof—it was tin, and

John Hartell (at left) and Frode Rambusch (at right, in straw hat) with their wives and the Hartells' daughter, out "on the town" in New York, 1893. Hartell and Rambusch had worked together in the 1880s in Vienna as decorative painters.

when I hit a chimney, a lot would bounce back on my face—overalls got some, too. When I was most interested in my work, the butler poked his head up from the skylight and said someone in the alley wants to see you. It was somebody, all right, but it was the last somebody I would care to see in the condition I was in, as it was my school-day sweetheart from the home town of Mystic, and was my face red as she said, "Why Freddie Rickeman, you said you were going to New York to learn to be an artist—the ones at home use a brush—in New York they use a mop. I won't tell anyone home she said." To help her to keep her promise, I spent a lot of my large salary taking her to shows, etc.

Well, greener days came—the others were only unusual like Los Angeles weather. We worked on one Catholic church—St. Gabriel's in New York—six months in Monsignor Farley's and nine months in a church in Harlem—129th Street. I think it was called All Saint's and many artists and painters were employed; Mr. Hendrik Olsen, I think his name was, being the foreman. He was Mr. Rambusch's lovely wife's brother. Never can I forget his kind treatment of me. He gave me every opportunity of advancement and didn't say too much. One day when Old Hansen was marbling some green columns and Monsignor Farley was watching him, I was washing the ceiling about 75 feet above them, so I let a dirty sponge fall on his head. Neither he nor Monsignor Farley could see me as drop clothes hid me. It spattered considerably. I didn't mind if they both got a little. Hansen did, because the next day we were calcimining the back of the organ, he was on the top plank and he gave me a full Dutch brush full of green, top of my head. He laughed a lot quietly, as Mr. Rambusch was on the other side of the organ.

Well, the firm prospered and decorated many mansions and theatres so I had more and more beer pails to carry for the men. They called it "rushing the growler," and one painter said I could rush a little faster if I would take a pole on each shoulder and string the cans along it[,] I wouldn't have to make so many trips. I told them they might play that tune on an apprentice in the Old Country but not on me. Even in China they would have cans about the same shape these were—mostly stovepipe elbows with different crooks following individual ideas as which one would hold more beer without the bartender noticing it.

One day I was gilding from a cushion in the lobby of the old Waldorf Astoria Hotel, when a big fat German hollered from under the scaffold and said, "what are you doing, boy?" I said "gilding." He said "I know it." I felt quite proud. A painter said "that's the walking delegate." That didn't bother me any—didn't know what it meant—but did later as he said "come down." I did, and just then, Mr. Rambusch came in. The delegate said "dot boy must have $4.00 a day for that work." Mr. Rambusch said "we can't pay him that." I was getting $12.00 a week—a lot, I thought.

Well, Mr. Rambusch had to discharge me. I think he only meant temporarily, but I was sort of proud and next day I went to Grovers Hall where they held union meetings and was told in the meeting they wanted no more apprentices or journeymen, either. There was a saloon downstairs, so I thought the right thing was to go downstairs, being it was a hot day, and forget my sorrow in beer. A young Jewish fellow named Charley Lewis came to me and said, "what are you drinking so much beer for?" I said "they won't let me join the union." He said "I'll see about that," and took me upstairs and told me to wait outside the room. He went inside and made one hell of a noise and lots of talk and the bunch came out, carried me in and made me a journeyman. So when I got outside I told Charley I was awful pleased—but where are we—right here—but really, where am I? No job—too young to be a journeyman, etc. He found me a job as a housepainter—$3.00 a day. I worked quite awhile at that and then got a job with K. J. Collins & Company through a friend, an Englishman, Frank Kuble. They made favors, etc., for banquets. We painted flowers, etc., on furniture, lampshades, etc. I liked the work. I didn't have to belong to the union and I only made $2.50 a day. It was about six months since I had seen Mr. Rambusch and I really missed him. As I was about to be laid off as the work was seasonable, I thought I'd better go see Mr. Rambusch and Mr. Pettit. They seemed as pleased to see me as I was to see them. Mr. Rambusch said "can't you in some way ask Collins if you can leave them?" (I felt they wouldn't weep too long at Collins if I asked them to sacrifice my services knowing full well I was to be fired pronto).

So I went back and received full journeyman's pay until the end of my apprenticeship. A Mr. David Paton was hired as a designer. He was a year or so older than I—a great landscape artist, too. We became great friends and he told me he was to go back to England in a few months. He had been sent here to do some decoration for his uncle, Thomas May, in London and was going back to work for him. Mr. May did work for Queen Victoria often. He studied in France for years and was a great artist, and when I got to London I often worked with them both—once in Buckingham Palace, St. Paul Ct. and was thankful for their work and instructions. Well, I worked some 3½ years in England, studying evenings at Westminster, Kensington, etc.

This ends the part I played with the good firm of Rambusch & Pettit after working for Campbell Smith—Waring & Gillow, Maple & Co., and some five years in Paris—and after traveling in Italy, Switzerland, etc., came back to the good old U.S.A. One day in Hollywood I was talking with a Jewish fellow about New York. He had newly arrived from there. He happened to say he had been working for Rambusch & Co. I heard off and on during the years that the firm still existed, yet I had never known for sure, as when in New York on our honeymoon Eva and I hadn't time to look up the firm. That was 32 years ago. I had always hoped to look up Mr. Rambusch, but the years passed and I was mostly traveling with stock companies in the west and seldom got to New York. This man told me Mr. Rambusch had passed away. I felt sad, as I had hoped one day to see him again. Common sense should have told me there was little chance of me meeting him again at my age.

I resolved then, as he told me, that Mr. Harold and Mr. Viggo carried on the firm; that I would visit them should I ever have the good fortune to be in New York again. So after some years my dream came true, and you can well think what a thrill it was to me when Charley Keck, a great sculptor and lifelong friend told me "Why Rambusch & Co. are only three blocks from here—why don't you run up and see them." I did, and had a greater thrill when I saw "The Rambusch Building" painted over the entrance. When I approached the elevator and thought when I entered it I would see the man who, as a baby boy (I was only a boy, too) I rocked to sleep when his dear dad and sweet lovely mother went out for an evening to a show, dance, etc. He had golden curls then; how will he look now—how will he receive me? Well, he and his brother, Viggo and Mr. McCarthy and all, from the heads of departments to the office girls and all employees gave me such a happy greeting and I will cherish my visit with them as one of the great spots of my life's happy memories.

Merry Christmas and a Happy New Year to you and all the firm of Rambusch & Co., and excuse the awful writing.

Respectfully,
F. Rickeman

APPENDIX D

List of Jobs (selected), 1926–1932

This list offers a random selection from Rambusch Decorating Company ledgers to indicate the range of cost and geographical location of theater commissions received by the firm. The original volumes reside in the Rambusch Archives, now located at Avery Architectural & Fine Arts Library, Columbia University. The five boroughs of the city of New York—Manhattan, Brooklyn, Queens, The Bronx, and Staten Island—are not given the state designation "NY."

*Asterisks denote entries with missing information.

1926 September

New Brandt Theatre, Brooklyn $4,700.00

1927 April

Sol[omon] Brill, *The Fresh Pond $6,000.00

Loew's Midland Theatre, Kansas City, MO $61,980.00

p/d $48,335

fixtures $6,510

metalwork $1,940

misc. $5,195

September

*Garsson (Chester Theatre), The Bronx $8,500.00

October

Loew's Midland (extras), Kansas City $2,685.23

December

Loew's State Capital Theatre, Syracuse, NY $26,000.00

1928 January

*Chapel State [Ohio Theatre], Columbus, OH $21,500.00

February

Trenton, NJ [*theater not listed] $11,250.00

March

B.F. Keith, Vaudeville, Exchange, [Manhattan] .... [*cost not listed]

State Theatre (decorating), Union City, NJ $370.00

Midway Theatre, Beacon, NY $25,000.00

Loew's State Theatre, Syracuse, NY $1,187.13

City Hall Theatre, Hartford, CT $6,000.00

June

Loew's State Theatre, Providence, RI $18,500.00

Loew's Palace Theatre, Washington, DC $5,000.00

October

Paramount Theatre, Brooklyn $50,000.00

Boyd Theatre, Philadelphia, PA $5,000.00

December

Paramount Theatre [*location not listed] $8,130.01

1929 March

Loew's Kings Theatre, Brooklyn $27,000.00

July

Saint George's Theatre, Staten Island $14,500.00
Strand Theatre, Brooklyn $7,000.00
Strand Theatre, Manhattan $9,500.00

August

Alvin Theatre, Pittsburgh, PA $9,100.00
Lyceum Theatre, New Britain, CT $7,300.00

September

Loew's Pitkin Theatre, Brooklyn $20,000.00
Apollo Theatre [*likely Manhattan] $55.00
Loew's Brooklyn Theatre, Brooklyn $167.08

October

Warner [Strand] Theatre, Syracuse, NY $12,000.00
Beacon Theatre, Manhattan $6,180.00

1930 January

Hollywood Theatre [*most likely Manhattan] $21,000.00

1931 October

Tremont Theatre, The Bronx $15,443.85

1931 November

Fox Audubon Theatre, Manhattan $486.00

1932 October

Trans-Lux Theatre, Manhattan $1,650.00
Rockefeller Center #10 Theatre, Manhattan $5,600.00

1932 November

Rockefeller Center #10 Theatre, Manhattan $6,000.00
Rockefeller Center #10 Theatre, Manhattan $4,191.11

1932 December

Radio City Theatre, Manhattan $4,500.00
Radio City Theatre, Manhattan $36,850.00

APPENDIX E

New York World's Fair, 1939: Partial List of Commissions

This list was compiled courtesy of Viggo F. E. Rambusch.

Key:
Name of building
Client
General contractor, architect, and/or designer (if known)
Work executed

***

American Telephone & Telegraph Company Building
Voorhees, Gmelin and Walker, architects
Vermilya-Brown Company, Inc., G.C.
"The Seven Ages of Man & the Bell System" façade, exhibition, and gilding

Art Museum
Harrison & Fouilhoux, architects
Lyonel Feininger, designer
Murals

Ballantine Gardens, Inc.
Ely Jacques Kahn & Scott & Tegan, architects
Thompson-Starrett, Inc.
Interior and exterior painting and murals

Board of Directors' Room
Board of Design
Mural map

Botany Worsted Mills Exhibition
Magill Smith, architect
Metal exhibition

Brass Rail Restaurants
Louis Allen Abramson, architect
Painting and decorating

Brazilian Pavilion
Lucio Costa & Oscar Niemeyer, and Soares, Filho and Paul Lester Wiener, architects
Hageman-Harris Co., Inc.
Painting and decorating

Business Systems and Insurance Building
Board of Design
John M. Sitton, designer of murals
Four murals (three metal and one painted) and exterior painting

"Casino of Nations"
Dowd & Wortmann Construction Co.
Interior and exterior painting

Communications Building
Board of Design
Painting and exterior painting

Consolidated Edison Building
Harrison & Fouilhoux, architects
Downlites and trough lighting

Cosmetics Building
Board of Design Interior
Painting and decorating

Court of States—Spanish Section
Board of Design
Painting

Danish Building
Tyge Hvass, architect
Boyd-Janoff Company, Inc.
Painting and decorating

Distilled Spirits Building
Witold Gordon, designer, and Morris Sanders, architect, for structural banner
Painting and thirty-foot murals

Electrical Products Building
Board of Design
Martha Axley, designer
Two painted murals

Ford Building
Albert Kahn, Inc., architects of special display (forty-five feet long), included Walter Dorwin Teague, designer animation, colored illumination, and other effects
Hegeman-Harris Company
Special display and Three-phase map

General Motors Building
Albert Kahn, architect of mobile mural and Norman Bel Geddes, designer of painting and decorating
Turner Construction Company
Mobile mural, painting, and decorating

Heineken Dutch Town, on the Zuiderzee
Louis A. Brown, architect
Painting and decorating

Icelandic Building
George A. Fuller Company
Painting and decorating

Johns-Manville Building
Shreve, Lamb & Harmon, architects
Hildreth Meière, designer of metalwork
Metal decoration

Marine Transportation Building
Board of Design
Lyonel Feininger, designer
Two painted murals

Medicine and Public Health, Science and Education Building Complex
Board of Design
Hildreth Meière, designer
Five murals (four painted and one metal)

Merrie England
J. T. Schless
Schless Construction Company
Painting and decorating

New York City Exhibitions
Architecture and Scientific Painting

Palestine Pavilion
Schwarzkopf and Lukach, Inc.
Painting and decorating

Polish Building
Jan Cybulski and Cross & Cross, architects
George A. Fuller, Company
Lighting, painting, and decorating

Schaeffer Building
Eggers & Higgins, architects
Painting

Switzerland Building
William Lescaze & John E. Weber, architects
William L. Crow Construction Co.
Interior and exterior painting

Temple of Religion
Clarence S. Stein, Alfred E. Poor, Oliver Reagan, architects
Murals

Time and Space Building
Henry M. Weitzner, Inc.
Interior painting

World's Fair Station
Board of Design (LIRR, IRT, BMT)
Entrance, platforms and ramps, and exterior painting

APPENDIX F

Rambusch Decorating Company: Design Studios and Workshops

The Rambusch Decorating Company was incorporated in December 1898 in the borough of Manhattan. (See Appendix B, Letter of Incorporation). It was established at 160 Fifth Avenue, also known as the Mohawk Building, which was designed by R. H. Robertson for the developer E. van Ingen. On the fifth floor of this building was the office of McKim, Mead & White.

Rambusch Design Studio	Rambusch Workshops
1898–1911 160 5th Ave. New York, NY	1898–1911, Paint Shop 22 6th Ave. New York, NY
1912–1946 2 West 45th St. New York, NY	1919–1921 East 42nd St. New York, NY
	1921–1926 343 East 44th St. New York, NY
	1926–1946 332 East 48th St. New York, NY
1947–1997 40 West 13th St. New York, NY	1947–1992, Art Metal and Lighting Fixture Shop 40 West 13th St. New York, NY
	1947–1998, Glass Shop 40 West 13th St. New York, NY
1997–2002 28 West 25th St. New York, NY	1993–1999, Art Metal shop and Lighting Fixture Shop 218–230 South Parkway Clifton, NJ
2003–present 160 Cornelison Ave. Jersey City, NJ	1999–present, All workshops 160 Cornelison Avenue Jersey City, NJ

Staff of the Rambusch Decorating Company, in front of offices at 40 West 13th Street, Manhattan, June 14, 1976.

APPENDIX G

Staff of the Rambusch Decorating Company, 1976

To list the names of all the people who, over a century, contributed their talent to the Rambusch Decorating Company would be difficult indeed. It would be an egregious error to allow them to go unacknowledged because their work has been a wellspring of collective activity that lies at the core of the company. In symbolic tribute to those who have gone before, and in recognition of those engaged in work in the late-twentieth century, the names of all Rambusch craftspeople, designers, and staff in 1976 are noted below. In the words of William Haley, who worked for the firm for thirty-five years, "I thought of Rambusch as a 'League of Nations' because of their diverse personnel." This statement could still be made today.

Rambusch employees, left to right:

1. Caesar Bongiorni
2. Vincent Stapleton
3. Richard Kraemer
4. James Hollis
5. Laura Rosen
6. Albert Wayner
7. Wesley Straughn
8. Joseph Costa
9. Albert Weiner
10. Alan Seif
11. George Carson
12. Arthur Turner
13. Pat Breheny
14. Albert Staudle
15. Frank Imperio
16. Barbara-Jo Utgard
17. Charles Weiss
18. James Alston
19. Jules Paisner
20. Stefan Scheidling
21. Edward Boegel
22. Dorothea McCarthy
23. Patsy D.Angio
24. Elisabeth Baltzer
25. Paul Romeo
26. Bruce Gutelius
27. Geri Bringman
28. Richard Zimmerman
29. Martin Zivotovsky
30. Robert King
31. Abraham Gruber
32. Ling Ling Hsu
33. Harold Rambusch
34. Johann Struna
35. Jose Gellinez
36. Walter Martens
37. Christopher Dillon
38. Viggo F. E. Rambusch
39. Viggo Bech Rambusch
40. Joseph Manzella
41. Donald Dynan
42. Robert Tucker
43. Leon Moderacki
44. Peter White
45. Alois Singer
46. Robert Rambusch
47. Joseph Heidelmeier
48. Michael J. Ducar
49. Peter Kusenda
50. Frances Carlotti
51. John McNicholas
52. Michael McNicholas
53. Salvatore Rotello
54. William Weber
55. Louis Bongiorni
56. George Garrison
57. Anthony DeStefano
58. Abraham Newerstein
59. Bernardo Lizcano
60. Manuel Feris
61. Leandro Velasco

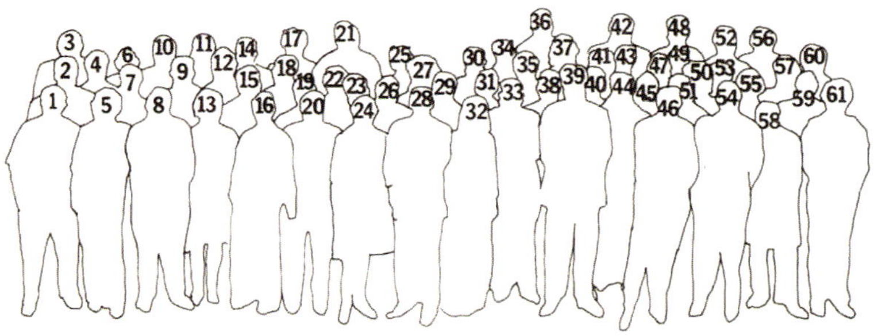

On June 14, 1976, the Rambusch staff gathered for this group portrait at the Rambusch building, 40 West 13th Street in New York.

Employees not in photograph:

Stephen Bridges
Michael Brown
Esther Mipaas
Willy J. Malarcher
Richard Millard
Ronald Millard
Howard Zucker
James Geraghty
Alfred Appio
James Casey
Victor Melin
David Burliuk
Edmund Golding
David Wilson
Hans Pesing
Italo Petronelli
Kevin Moss
P. O'Donnell
R. Stoner
Vincent Cirlincione
Huarchie Green
Cliff Young

Catha Jackson Grace

ABOUT THE AUTHOR AND EDITOR

Catha Jackson Grace was graduated cum laude from Smith College. She was an early Fellow in the Winterthur curatorial program for American decorative arts. A few years later, she received an M.A. in American Studies from New York University.

Mrs. Rambusch was hired in 1973 by the AIA as executive director of the Committee for the Preservation of Architectural Records (COPAR) to create a national program. This work was originally funded by a three-year grant from the National Endowment for the Humanities. In September 1988 she received the Public Service Award from Donald Paul Hodel, the US Secretary of the Interior. In 1980, at the AIA annual conference in Cincinnati, Ohio, she accepted the AIA Silver Medal for the COPAR project. In 1990, she became the executive director of the Catalogue of Landscape Records at Wave Hill, in the Bronx. Both projects were national in scope.

As the archivist for the Rambusch Decorating Company, she gathered and organized information relating to the company's body of work from its first 100 years. Her husband was employed by, and eventually led, the firm during the second half of this period. Two of their five children currently own and manage the firm. At the time of publication, she served as president of the New York Archival Society.

Barbara S. Christen is an architectural historian and editor with specializations in the work of American architect Cass Gilbert and the history of campus and preservation planning. She organized the first national symposium to reevaluate Gilbert's contributions to the American landscape and subsequently co-edited *Cass Gilbert, Life and Work: Architect of the Public Domain*. Further publications and research have addressed the architect's career in many cities. She has edited several publications for the National Gallery of Art and other museums. Previously, she collaborated on several projects with Catha Jackson Grace, including *The Landscape and Architecture of Laurel Lodge: A Little-Known Early 20th-century Summer Estate on Long Island's North Shore*.

At the Council of Independent Colleges (CIC), she developed and led the CIC Historic Campus Architecture Project, an inventory of historic campus architecture and landscape design regarding more than 2000 cultural heritage sites at nearly 400 campuses of independent colleges and universities across the United States. She received her Ph.D. in art and architectural history from the City University of New York Graduate Center.

CREDITS

All reasonable efforts have been made to trace the copyright holders of the visual material reproduced in this book. The publisher and the Rambusch Decorating Company apologize to anyone who has not been reached. Errors and omissions should be brought to our attention and will be corrected in future editions.

Rambusch Decorating Company: figs. 1–5, 1–14, 2–5, 2–9, 2–11, 2–12, 2–13, 2–14, 2–15, 2–17, 3–4, 3–6, 3–7, 3–10, 3–24, 3–28, 3–30, 3–32, 3–33, 4–2, 4–3, 4–4, 4–7, 4–8, 4–9, 4–10, 4–14, 4–18, 4–19, 4–22, 4–23, 4–24, 4–25, 4–31, 4–32, 5–9, 5–11, 5–14, 5–15, 5–16, 5–17, 5–18, 5–19, 6–1, 6–6, 6–7, 6–9, 6–13, 6–14, 6–16, 7–11, 7–13, 7–14, 7–15, 7–20, 7–27, 7–28, 8–1, 8–5, 8–7, 8–8, 8–9, 8–11, 8–16, 8–17, 8–18, 9–1, 9–2, 9–3, 9–4, 9–5, 9–6, 9–11, 9–12, 10–1, 10–4, 10–5, 10–6, 10–7, 10–9, 10–10, 10–12, 10–15, 10–16, 10–19, 10–20, 11–3, 11–4, 11–5, 11–6, 11–7, 11–8, 11–9, 11–12, 11–13, 11–14, 11–15, 11–16, 11–17, 11–19, 11–20, 11–22, 11–23, 12–2, 12–3, 12–4, 12–5, 12–6, 12–7, 12–8, 12–10, 12–11, E–3, E–4, E–5, E–6, E–8, E–9, pp. 223–225, p. 228, pp. 238–239; ***American Architect:*** 2–4, 2–16, 3–20; **Anderson:** 7–10; **Victor G. Anderson:** 8–4, 9–8, 9–9, 9–10; **Edward Bierstadt:** 11–2; **Tom Bonner Photography:** E–7; **Richard W. Burry:** 10–2, 10–3; **©The Christian Science Board of Directors:** 5–20; **Leland A. Cook:** 1–1, 1–4, 1–6, 1–8, 1–10, 1–13, 2–8, 2–16, 3–2, 3–5, 3–8, 3–9, 3–11, 3–14, 3–15, 3–18, 3–19, 3–25, 3–26, 3–29, 4–12, 4–13, 4–20, 4–27, 4–28, 4–30, 5–5, 5–7, 5–8, 6–2, 6–10, 7–7, 7–8, 7–9, 7–12, 7–18, 7–19, 7–22, 8–2, 8–3, 8–6, 9–7, 10–8, 10–11, 11–21; **Ray B. Dame:** 6–8; **DeLuxe Studio:** 7–24; **Hildreth Meière Dunn, courtesy of the International Hildreth Meière Association:** cover, 8–10; **Drix Duryea:** 2–6; **Courtesy of The Mary Baker Eddy Collection for the Christian Science Board of Directors:** 10–18; **Richard Garrison:** 8–14, 8–15; **David Gavasheli, Rambusch Decorating Company:** p. 3, 1–2, 1–3, 1–7, 1–16, 2–1, 2–7, 3–12, 3–23, 8–13, 9–13, 10–13, E–2; **Samuel H. Gottscho:** 2–3; **Mark Emerson Hamilton:** 3–1, 3–3, 3–13, 3–17, 4–21; **Louis Hansen Family Archives, Hørsholm, Denmark:** 1–11, 1–12; **James A. Hasler, Rambusch Decorating Company:** E–11; **Hawai'i Community Foundation:** 4–29; **John E. Hood:** 7–25; **Horn & Hardart:** 6–11, 6–12; **Hudson River Museum:** 11–2; **Keystone View Co.:** 4–11; **Courtesy of Legislative Library of British Columbia, Alan J. Hodgson fonds:** 12–1, 12–9; **Fay S. Lincoln:** 5–1, 5–6, 5–10; **Fay S. Lincoln photograph collection, 01628, Eberly Family Special Collections Library, Pennsylvania State University:** 2–10, 5–2, 5–12, 10–17; **Martini:** 7–23; **Image copyright ©The Metropolitan Museum of Art. Image source: Art Resource, NY:** 4–16, 4–17; **Richard Millard:** 5–13; **Dan Miller Photography:** 11–18; **Newark Museum of Art:** 11–10, 11–11; **William K. Pedersen:** 1–9, p. 226; **Edwin P. Rambusch, Rambusch Decorating Company:** 1–15, 3–27; **Martin V. Rambusch, Rambusch Decorating Company:** 2–2, 5–4, 7–26, 10–21, 12–12; **Viggo Bech Rambusch, Rambusch Decorating Company:** p. 240; **Mark Ross:** 6–15; **Thurman Rotan:** 6–3, 6–4, 6–5; **Archives of Saint Peter Cathedral:** 11–1; **Albin F. Schneider:** 3–16, 3–21, 3–22, 4–1, 4–5, 4–6; **Schutz:** 7–16, 7–17; **Martin Shannon:** 5–3, 8–12; **Kevin Simonson, Rambusch Decorating Company:** E–1, E–10; **Source unknown:** 3–31; **©Jan Staller:** 4–26; **Ezra Stoller/Esto:** 10–14; **Theatre Historical Society of America:** 7–21; **Theatre Historical Society of America, Collection of Michael R. Miller:** 7–1, 7–2, 7–3, 7–4, 7–5, 7–6; **Kristin von Thelen:** 4–15; **Paul T. Whyte:** 5–21.

INDEX

Note: Page numbers in italic type indicate illustrations.

Abraham Lincoln window, Valley Forge Military Academy, Gettysburg, PA, 90, *90*

Abramson, Louis Allen, Brass Rail Restaurants, New York World's Fair (1939), 233

Academy Awards, 73

acid etching, 52, 62, 92

Advisory Council on Historic Preservation, 98

Aesthetic movement, 41

Agnes, Saint, 37

Ahlschlager, Walter W., 115; Roxy Theatre, Manhattan, 117, 121, 124, *124*

Alabama State Capitol, Montgomery, 83

Albert, Prince, 131

Alex. Brown & Sons, Baltimore, MD, dome restoration, 98, *99*

Alhambra theater, Manhattan, *114*, 115

Alnwick Hall, Convent Station, NJ, 191

Alston, James, 239

aluminum, 52, 73

Aluminum Corporation of America (ALCOA), 52

Alvin Theatre, Pittsburgh, PA, 232

Ambrose, Saint, 36

Ambry (or Holy Oils) Cabinet, Church of Our Lady of Lourdes, Manhattan, 48, *49*

Americana Hotel, Fort Worth, TX, 110, *111*

American Airlines Terminal, John F. Kennedy Airport, Queens, *Stained-glass window*, 93, 94

American Architect and Architecture (magazine), 56

American Fine Arts Society, 20

American Institute of Architects, 185

American Museum of Natural History, New York, NY, 26

American Security and Trust Company, Washington, DC, bronze lamp standards, 45, *47*

American Telephone and Telegraph Company, 191. *See also* New York World's Fair (1939): AT&T Building

American Theatre, Manhattan, 22, 115

American Water Color Society, 26

Amtrak, 191

Andersen (Danish master painter), 17

Anderson, Victor G., 71, 151–52; *Design for Wall Decoration*, *150*, 151; instructional panel for operators of sixty-inch anti-aircraft searchlights, 147, *147*; *Patent drawing: Mark I Downlite*, *72*; President's Demonstration Room, Sperry Gyroscope Company, 151–52, *151*

Angel, *70*

angels, 41

Angio, Patsy D., 239

Annulites, 27

Annunciation of the Blessed Virgin Mary Church, McSherrytown, PA, 33, *34*

Anthony, Wilfred A., 53; candlesticks, Church of Saint Vincent Ferrer, Manhattan, *50*, 52

anti-aircraft searchlights, 13, 147, 148, 151

Apollo Theatre, Manhattan, 232

Appio, Alfred, 239

apprentices, 11, 87–88, 142, 227–29

architects, role of, 7, 10–11, 28, 119, 127, 142, 143

Architectural Forum (magazine), 118–19

Architectural League of New York, 20, 33, 62, 77, 104

Archives of American Art, Smithsonian Institution, Washington, DC, 155

Arizona Territorial Capitol, Phoenix, AZ, scale drawing of sconce, *190*, 191

Armstrong, D. Maitland, 26

Arnold & Locke, 18, 195, 221, 227

Art Deco, 60, 71, 103–4, 119

art metal, 12, 22, 44–64

Art Moderne, 77, 108, 119

Art Nouveau, 38, 41, 101, 106

Arts and Crafts movement, 49

Art Students League, New York, 26, 34

Aston, William M., 75

Astor, John Jacob, 188

Atlantic Coast Line Railroad, 172

atmospheric theaters, 119, 171, 196

Auburn Schine Theatre, Auburn, NY, 119, *123*

Augustine, Saint, 36

Aura lighting fixture, 77, *78*

Available Light, 217

Axley, Martha, *Mural*, Electrical Products Building, New York World's Fair (1939), 141, *141*, 234

Babson, Seth, Crocker Art Museum, Sacramento, CA, *184*, 185, *185*

Bacardi Rum Company, Cataño, PR, *Trompe l'oeil mural*, 200, *200*

Balboa, Panama, 196

Baldachin, House of the Good Shepherd, Troy, NY, 56, *57*

baldachins, 54–58

Balducci, Louis, 171

Baldwin, Benjamin, Reflections Restaurant, Americana Hotel, Fort Worth, TX, 110, *111*

Ballantine, John H., 177

Ballantine House, Newark, NJ, 177, 182–83, 185, 188; dining room, *183*; library, *182*

Baltimore Cathedral. *See* Basilica of the Assumption, Baltimore, MD

Baltzer, Elisabeth, 239

Bamberger's department store, Newark, NJ, 106, *108*

Banco Popular, San Juan, PR, 196

Bangor Naval Base, Bremerton, WA, 152

Barrie, John Peter, 166

Bartel, Jose, 22

Bartholdi, Frédéric Auguste, Statue of Liberty torch and flame, *213*

Basilica of the Assumption, Baltimore, MD, *21*, 21–22; *Mural study*, 34, *35*

Basilica of the National Shrine of the Immaculate Conception, Washington, DC, 11; *Garland with flowers and Marian symbols*, 3, *244* (detail); Great Upper Church, 11, 27, 208, *209*, *210*; *Rose window*, South Gallery, 87, *87*; Trinity dome, 208, *209*, *210*, 212; Trinity dome model, *27*

Bates College, 207

Batik banners, chapel of US Coast Guard Academy, New London, CT, 152, *153*

Battersea Polytechnic, London, England, 26

Battle Hall, University of Texas, Austin, 79

Bauhaus, 28, 39

Baumann, Cajetan J. B., 200

Beacon Theatre, Manhattan, 232

Beatrix, Princess of the Netherlands, 61

Beaux-Arts tradition, 39, 98, 142, 214

Bech, Gudrun Harriet, 24, 26

Becker, Ralph, 108

Bedi-Makky Art Foundry, *FDNY Memorial Wall of 09.11.01*, *211*

Beman, Solon Spencer, First Church of Christ, Scientist, Boston, MA, 169–70, *170*
Benedict, Saint, 37
Bergethon, Per, 86, 94
Bernhardt, Gustave, 85, 86; *Virgin Mary, with Saints*, Church of the Assumption of the Blessed Virgin Mary, Detroit, MI, *84*, 85
Bernini, Gian Lorenzo, baldachin, Saint Peter's Basilica, Rome, Italy, 54
Beverly Theatre, Washington, DC, 119, *123*
Bicentennial (US, 1976), 175, 176, 192
Bierstadt, Edward, *Library and parlor*, Glenview, Yonkers, NY, 176, *176*
Billy Rose Theatre, Manhattan, 128
Birnbaum, Charles A., 219
Bishop, Mrs. Kenneth (Mary), 129
bishop's crosier, illustrated in Robert Stiassny, *Michael Pachers St. Wolfganger Altar*, 55, *55*
Bisso, Joe, *23*, *132*
Black-out Ventilators, 148, *149*
Blenko, 90
Blessed Stanley Rother Oratory, Cathedral of Our Lady of Perpetual Help, Oklahoma City, OK, *206*, 208
BMT subway line, 133
Boca Raton Hotel, The Cloister Inn, Boca Raton, FL, 106, *107*
Boegel, Edward, 239
bonded bronze, 45, 48
Bongiorni, Caesar, 239
Bongiorni, Louis, 239
Boniface, Saint, 36
Book of Kells, 41, 189
Boomer, Lucius, 104–6
Bowery Savings Bank, Manhattan, 166
Boyd-Janoff Company, 234
Boyd Theatre, Philadelphia, PA, 231
Brandston, Howard, 214
Brandt, William, 115
Breheny, Pat, 239
Brevetti, Albert C., 157
Brewer Building, lobby interior, with pendant light fixtures, Honolulu, HI, *77*, *79*
Bridges, Stephen, 87, 239
Brigham, Charles, First Church of Christ, Scientist, Boston, MA, 169–70, *170*
Brill, Solomon "Sol," 115, 231
Bringman, Geri, 239
Broadhurst Theatre, Manhattan, 129
Broadway Theatre, Brooklyn, 115
The Bronx Theatre, The Bronx, 115
bronze, 45, 48, 212
Brooklyn Edison Company, 79
Brooklyn Paramount Theatre, Brooklyn, 128
Brown, Louis A., Heineken Dutch Town, on the Zuiderzee, New York World's Fair (1939), 141, *142*, 234
Brown, Michael, 239
Bruun, Sven W., *79*, 83, 134
Buchanan Center for the Performing Arts, ceiling lighting in lobby, University of Wyoming, Laramie, *81*, 83
Bunshaft, Gordon, 28
Bureau International des Expositions, 131
Burliuk, David, 239; *Sconce*, scale drawing for Arizona Territorial Capitol, Phoenix, AZ, *190*, 191
Busch Gardens, Williamsburg, Virginia, 48
Buti, Lori, 219
Byzantine-inspired lantern, *66*, *68*

Café Savarin, Manhattan, 102–3, *102*
Cain, Farrell & Bell, restoration of New York Academy of Medicine, Manhattan, 189–90, *189*
Calder, Alexander, 169
camouflage, 145–47
Campbell Smith, 229
candlesticks, 12, 48–52; Cathedral of Saints Peter and Paul, Philadelphia, PA, *50*, 52; ceramic, *51*, 52, 152, *152*; Church of Our Lady of Lourdes, Manhattan, with crucifix, 12, 49, *51*; Church of Saint Vincent Ferrer, Manhattan, *50*, 52; Church of the Epiphany, Manhattan, *50*, 52; Church of the Heavenly Rest, Manhattan, with crucifix, 52, *53*; made during World War II, *51*, 52, 152, *152*; Saint Francis School, Athol Springs, NY, *51*, 52
capitols. *See* public spaces
Carlotti, Frances, 239
Carlson, S. Lee, 191
Carnegie, Andrew, 10, 34
Carolina Theatre, Greensboro, NC, 129
Carroll, John, 34
Carroll House Chapel, Washington, DC, 87
Carson, George, 239
Cartier, 58
Casey, James, 239
Casino Theatre, Brooklyn, 115
Cathedral Basilica of Saints Peter & Paul, Philadelphia, PA, 43, *43*, 65, 200; candlestick, *50*, 52
Cathedral of Our Lady of Perpetual Help, Oklahoma City, OK, Blessed Stanley Rother Oratory, *206*, 208
Cathedral of Prince Edward's Island, 195
Cathedral of Saint Ignatius Loyola, Palm Beach Gardens, FL: *Saint Francis of Assisi*, garden, 41, *41*; tabernacle niche, *40*, 41
Cathedral of Saint John the Divine, Manhattan, 85–86
Cathedral of Saint Joseph, Hartford, CT: baldachin, 58, *59*; ostensorium, 54, *54*
Cathedral of Saint Peter, Scranton, PA, 66
Catherine the Great, 61
Catholic Church. *See* Roman Catholic Church
Catholic University, 24, 28
Cecilia, Saint, 37
Centennial Exhibition (Philadelphia, 1876), 131
Central Synagogue, Manhattan, 175–76
Century Association, Manhattan, 101
Century of Progress Exposition (Chicago, 1933), 131
Chapel State Theatre. *See* Ohio Theatre
Chatham Trust Company, 191
Chester Theatre, The Bronx, 231
Chicago Public Library, Chicago, IL, 192, *193*
Child's Restaurant, Manhattan, 106, *108*
Christen, Barbara S., 219
Christensen, C. G., 18
Christian, Frederick W.: *Mary Magdalene and Claire of Assisi: cames pattern*, study for chapel, Sisters of Saint Martha, Antigonish, NS, 88, 90, *90*; ostensorium, Cathedral of Saint Joseph, Hartford, CT, 54, *54*
Christian Science Publishing Society. *See* Mary Baker Eddy Library
Christ the King Church, Rutland, Vermont, *Stations of the Cross*, 48, *49*
Churchill, Chester Lindsay, Mary Baker Eddy Library, Boston, MA, 86, 94, 96, *97*
church interior design and decoration, 11–12, 18, 19, 22, 30–44
Church of Our Lady of Lourdes, Manhattan: ambry (or holy oils) cabinet, 48, *49*; candlesticks and crucifix, 12, 49, *51*
Church of Our Lady of Victory, Manhattan, *Stained-glass window* sketch, 90, *90*
Church of Saint Louis, Louisville, OH, redesign of sanctuary interior, 36, *37*, 39, 41
Church of Saint Paul the Apostle, Manhattan, ciborium, 48, *48*
Church of Saint Peter, Staten Island, 37–38, 41
Church of Saint Vincent Ferrer, Manhattan, candlestick, *50*, 52
Church of the Assumption of the Blessed Virgin Mary, Detroit, MI, *Virgin Mary, with Saints*, *84*, 85
Church of the Epiphany, Manhattan, candlestick, *50*, 52
Church of the Heavenly Rest, Manhattan, candlesticks and crucifix, 52, *53*
Church of the Immaculate Heart of Mary, Scarsdale, NY, ostensorium, 53–54
Church of the Redeemer, Brooklyn, 22
Ciborium, Church of Saint Paul the Apostle, Manhattan, 48, *48*
Cincinnati Grand Opera House, Cincinnati, OH, 115, 189
Cirlincione, Vincent, 239
City Hall Theatre, Hartford, CT, 231
Clarence M. Mitchell Courthouse, Baltimore, MD, 98
Claridge Hotel, Manhattan, 101
Classic Lanterns, 27
Clinton, Charles W., Glenview, Yonkers, NY, 176–77, *176–81*
cloisonné, 48
Cluster lantern fixture, *66*, *68*

Cochrane and Piquenard, Illinois State Capitol, Springfield, IL, 157, *160*
Coleman, Clifford and Melissa, Milton Hershey School, Founders Hall, Hershey, PA, 166–67, *166*
Coleman, John, 110
Colonial Revival style, 90
Colonial Theatre, Manhattan, 115
Colorado State Capitol, Denver, CO, 157
Columbia College, 24
Columbia Graduate School of Architecture, Planning and Preservation, 207
Comes, John Theodore: Annunciation of the Blessed Virgin Mary Church, McSherrytown, PA, 33, *34*; Saint Agnes Church, Cleveland, OH, 33
Concha, Luis Cardinal, 198
Connick, Charles J., 86
Connick Studios, 88
Consolidated Edison: pavilion, New York World's Fair, 138, *140*, 234; Sidewalk Lighting Program, *82*; Waterside steam plant turbine room, 73
Cooper, Peter, 71
Copenhagen Engineering School, Denmark, 26
Corbett, Harrison & MacMurray, 124
Corbett, Harvey Wiley, Metropolitan Life Insurance Company North Building, Manhattan, 45, *46*
Cornelius, Robert, 192
Corn Exchange Bank, Manhattan, 163
Costa, Joseph, 239
Costa, Lucio, Brazilian Pavilion, New York World's Fair (1939), 233
courthouses. *See* public spaces
Coventry Cathedral, Coventry, UK, 202
craft/craftsmanship: diminished role of, 20, 28, 119, 142–43; institutional structure for, 11; Rambusch's reputation for, 9–11, *23*, 24, 28, 56, 58, 66, 98, 113, 127, 138, 197–98, 204, 214, 239, *239*; skill and role of, *7*, 9, 127, 141–43, 197. *See also* guild system
Crescent Theatre, Brooklyn, 115
Crocker, Edwin Bryant, 185
Crocker Art Museum, Sacramento, CA, gallery decoration, *184*, 185, *185*
Cross & Cross, Polish Building, New York World's Fair (1939), 234
Crovatto, Costante, 11, 26, 110
Crovatto Mosaics, 26
Curtis, Philip H., 182
Cybulski, Polish Building, New York World's Fair (1939), 234

Daly, Leo A. *See* Leo A. Daly, Architects
Daly, Leo A., Jr., 203
Daly, Leo A., III, 203
Danish Design School, Royal Danish Academy of Art, Copenhagen, Denmark, 17
Danish immigrants, 9–11
Danish language, 11, 22
D'Ascenzo Studios, 86, 108
DayBrite, 27
Delmonico's Restaurant, 191
Depression, 20, 53, 106, 117, 124, 127
Derujinsky, Gleb, 56
designers, role of, 10–11, 142
Deskey, Donald, Radio City Music Hall, Manhattan, 117, 124–25, *125*, 127
Despont, Thierry, 214
DeStefano, Anthony, 239
Dijk, Peter van, 166
Dillon, Christopher, 239
dining out, 104, 106
Dinkeloo, John, Great Hall, Metropolitan Museum of Art, Manhattan, 73, *74*, *75*
Diocesan Building Commission, 22
The Doctors of the Church, *88*
Dominic, Saint, 37
Doney, Thomas, 192
Dornin, Anne, Ohio Theatre, Columbus, OH, 129, *129*
Dowd & Wortmann Construction Co., 233
Dowling, Robert, 61
Downlites, 12, 26–28, 71, *72*, 73, *74*, *75*, 119, 141, 212, 214. *See also* Mark IV Downlites
Doyle, Gerald, restoration of Arizona Territorial Capitol, Phoenix, AZ, *190*, 191
D. S. Hess Company, 177
Ducar, Michael, 48, 239; "Little Old New York," McGraw-Hill Building, Manhattan, 171
Durban, South Africa, 196
Dutch metal, 32, 177, 185
Dynan, Donald, 239

Eastlake style, 176–77
eating out, 104, 106
Eberson, Drew, 196
Eberson, John, 119, 196; Auburn Schine Theatre, Auburn, NY, 119, *123*; Beverly Theatre, Washington, DC, 119, *123*; Pitkin Theatre, Brooklyn, 119, *122*; Silver Spring Theatre, Silver Spring, MD, 119, *122*, *123*
Echo Box, 13, 148, *148*
Ecole des Beaux Arts, Paris, France, 142. *See also* Beaux-Arts tradition
Eddy, Mary Baker, 169. *See also* Mary Baker Eddy Library
Edison, Thomas Alva, 65
Edward F. Caldwell & Company, 79; vase for Waldorf-Astoria, Manhattan, *105*
Eggers, Otto: candlestick, Cathedral Basilica of Saints Peter and Paul, Philadelphia, PA, *50*, 52; Church of Our Lady of Victory, Manhattan, 90, *90*
Eggers & Higgins: Cathedral Basilica of Saints Peter & Paul, Philadelphia, PA, 43, *43*, 65, 200; Cathedral of Saint Joseph, Hartford, CT, 54, *54*, 58, *59*; Schaeffer Building, New York World's Fair (1939), 234
Eggers Group, 61
Eidlitz, Leopold, Temple Emanu-El, Manhattan, 175
Eken, Andrew J., 163
El Convento, San Juan, PR, 202
Elks Club, Brooklyn, 102
Elongated lantern fixture, 66, *69*
Elskus, Albinas, 11, 88
Ely Jacques Kahn & Scott & Tegan, Ballantine Gardens, New York World's Fair (1939), 233
Embury, Aymar, United Nations early headquarters, Lake Success, NY, 60–61, *60*
Emery Roth and Son, 186
Empire State Building, Manhattan, 162–63, *162*
Empire Theatre, Brooklyn, 115
Engle, Claude, *Experimental mock-up of lighting fixtures*, for National Gallery of Art, East Building, Washington, DC, *168*, 169
Erikson, Leif, 9

Farley, John Murphy, 228
FDNY Memorial Wall of 09.11.01, FDNY Ten House, Ground Zero, Manhattan, 13, *211*, 212
Federal Historic Preservation Tax Incentives program, 175
Federal Reserve Building, Manhattan, armillary spheres, 62, *63*
Federal Seaboard Terra Cotta Corporation, 55
Feininger, Lyonel: mural, Marine Transportation Building, New York World's Fair (1939), 133, 234; murals, Art Museum, New York World's Fair (1939), 233
Feris, Manuel, 239
Ferlin, Edward, 62; ciborium, Church of Saint Paul the Apostle, Manhattan, 48, *48*; ostensorium, Church of the Immaculate Heart of Mary, Scarsdale, NY, *53*; ostensorium, Saint Michael's Church, Jersey City, NJ, 53, *53*; ostensorium, Saint Raphael's Church, Pittsburgh, PA, 53, *53*
Fernbach, Henry: Central Synagogue, Manhattan, 175–76; Temple Emanu-El, Manhattan, 175
Ferri, Roger, Reflections Restaurant, Americana Hotel, Fort Worth, TX, *111*
Fiedler, Arthur, 169
Field Museum of Natural History, Chicago, IL, 94
Fifth Avenue Theatre, Manhattan, 221
Fire Department of New York. *See* FDNY Memorial Wall of 09.11.01
First Church of Christ, Scientist, Boston, MA, 169–70, *170*. *See also* Mary Baker Eddy Library
flashed glass, 91–92
Fleur-de-lis sheets, *44*, 45
Florence, Italy, 26
Florida, 106
Ford Motor Building, New York World's Fair (1939), 134, *134*, *135*

Forum of the Twelve Caesars, Rockefeller Center, Manhattan, 108, 110, *110*
Foscato, Vittorio, 11, 26
Fox, 115
Fox Audubon Theatre, Manhattan, 232
Francis, Saint, 37
Franciscan Monastery of the Holy Land in America, Washington, DC, sketch of altar proposal and baldachin as built, 56, *57*
Franklin, Benjamin, 138
French, Daniel Chester, 170
fresco painting, 32–34
Fulton Theatre, Brooklyn, *114*, 115
Funke, Wilhelm, 26

Gade, George, Rochester Art Museum, NY, 32
Garland with flowers and Marian symbols, *3*, *244* (detail)
Garrison, George, 239
Gate of Heaven, from *Garland with flowers and Marian symbols*, *256* (detail)
Gates, Metropolitan Life Insurance Company North Building, Manhattan, 45, *46*
Gates, Rothafel House, Manhattan, 62, *62*
Gaudreau, Inc., 61
Gavasheli, David, 219
Gavasheli, Mati, 219
Geddes, Norman Bel, General Motors Building, New York World's Fair (1939), 133–34, 138, *133*, 234
Gellinez, Jose, 239
General Motors Building, Caracas, Venezuela, exterior mosaic mural, 198
General Society of Mechanics & Tradesmen, New York, NY, 26
George A. Fuller Company, 234
George A. Schastey, 221
Geraghty, James, 239
Gibson, Peter, 87
Gibson Art Glass and Decorating Company, 19, 85, 221
Gilbert, Cass: Battle Hall, University of Texas, Austin, *79*; US Courthouse, Foley Square, Manhattan, 157, *161*, 162
Gillmor, Reginald, 151–52
Glaenzer, George A., 104
glass block, 91
Glenbow Art Museum, Calgary, AB, 196
Glenview, Yonkers, NY, 176–77, *176–81*; dining room, *181*; library and parlor, *176*
Glisson, Tom, *Two scale models of war memorials for New York Life Insurance Company veterans*, *154*, 155
Gluck, Alma, 191
Golding, Edmund, 239
Gonzalez-Rio, Jesus, 83
Goodhue, Bertram Grosvenor, 147; Church of Saint Vincent Ferrer, Manhattan, 52; Nebraska State Capitol, Lincoln, NE, *156*, 157; Saint Bartholomew's Church, Manhattan, *30*, 31, 90–91
Goodhue, Harry, 86
Gordon, James Riely, Arizona Territorial Capitol, Phoenix, AZ, *190*, 191
Gordon, Witold, *Distilled Spirits Exhibition*, Distilled Spirits Building, New York World's Fair (1939), 138, *140*, 234
Gothic style, 33, 37, 39, 43, 52, 53, 66, 172, 175, 188
Gozzoli, Benozzo, 32
Grace, Catha Jackson, 207, *240*
Grand Central Terminal, Manhattan: Greybar Arcade, 169; Main Concourse, 75, *76*, *77*, 94
Granite Club, Toronto, ON, 196
Great Exposition (London, 1851), 131
Great Northern Railroad, 192
Green, Huarchie, 239
Gregory, Saint, 36–37
Griffin, Percy, Alnwick Hall, Convent Station, NJ, 191
grisaille, 85, 88, 90, 91
Gruber, Abraham, 239
Grundtvig, Frederik Lange, 9–10
Grundtvig, Nikolai Frederik Severin, 9
Grundtvigianism, 10, 11, 17
Gugler, Slee and Bryson, Business Systems and Insurance Building, New York World's Fair (1939), 138, *139*
guild system, 11, 87–88
Guinness Book of Records, 94
Gutelius, Bruce, 239

Hake, Harry, Thomas J. Moyer Judicial Center, Columbus, OH, *156*, 157, *158–59*
Haley, William "Bud," 86–87, 239; letter describing camouflage, 13, 145, *146*; *Noah's Ark*, *86*, 87; *Paint truck and scale grids, in ca. 1943*, 13, *144*, 145; *Saint Mark and Saint John*, Saint Agatha's Church, Brooklyn, *86*, 87
halogen lights, 26, 73
Hamersky, Bohdan, *Sconce*, scale drawing for James J. Hill House, St. Paul, MN, *191*, 192
Hamlin, Talbot F., 43
Hammer, Trygve, 26, 102
Hand, Learned, 162
Hanna, Mark, 115
Hansen, Hans Peter, 34
Hansen, Louis, 23; *Study for Mercury, The Spirit of Communication*, Consolidated Edison Building, New York World's Fair (1939), 138, *140*
Hardenbergh, Henry J., 20, 104; Plaza Hotel, Manhattan, 110
Harney, George Edward, Ballantine House, Newark, NJ, 177, 188
Harrison, Wallace K., 124–25
Harrison & Fouilhoux: Art Museum, New York World's Fair (1939), 233; Consolidated Edison Building, New York World's Fair (1939), 138, *140*, 234
Hart, David H., restoration of the Utah State Capitol, Salt Lake City, UT, 214, *215*, *216*, 217
Hartell, John, *228*
Harvard Club, Manhattan, 101
Haskell & Considine, Saint Ann's Church, Hornell, NY, 36, *37*
Hatch Memorial Band Shell, Boston, MA, 169, *169*
H. C. King & Associates, 27
Hegeman-Harris Company, 198, 234
Heidelmeier, Joseph, 239
Heinigke, Otto, 86
Hellmuth, Yamasaki and Leinweber, Lambert Airfield, St. Louis, MO, 167, *168*
Helmsley, Harry, 186–87
Helmsley, Leona, 187
Helmsley Palace Hotel, Manhattan, 186–88. *See also* Villard Houses
Helving, Francis, 34, 102
Hencken, George D., 20
Hencken, William F., 20, *21*, 22, 85
Henry M. Weitzner, Inc., 235
Hershey, Milton S. and Catherine S., 166
Herter Brothers, 21, 221
Herts Brothers, 221
Hewitt, Abram, 71
high-intensity discharge (HID) lamps, 75, *79*
high modernism, 39–40
Hill, Homer, *Trompe l'oeil mural*, Bacardi Rum Company, Cataño, PR, 200, *200*
Hill, James J., 192
Hippodrome Theatre, Manhattan, 128
Hodgson, Alan, restoration of Legislative Assembly of British Columbia, Parliament Buildings, Victoria, BC, *194*, 195, 196, 200, *201*, 202
Hollis, James, 239
Hollywood Theatre, Manhattan, 119, *120*, *121*, 232
Holy Angels' Church, St. Thomas, ON, 195, *197*
Holy Child Jesus Church, Richmond Hill, Queens, 86
Holy Cross Church, Omaha, NE, baldachin, 58, *58*
Holy Name Church, Columbus, OH, 33, *33*
Holy Trinity Lithuanian Roman Catholic Church, Newark, NJ, baldachin, 55–56, *56*
Hood and Fouilhoux, 124
Horn & Hardart, Manhattan, 106, 108, *109*
Hotel McAlpin, Manhattan, 101, 104
hotels, 101, 104–7, 110
House of the Good Shepherd, Troy, NY, baldachin rendering and face of tympanum, 56, *57*
Hoving, Thomas, 73
Hsu, Ling Ling, 239
Hubbell & Mink, 101, 103
Hudson River Museum. *See* Glenview
Huntington Station Theatre, Huntington

Station, NY, *126*, 127
Hvass, Tyge, Danish Building, New York World's Fair (1939), 234

I. E. Ahmed and Mohammed Saleh Kaki Company, 204
Ignatius, Saint, 37
Illinois State Capitol, Springfield, IL, 157, *160*
Illuminated Engineering (magazine), 79
Illuminating Engineering Society, 12, 27, 28, 73
Imperio, Frank, 239
Indianapolis War Memorial, 86
International Style, 20, 40, 52, 75, 93, 142
IRT subway line, 133

Jacobs, Robert, 94
James J. Hill House, St. Paul, MN, scale drawing of sconce, *191*, 192
Jansson, Otto, 195, 196
Jedda Airport, Saudi Arabia, Royal Reception Lounge, *203*, 204
Jefferson, Thomas, Virginia State Capitol, Richmond, VA, 157
Jefferson Theatre, Manhattan, 24, *114*, 115, 129
Jensen, Georg, 101
Jerome, Saint, 36
Jerusalem, Israel, 200
Johannesburg, South Africa, 196
John B. McElfatrick & Son, Alhambra, Manhattan, *114*, 115
John Bond Trevor House. *See* Glenview
Johnson, Donald, Saint Mary's Church, Rockville, MD, 58, *58*
Joy, Russell, *Floor mosaic*, Saint Andrew Avellino Roman Catholic Church, Flushing, Queens, 38, *38*
J. Paul Getty Museum, Los Angeles, CA, *213*, 214
J. Supor & Son, *213*
Jubilee Auditorium, Calgary, AB, 196
Jubilee Auditorium, Edmonton, AB, 196

Kahn, Albert: Ford Motor Building, New York World's Fair (1939), 134, *134*, *135*, *136*, 234; General Motors Building, New York World's Fair (1939), 133–34, 138, *133*, 234
Kahn and Jacobs, American Airlines Terminal, John F. Kennedy Airport, Queens, *93*, 94
Kann & Ammon, 98
Kaplan, Joseph, 98
Keck, Charley, 229
Keely, Patrick Charles, 22; Saint Peter Cathedral, Erie, PA, *174*, 175
Keister, George, Jefferson Theatre, Manhattan, 24, *114*, 115, 129
Keith, B. F., 231
Keller, Dayle, 219
Kemp Bunch & Jackson, 61
Kennedy, Eugene, 53
Kennedy Center, Washington, DC, 169
Kimball, Francis, H., Fifth Avenue Theatre, Manhattan, 221
King, Robert, 239
Kirby, Petit & Green, 101
Kirkleigh Villa, Baltimore, MD, 86
K. J. Collins & Company, 229
Kletting, Richard, Utah State Capitol, Salt Lake City, UT, 214, *215*, *216*, 217
Koehl, William A., Church of Saint Louis, Louisville, OH, 36, *37*
Kosciuszko, Tadeusz, 138
Kraemer, Richard, 239
Krol, John Cardinal, 200
Kuble, Frank, 229
Kusenda, Peter, 239

La Farge, John, 21, 26, 96, 98, 186
Lamb, Karl Barre, 85
Lamb, Thomas White, 118, 119, 124, 125, 196; Jefferson Theatre, Manhattan, 24, *114*, 115; Loew's 175th Street Theatre, Manhattan, 119, *119*; Loew's State Theatre, Syracuse, NY, 118, *118*; Loew's Theatre, Columbus, OH, 128–29, *129*; Strand Theatre, Manhattan, 115
Lambert Airfield, St. Louis, MO, ticket-area lighting, 167, *168*
Langley, Henry, Holy Angels' Church, St. Thomas, ON, 195, *197*
languages, spoken in the Rambusch studios, 11, 22
Lantern light fixtures, 66, *68*
Larsen, Axel, *23*, 22; Instructional panel for operators of sixty-inch anti-aircraft searchlights, 147, *147*
Lathrop, Francis, 21
Latrobe, Benjamin Henry, Basilica of the Assumption, Baltimore, MD, 21–22
Laub, D. C., 18; letter of recommendation, *19*
Laub, Knud, 22, 101; *Baldachin*, 55, *55*; pitcher, *44*, 45
Law, Bernard Cardinal, 62
Lawrence, Saint, 37
Lawrence, Stacee Gravelle, 219
Lazarus, Emma, 214
LeBrun, Napoleon, Cathedral Basilica of Saints Peter & Paul, Philadelphia, PA, 52, 200
Le Corbusier, Notre-Dame du Haut, Ronchamp, 52
Legislative Assembly of British Columbia, Parliament Buildings, Victoria, BC, *194*, 195, 196, 200, *201*, 202
L'Enfant Plaza Hotel, Washington, DC, *Mural*, 110, *110*
Lenore Hotel, Manhattan, 101
Leo A. Daly, Architects, 61, 202–3; Holy Cross Church, Omaha, NE, 58, *58*; National Guard Headquarters, Riyadh, Saudi Arabia, *202*, 203
Lescaze, William Edmund, Switzerland Building, New York World's Fair (1939), 133, 234
Lever House, Manhattan, 28, 73
Lewis, Charley, 229
Liccioli, Mario, 26, 197–98
lighting, 12, 22, 26–28, 45, 64–83, 119, 141, 148, 152, 191, 212, 214. *See also* anti-aircraft searchlights
lighting fixture, Saint Vincent de Paul, Bayonne, NJ, 66, *69*
Lighting fixture with shield, 66, *66*
Light shield for a one-bulb lamp, *64*, 65
Lincoln Memorial, Washington, DC, 170–71
Link, Weber & Bowers, Saint Boniface Church, Pittsburgh, PA, 55, *55*
Linn, Charles D., 219
Lister, Joseph, 138
Lite Paks, 27, *72*, *77*, *79*
Liturgical Commission, 22
Lizcano, Bernardo, 239
L. Marcotte and Company, 221
Locsin, Mario, 62
Loewe, Frederick, 62
Loew's 175th Street Theatre, Manhattan, 119, *119*
Loew's Brooklyn Theatre, Brooklyn, 232
Loews Corporation, 110
Loew's King Theatre, Brooklyn, 231
Loew's Midland Theatre, Kansas City, MO, 117, *118*, 231
Loew's Palace Theatre, Washington, DC, 231
Loew's State Theatre, Providence, RI, 231
Loew's State Theatre, Syracuse, NY, 231; *Mural of Wedding Procession of Maharaja's Daughter*, 118, *118*
Loew's Theatre, Columbus, OH, 128–29, *129*
Loew's Theatres Incorporated, 117, 196
Loew's Woodside Theatre, Queens, 128
Long, Birch Burdette: *Sanctuary: interior* (rendering), 33, *34*; *Sanctuary: interior* (watercolor sketch), 34, *34*
Long Island Railroad, 133
Lotte Plaza Hotel. *See* Villard Houses
Lovers Lane United Methodist Church, Dallas, TX, *Nave window*, 94, *94*
Lumen Award, 73, 166
Lyceum Theatre, New Britain, CT, 232

Maas, Arnold Johannes Wilhelmus (Marcolino "Marco"), 11, 88
Mack Jenny and E. F. Tyler, 108
Maginnis, Charles D., 19, 90; Christ the King Church, Rutland, Vermont, 48
Maginnis and Walsh (later Maginnis, Walsh and Kennedy), 53; Basilica of the National Shrine of the Immaculate Conception, Washington, DC, 3, 11, *27*, 87, *87*, 208, *209*, *210*, 212
Main Street Project, 129

Maison Jansen, Paris, France, 105
Malarcher, Willy J., 239
Mandel, Alsa, 200
Mannerism, 41
Manzella, Joseph, 239
Map for the Southern Railroad, for the Atlantic Coast Line Railroad, Jacksonville, FL, 172, *172*
Maple & Co., 229
Mapparium, Mary Baker Eddy Library, Boston, MA, 86, 94, 96, *97*
marble, 26
Mark, Mitchell, 115
Mark, Moe, 115
Mark IV Downlites, 26, 73
Markussen (Danish master painter), 17
Martens, Walter, 239
Mary Baker Eddy Library, Boston, MA, Mapparium, 86, 94, 96, *97*. *See also* First Church of Christ, Scientist
Masonite, 70, 152, 195
Mater Ecclesiae, Vatican Gardens, Vatican City, 204, *205*
Mathiasen Brothers, 55
May, Thomas, 229
Mayers, Murray and Phillip: library, Oriental Institute, University of Chicago, IL, 163, *163*; Medicine and Public Health, Science and Education Building, New York World's Fair (1939), *132*, 133, 134, *137*, 138, *139*, 234
McCarthy, Dorothea, 239
McCarthy, Michael, 11, 145, 227, 229
McElfatrick, William H., Fulton Theatre, Brooklyn, *114*, 115
McGraw-Hill Building, Manhattan, 171
McHamon, Joseph H., 48
McKim, Mead & White, 237; Bowery Savings, Bank, Manhattan, 166; Newark Station, Newark, NJ, 191–92; Villard Houses, *112*, 113, 186–88, *186*
McNicholas, John, 239
McNicholas, Michael, 239
Meany, Edward P., 191
Meany, Rosaline, 191
Meière, Hildreth, 90–91, 142–43, 155, 172; *Dragon of Ignorance*, 138, *138*; House Chamber: gilded frieze, Nebraska State Capitol, Lincoln, NE, *156*, 157; Mural over entrance and other murals, Medicine and Public Health, Science and Education Building, New York World's Fair (1939), *132*, 133, 134, 138, *139*, 234
Melin, Victor, 177, *180*, 239
Mellon family, 53
mercury-vapor lamps, 73, *75*
Messel, Oliver, 128
metalwork. *See* art metal
Metropolitan Cathedral of Medellín, Colombia, 198–99, *198*
Metropolitan Life Insurance Company, Manhattan: Board of Directors Room, 186; gates of North Building, 45, *46*
Metropolitan Museum of Art, Manhattan, 48, 71; Great Hall, 73, *74*, *75*
Metropolitan Transportation Authority (MTA), 75
Midway Theatre, Beacon, NY, 231
Mies van der Rohe, Ludwig, 94
Milken, Michael, 217
Milken Center for Advancing the American Dream, Washington, DC, 217
Millard, Richard, 88, 239; *Portrait of Pia Zadora*, 93, *93*
Millard, Ronald, 239; decoration of gallery, Crocker Art Museum, Sacramento, CA, *184*, 185, *185*; decoration of Villard Houses, *186*; *Mural*, L'Enfant Plaza Hotel, Washington, DC, 110, *110*; *Trompe l'oeil mural*, Bacardi Rum Company, Cataño, PR, 200, *200*
Milton Hershey School, Hershey, PA, Founders Hall, grand rotunda depicting floor medallion, 166–67, *166*
Miotto, Stephen, 26
Miotto Mosaic Art Studios, 26
Mipaas, Esther, 239
USS *Missouri*, 13, 148, *148*
Mizner, Addison, 106
Mock, Robert C., Trans World Airlines terminal, LaGuardia Airport, Queens, 167, *167*
Model of Baptistery, Saint Bartholomew's Episcopal Church, Manhattan, *30*, 31
Moderacki, Leon, 239
modernism, 52, 58. *See also* high modernism; International Style
Moe, Alphonse, *23*; ciborium, Church of Saint Paul the Apostle, Manhattan, 48, *48*; ostensorium, Saint Raphael's Church, Pittsburgh, PA, 53, *53*
Mohawk Building, Manhattan, 237
Mohawk Industries, 124
Moore McCormack Steamship Lines, 172
More, Thomas, 91
Morgan & Milliman, House of the Good Shepherd, Troy, NY, 56, *57*
Moriarity, Bill, 195
Morrison's cafeteria, Manhattan, 106
Morton, Johannes, 33; apsidal mural, Holy Name Church, Columbus, OH, 33, *33*; chancel mural, Saint Patrick's Roman Catholic Church, Bay Shore, NY, 32–33, *32*
Moskowitz, H., 196
Moss, B. S., 115
Moss, Kevin, 239
Mount Vernon Ladies' Association, 175
movie houses. *See* theaters and movie houses
Muller, Theodor Carl, 43; *Sconce with fluorescent and incandescent lamps*, 77, *77*
Mural of Wedding Procession of Maharaja's Daughter, Loew's State Theatre, Syracuse, NY, 118, *118*
Museum of the Moving Image, 70

National Academy, 227
National Council of Churches, 197
National Gallery of Art, Washington, DC: experimental mock-up of lighting fixtures for East Building atrium, *168*, 169; lighting for East Building atrium, 73, *73*
National Guard Headquarters, Riyadh, Saudi Arabia, chandeliers and sconces, *202*, 203
National Historic Landmarks, 192
National Historic Preservation Act, 175
National Museum of the US Air Force, Wright-Patterson Air Force Base, OH, 172
National Trust for Historic Preservation, 129
Naval Headquarters, Riyadh, Saudi Arabia, 203
Naval Reception Facility, Jeddah, Saudi Arabia, 203
Nazareth Chapel, Capetown, South Africa, 196
Neandross, George, 26
Neandross, Knud, 26
Neandross, Leif, 12–13, 26, 106, 108, 134, 145; *Advertisement, depicting an example of a painted ceiling*, 163, *164*; candlesticks, Church of the Epiphany, Manhattan, *50*, 52; *The Cloister Inn: main lobby*, Boca Raton Hotel, Boca Raton, FL, 106, *107*; *Downstairs dining room*, Saltzman's Restaurant, Manhattan, 103, *103*; flatware, made for the Norse Grill, The New Waldorf-Astoria, Manhattan, 105, *106*; *Grand Rotunda, depicting floor medallion*, Milton Hershey School, Founders Hall, Hershey, PA, 166, *166*; Loew's Midland Theatre, Kansas City, MO, 117, *118*; *Main dining room: ceiling detail*, Saltzman's Restaurant, Manhattan, 104, *104*; *Main dining room: column detail*, Saltzman's Restaurant, Manhattan, 104, *104*; *The New Waldorf-Astoria: Park Avenue entrance*, *100*, 101, 105, *105*; *Partial view of theater*, Roxy Theatre, Manhattan, 121, *124*; *Proscenium arch*, Hollywood Theatre, Manhattan, 119, *121*; *Sanctuary: interior* (watercolor sketch), *34*; *Sanctuary: interior*, Saint Pancras Church, Glendale, Queens, 34; *Sanctuary: nave, after renovation*, Saint Mary's of the Lake, North Bay, ON, 195, *197*
Neandross, Sigurd, 26
Nebraska State Capitol, Lincoln, NE, House Chamber: gilded frieze, *156*, 157
needlework, 26
Neumann, John, 200
Newark Museum of Art, Newark, NJ, 177
Newark Station, Newark, NJ, 191–92
New Brandt Theatre, Brooklyn, 231
Newerstein, Abraham, 239
New Kensington Collection of candlesticks, 52
New York Academy of Medicine, lobby with Pan-a-lux lighting, Manhattan, 79, *80*
New York Life Insurance Company, Manhattan, 155; gilded spire, 172, *173*

New York State Capitol, Albany, NY, 157, *160*
New York World's Fair (1939), 12, 130–43, 147; AT&T Building, 141, 233; Art Museum, 233; Ballantine Gardens, 233; Board of Design, 133, 233, 234, 235; Board of Directors' Room, 233; Board of Governors' Room, 133; Botany Worsted Mills Exhibition, 141; Brass Rail Restaurants, 233; Brazilian Pavilion, 233; Business Systems and Insurance Building, 138, *139*, 233; "Casino of Nations," 233; Chapel of the Good Shepherd, Vatican Pavilion, 141; Communications Building, 233; Consolidated Edison Building, 138, *140*, 234; Cosmetics Building, 234; Court of States–Spanish Section, 234; Danish Building, 234; Distilled Spirits Building, 138, *140*, 234; Electrical Products Building, 141, *141*, 234; Ford Motor Building, 134, *134*, *135*, *136*, 234; General Motors Building, 133–34, 138, *133*, 234; Heineken Dutch Town, on the Zuiderzee, 141, *142*, 234; Icelandic Building, 234; Johns-Manville Building, 138, 141, 234; Marine Transportation Building, 133, 234; Medicine and Public Health, Science and Education Building, *132*, 133, 134, *137*, 138, *139*, 234; Merrie England, 141, *143*, 234; New York City Exhibitions, 234; Palestine Pavilion, 234; partial list of commissions, 233–35; plan, *130*; Polish Building, 234; Russian Building, 141; Schaeffer Building, 234; Switzerland Building, 133, 234; Temple of Religion, 234; Time and Space Building, 235; World's Fair Station, 235
Nicholas, Joep, 11, 88
Nicolai and Faro, Time and Fortune Building, Century of Progress Exposition (Chicago, 1933), 131
Nielson, Einar, 141
Niemeyer, Oscar, Brazilian Pavilion, New York World's Fair (1939), 233
9/11 attacks, 13, 212
Nordic design, 38, 101, 105. *See also* Scandinavian design

O'Brien, S. J., Instructional panel for operators of sixty-inch anti-aircraft searchlights, 147, *147*
Oddi, Joseph A., *FDNY Memorial Wall of 09.11.01*, *211*, 212
O'Donnell, P., 239
Ohio State American Institute of Architects Award for Restoration, 166
Ohio State Capitol, Columbus, OH, 157
Ohio Theatre, Columbus, OH, 129, *129*, 231
Ohms, Hugo, 34
Olsen, Hendrik, 228
Olsen, Henry, *23*
Olsen, Valborg. *See* Rambusch, Valborg Olsen
Orpheum Theatre, Jersey City, NJ, *114*, 115
Orr, Douglas W., Saint Thomas More Chapel, Yale University, New Haven, CT, 92–93, *92*
Osadca, Apollinaire (Paul), 54
ostensoria, 52–54; Cathedral of Saint Joseph, Hartford, CT, *54*; Saint Michael's Church, Jersey City, NJ, *53*; Saint Raphael's Church, Pittsburgh, PA, *53*
Our Lady of Good Counsel Church, Brooklyn, 41
Our Lady of the Blessed Sacrament, Harrisburg, Pennsylvania, 24
Overbeck, Margarete, *Bloc de Cor: Morning glory design*, 91, *91*

Pahlavi, Ashraf ol-Molouk, 93
painting techniques, 31. *See also* fresco painting
Paisner, Jules, 239
Pan-a-lux, 27, 79
Panama Canal Zone, 196–97
Paramount Theatre, Brooklyn, 231
Parsons School of Design, 207
Pasteur, Louis, 138
patents, 9, 10, 12, 26, 27, 71, 73, 77, 91, 119, 148, 212
Paton, David, 229
Patrick, Saint, 36
Pei, I. M., National Gallery of Art, East Building, Washington, DC, 73, *73*, 169
Pelli, César, World Financial Center, Manhattan, 163, *165*
Pennsylvania Station, Baltimore, MD, 98
Pennsylvania Station, New York, NY, demolition of, 40
Penn Theatre, Titusville, PA, *126*, 127
Perry, James, 200
Pesing, Hans, 239
Peterson, Stanley, lighting for Mother Church, First Church of Christ, Scientist, Boston MA, 169–70, *170*
Petit, John J., 101–2, 104; Café Savarin, Manhattan, 102–3, *102*
Petronelli, Italo, 239
Petrovics, Joseph, *FDNY Memorial Wall of 09.11.01*, *211*, 212
Pett, Robert N., Utah State Capitol, Salt Lake City, UT, *215*, *216*, 217
Pettit, H. McEwen, 19, *19*, 214, 229
Phelps Construction, 214
Picklington Glass, 96
Pinar, Robert, 88
Pitkin Theatre, Brooklyn, 119, *122*, 196, 232
Plaza Hotel, Manhattan, 110
Plumbob lighting fixtures, *23*, 34, 66, *67*
Plymouth Theatre, Manhattan, 129
Pontoppidan, Aage, *23*
Poor, Alfred Easton, 45, 79; Temple of Religion, New York World's Fair (1939), 234
Pope, John Russell, 22
Potter, Adelbert, 79
Pottier & Stymus, 21, 221
pounce method, 31–32
Pratt Institute, 24, 227
preservation, 129, 175. *See also* restoration
Pro-Cathedral of the Assumption. *See* Saint Mary's of the Lake Cathedral
Prudential Insurance Company, 61–62
Pruitt & Brown, R.C.A. Building, Manhattan, *108*
public spaces, 156–73
Puerto Rico, 199–200
Puhl-Wagner-Heinersdorff, *Virgin Mary, with Saints*, Church of the Assumption of the Blessed Virgin Mary, Detroit, MI, *84*, 85

radar, 13, 148
Radio City Music Hall, Manhattan, 117, 124–25, *125*, 127, 232
Rambusch, Edward Vilhelm August, 12, 26–27, 71, *82*, 83, 170–71, 212; *Patent drawing: Mark I Downlite*, *72*
Rambusch, Edwin Peter, *27*, 28, 207, 217
Rambusch, Frode Christian Valdemar, 9–12, 17–22, 24, 37, 65, 85, 98, 101, 115, 129, 138, 189, 195, 207, 217, 221, 227–29; *Childhood sketchbook drawings*, 12, *16*, 17; *Church interior*, 17, *17*; passport of, *18*; photographs of, *19*, *228*; portrait of, *21*
Rambusch, Harold William, 20, 22, 24, *25*, 28, 33, 119, 121, 124, 125, 131, 227, 229, 239; candlesticks and cross, Church of the Heavenly Rest, Manhattan, 52, *53*
Rambusch, Martin Viggo, *27*, 28, 207, 212, 217
Rambusch, Robert Edward, 24, 28, 239
Rambusch, Sigurd, 19
Rambusch, Valborg Olsen, 10, 18, 20, 227, 228
Rambusch, Viggo Bech Ansgar, 26, 28, 61, *77*, 207, *210*, 217, 219, 239; concept designer, FDNY Memorial Wall of 09.11.01, *211*; model of armillary sphere, one-quarter size, Federal Reserve Bank, Manhattan, 62, *63*; ostensorium, Cathedral of Saint Joseph, Hartford, CT, 54, *54*; photographs of, *27*
Rambusch, Viggo Frode Edvard, 24, *25*, 26, 28, 94, 219, 229, 239
Rambusch, William, 24
Rambusch & Pettit, Interior Decorators, 18–20, 221, 229; letterhead stationery, *18*, *20*; studio interior, *19*, *226* (detail)
Rambusch Company of Canada, 195–96, 202
Rambusch Decorating Company: advertisements, 12, *21*, 21–22, *24*, *36*, *42*, *43*, *69*, *70*, *108*, 118–19, *119*, 148, *149*, *161*, 163, *164*; Artwork and Liturgical Environments Studio, 207, 208; Custom Lighting Studio, 207, 212, 214, 217; distinctive characteristics of, 9, 10; Engineered Lighting Studio, 207, 212, 214, 217; founding and early years of, 9–10, 20–22, 85; letter of incorporation, *223–25*; library of, 10, 54–55; locations of design studios and workshops, 21, 22, 24, 26, 227, 237; reputation of, 11, 22 (*see also* craft/craftsmanship: Rambusch's reputation for); shops within, 11, 22, *23*, 24, *24*, 26–28, 66, 86, 207–17, 237; sign for, *44*, 45; staff in front of offices (1976), *238*, 239; Stained Glass and Mosaics Studio, 207, 208, 212

Rambusch Glass and Decorating Company. *See* Rambusch Decorating Company
Ramsey, Edward A., Holy Name Church, Columbus, OH, 33, *33*
Rand McNally, 96
Raphael, 53
Rapp, C. W., 115
Rapp, George L., 115
Rasmussen, Ejner, *23*
Ratner, Abraham, 88
Rattenbury, Francis M., Legislative Assembly of British Columbia, Parliament Buildings, Victoria, BC, *194*, 195, 196, 200, *201*, 202
Reagan, Oliver, Temple of Religion, New York World's Fair (1939), 234
Reed, Henry Hope, *7*
Reed & Stem, Grand Central Terminal, Manhattan, *75*, *76*, *77*, 94, 169
Reflections Restaurant, Americana Hotel, Fort Worth, TX, 110, *111*
Reilly, Paul C., 61
Reinhard & Hofmeister, 124
Reisenweber's Restaurant, Manhattan, 101–2
Renwick, James, Jr., Saint Patrick's Cathedral, Manhattan, 22, 186
repoussé decoration, 12, 33, 45, 48, 49, 51, 56, 62, 66, 67, 141, 213
Restaurant Associates, 108
restaurants, 101–4, 106–10
restoration, 79, 96, 98, 113, 124, 129, 166, 174–95, 214. *See also* preservation
Rhodes, James, 188
Rickeman, Frederick "Fred" R., 11, *19*, *226*, 227–29
Rickey, Branch, 11
Rieger, Jan, *Whale-oil lighting fixtures in Old Senate Chamber*, 192, *192*
Rigaumont, Victor A., Penn Theatre, Titusville, PA, *126*, 127
Riklis, Meshulam, 93
Riley, Chauncey W., Banco Popular, San Juan PR, 196
Rinaldi, Lucien, 86
Ritz-Carlton, Manhattan, 110
Roberts & Schaefer, Lambert Airfield, St. Louis, MO, 167, *168*
Robertson, R. H., Mohawk Building, Manhattan, 237
Rochambeau, Comte de, 138
Roche, Kevin, Great Hall, Metropolitan Museum of Art, Manhattan, *73*, *74*, *75*
Rochester Art Museum, Rochester, NY, 32
Rockefeller Center, Manhattan, 124
Rockefeller Center #10 Theatre, Manhattan, 124, 232
Rohling, Geraldine M., 219
Roman Catholic Church: American roots of, 34; didactic function of decoration in, 34, 36–37; Frode Rambusch's conversion to, 22; patronage of, 11; reforms in, 39, 40. *See also* church interior design and decoration
Romeo, Paul, 239
Röntgen, Wilhelm, 66
Rose, Billy, 127–28
Rosen, Laura, 239
Rosenblatt, Arthur, 73
Rossi, Walter R., 212
Rotello, Salvatore, 239
Roth, Leland M., *7*
Rothafel, Samuel Lionel "Roxy," 62, 121, 125
Rothafel House, Manhattan, 62, *62*
Rother, Stanley, *206*, 208
Roxy Theatre, Manhattan, 117, 121, 124, *124*
Royal Court painters, 28
Royal Danish Academy of Art, Copenhagen, Denmark, 17, 22
Ruskin, John, 49

Sacred Heart Chapel, Tokyo, Japan, 199
Saint Agatha's Church, Brooklyn, *Saint Mark and Saint John*, *86*, 87
Saint Agnes Church, Arlington, VA, ostensorium, 53
Saint Agnes Church, Cleveland, OH, 33
Saint Agnes Church, Tonawanda, NY, 85
Saint Andrew Avellino Roman Catholic Church, Flushing Queens, 38, *38*
Saint Andrew's Cathedral, Victoria, BC, 188–89
Saint Anne's Church, Brooklyn, 18
Saint Ann's Church, Hornell, NY, 36, *37*
Saint Bartholomew's Episcopal Church, Manhattan, 31, 90–91; Model of Baptistery, *30*, 31
Saint Boniface Church, Pittsburgh, PA, 55, *55*
Saint Clement's, Rome, Italy, 32–33
Saint Clement's Eucharistic Shrine, Boston, MA, 53
Saint Francis of Assisi, Garden of Cathedral of Saint Ignatius Loyola, Palm Beach Gardens, FL, 41, *41*
Saint Francis of Assisi, Saint Francis of Assisi Church, Neligh, NE, 92, *92*
Saint Francis of Assisi, Saint Thomas More Chapel, Yale University, New Haven, CT, 92–93, *92*
Saint Francis School, Athol Springs, NY, candlestick, *51*, 52
Saint Gabriel's Church, Manhattan, 228
Saint-Gaudens, Augustus, 145, 186
Saint-Gaudens, Homer Schiff, 145
Saint George's Theatre, Staten Island, 232
Saint Ignatius Loyola Church, Manhattan, 110
Saint Jerome's Church, The Bronx, 41
Saint John's Cemetery, Brooklyn, *Te Deum window*, 88, *89*, 90
Saint John's Seminary, crypt of Saint John the Evangelist Chapel, Brighton, MA, 91
Saint Martin of Tours Church, Brooklyn, 36, *36*, 41
Saint Mary's Church, Rockville, MD, 58, *58*
Saint Mary's Hospital, Rochester, MN, 198
Saint Mary's of the Lake Cathedral, North Bay, ON, 195, *196*, *197*
Saint Michael's Church, Jersey City, NJ, ostensorium, 53, *53*
Saint Michael's Monastery Church, Union City, NJ, 19, 85
Saint Pancras Church, Glendale, Queens, 33–34, *34*
Saint Patrick's Cathedral, Manhattan, 22, 186
Saint Patrick's Church, Halifax, NS, 195
Saint Patrick's Roman Catholic Church, Bay Shore, NY, 32–33, *32*
Saint Peter Cathedral, Erie, PA, *174*, 175
Saint Peter's Basilica, Rome, Italy, 200
Saint Raphael's Church, Pittsburgh, PA, ostensorium, 53
Saint Raymond's Church, The Bronx, 24, *25*, 217
Saint Sebastian Church, Woodside, Queens, 128, *128*
Saint Stephen Church, Winooski, VT, 85
Saint Stephen's Episcopal Church, *The Life of Christ*, Durham, NC, *76*, 94, *95*
Saint Thomas More Chapel, Yale University, New Haven, CT, *Saint Francis of Assisi*, 92–93, *92*
Saint Wolfgang pilgrimage church, St. Wolfgang im Salzkammergut, Austria, 55
Saltzman's Restaurant, Manhattan, 103–4, *103*, *104*
Sanctuary of Monserrate, Colombia, 199
Sanders, Morris, Distilled Spirits Building, New York World's Fair (1939), 138, *140*, 234
Santos, Joaquin: baldachin, Cathedral of Saint Joseph, 58, *59*; baldachin, Franciscan Monastery of the Holy Land in America, Washington, DC (sketch of altar proposal and baldachin as built), 56, *57*; baldachin, Holy Cross Church, Omaha, NE, 56, 58, *58*; baldachin, Saint Mary's Church, Rockville, MD, 58, *58*; instructional panel for operators of sixty-inch anti-aircraft searchlights, 147, *147*; ostensorium, Saint Agnes Church, Arlington, VA, 53; scale model of wood carving for baldachin, Metropolitan Cathedral of Medellín, Colombia, *198*, 199; *TF-360 Theatre Lighting Fixture* (bronze), 71, *71*; *TF-360 Theatre Lighting Fixture* (drawing), 71, *71*
Saudi Arabia, 202–4
Scandinavian American Steamship Lines, 33
Scandinavian design, 102, 103, 105. *See also* Nordic design
Scheidling, Stefan, *187*, 188, 239; candlesticks, Church of the Epiphany, Manhattan, *50*, 52; candlesticks and cross, Church of the Heavenly Rest, Manhattan, 52, *53*
Scheurle, Hermann, ostensorium, Saint Agnes Church, Arlington, VA, 53
Schless, J. T., Merrie England, New York World's Fair (1939), 141, *143*, 234
Schless Construction Company, 234

Schoen, Eugene, 101, 131; Saltzman's Restaurant, Manhattan, 103–4, *103*, *104*

Schoen, Lee, 101; Saltzman's Restaurant, Manhattan, 103–4, *103*, *104*

Schrafft's cafeteria, Manhattan, 106

Schultze and Weaver: Breakers, Palm Beach, FL, 106; The Cloister Inn, Boca Raton Hotel, Boca Raton, FL, 106, *107*; Waldorf-Astoria Hotel, Manhattan, 105

Schumann Sons Jewelry Shop, Manhattan, 103

Schwarzkopf and Lukach, 234

S. Diehm Company, 26

Seaboard National Bank, Manhattan, 163

Seaman's Church, Brooklyn, 18

searchlights. *See* anti-aircraft searchlights

Second Vatican Council. *See* Vatican II

Seif, Alan, 239

Sekinger, Harold, Cathedral of Saint Ignatius Loyola, Palm Beach Gardens, FL, *40*, 41, *41*

Shinn, Everett, 110

Shovelites, *27*, 152

Shreve, Lamb & Harmon: Empire State Building, Manhattan, 162–63, *162*; Johns-Manville Building, New York World's Fair (1939), 138, 141, 234

Sign, for Rambusch Decorating Company, *44*, 45

Silver Spring Theatre, Silver Spring, MD, 119, *122*, *123*

Simonson, Kevin, 219

Singer, Alois, 239

Sisters of Saint Martha, Antigonish, NS, 195; *Mary Magdalene and Claire of Assisi: cames pattern*, study for chapel, 88, 90, *90*

Sitton, John M., *Genius of Progress* and other murals, Business Systems and Insurance Building, New York World's Fair (1939), 138, *139*, 233

S. J. O'Brien, 22, 65

Skidmore, Owings & Merrill (SOM), 191; Lever House, Manhattan, 28, 73; United Nations early headquarters, Lake Success, NY, 60–61, *60*

Slott-Møller, Harold, *Frode Christian Valdemar Rambusch*, *21*

Small, G. Milton, Saint Stephen's Episcopal Church, Durham, NC, 94, *95*

Smed, Peer, 65; pitcher, *44*, 45, 65

Smithsonian Institution. *See* Archives of American Art

Soares, Filho and Paul Lester Weiner, Brazilian Pavilion, New York World's Fair (1939), 233

SOM. *See* Skidmore, Owings & Merrill

Sønder Omme, Denmark, 11, 17

Sowers, Robert, 88; *Stained-glass window*, American Airlines Terminal, John F. Kennedy Airport, Queens, *93*, 94

Spence, Basil, 202

Sperry Gyroscope Company, 13, 147, 148, 151; President's Demonstration Room, 151–52, *151*

Spicer (captain), 227

stained glass, 12, 26, 84–99

Stained-glass window, sketch for Church of Our Lady of Victory, Manhattan, 90, *90*

Stanley, Thomas E., Lovers Lane United Methodist Church, Dallas, TX, 94, *94*

Stanton Theatre, Philadelphia, PA, *116*, 117, *117*

Stapleton, Vincent, 239

Starrett Brothers and Eken, 163

State Theatre, Union City, NJ, 231

Statue of Liberty, 13, *213*

Statue of Liberty Museum, Liberty Island, Upper New York Bay, *213*, 214

Staudle, Albert, 239

Steen, Olava, 24

Stein, Clarence S., Temple of Religion, New York World's Fair (1939), 234

Steinback, Gustave E.: Saint Pancras Church, Glendale, Queens, 33–34, *34*; Saint Patrick's Roman Catholic Church, Bay Shore, NY, 32–33, *32*

stencil decoration, 31

Stephen, Saint, 37

Sterling Forest Gardens, Tuxedo, NY, *Raintree Fountain*, 61, *61*

Stewart, Allan, 176–77, *178*, *179*, *180*

Stiassny, Robert, *Michael Pachers St. Wolfganger Altar*, illustration of bishop's crosier, 55, *55*

St. Michael's College, University of Toronto, 28

Stone, Edward Durell: Kennedy Center, Washington, DC, 169; Radio City Music Hall, Manhattan, 117, 124–25, *125*, 127; US Embassy, New Delhi, India, rendering of the seal of the United States, 199, *199*

Stoner, R., 239

Stork Club, Manhattan, 101

Strand Theatre, Brooklyn, 232

Strand Theatre, Manhattan, 70, 115, 232

Straughn, Wesley, 239

Struna, Johann, 239

Swanke Hayden Connell Architects, 61, 166; American Security & Trust Company entrance, Washington, DC, 45, *47*

Sweet's Indexed Catalogue of Building Construction, 21, 101, 115, 163

tabernacles, 39–41, *40*

Teague, Walter Dorwin: *Highways of 1903, 1939, and 1969*, Ford Motor Building, New York World's Fair (1939), *135*, 234; *Highways of 1969*, Ford Motor Building, New York World's Fair (1939), *134*, 234; *Model of an automobile engine*, Ford Motor Building, New York World's Fair (1939), 134, *136*, 234

Technology and Conservation (magazine), *186*, 187

Te Deum window, Saint John's Cemetery, Brooklyn, 88, *89*, 90

Tennessee Theatre, Nashville, TN, 127, *127*

theaters and movie houses, 114–29

Theatre Fixture #1, *72*

Theatre-Fixture 360 (TF-360), 71, *71*, *79*

Thomas, A., *Mural study*, Basilica of the Assumption, Baltimore, MD, 34, *35*

Thomas J. Moyer Judicial Center, Columbus, OH, grand concourse, *156*, 157, *158–59*

Thompson-Starrett, 233

thread of design, 207–8

Tiepolo, Giovanni Battista, 39

Tiffany, Louis Comfort, 21, 26, 65, 86, 96, 167, 186, 187

Tiffany Studios, 21, 26, 221

Tiffin tea shops, 101

Time (magazine), 94, *96*

Trans-Lux Corporation, 171

Trans-Lux Theatre, Manhattan, 232

Trans World Airlines terminal, LaGuardia Airport, Queens, 167, *167*

Tremont Theatre, The Bronx, 232

Trevor, John Bond, 176

Trinity Church, Manhattan, 188

Trinity Dome model, Great Upper Church, Basilica of the National Shrine of the Immaculate Conception, Washington, DC, *27*

trompe l'oeil, 34, 101, 119, 128, 187, 200

Tucker, Robert, 239

Tulane University, 207

Tulk, Alfred, 34, 58; *Designs for the Stations of the Cross* (drawing), Christ the King Church, Rutland, VT, 48, *49*; *Jesse Tree*, ceiling mural, Saint Ann's Church, Hornell, NY, 36, *37*; *Panorama, Observation Deck*, Empire State Building, Manhattan, *162*; *Stations of the Cross* (bronze and vitreous enamel), Christ the King Church, Rutland, VT, 48, *49*

Turner, Arthur, 239

Turner Construction Company, 234

Uccello, Paolo, 32

Union Bank of Commerce, Cleveland, OH, 166

Union League Club, Manhattan, 101

United Nations early headquarters, General Assembly Chamber, map mural, 60–61, *60*

United Service Organizations (USO), 155

United States Capitol, East Front Extension, Washington, DC, *79*, 83

United States Military Academy, West Point, NY, Cadet's Chapel chancel window, 86

University of Chicago, Chicago, IL, library of Oriental Institute, 163, *163*

Upjohn, Richard, Trinity Church, Manhattan, 188

Urban, Joseph, 131

US Army Corps of Engineers, 13, 28, 145, 147, 155, 202–3

US Capitol: carved wooden patterns used to fabricate lighting fixtures for, 45, *46*; restoration of Old Senate Chamber, 192, *192*

US Coast Guard Academy, New London, CT, banners in chapel, 152, *153*
US Courthouse, Foley Square, Manhattan, 157, *161*, 162
US Department of Transportation, 98
US Embassy, New Delhi, India, rendering of the seal of the United States, 199, *199*
USO. *See* United Service Organizations
US Postal Service "Forever" Stamp, commemorating the USS Missouri, 148, *148*
US War Department Office of the Chief of Engineers, 145
Utah State Capitol, Salt Lake City, UT, 214, *215*, *216*, 217
Utgard, Barbara-Jo, 239

Valley Forge Military Academy, Gettysburg, PA, *Abraham Lincoln window*, 90, *90*
van Ingen, E., 237
Vatican II, 39, 40
Vatican Gardens, Vatican City, *Mater Ecclesiae*, 204, *205*
Vaughan, Herbert Alfred Henry, *Directions for the Use of Altar Societies and Architects*, 39
Velasco, Leandro, 11, 88, 94, 200, 202, 239; cover of *Time*, 94, *96*; *The Life of Christ*, Saint Stephen's Episcopal Church, Durham, NC, *76*, 94, *95*; *Trinity dome*, Basilica of the National Shrine of the Immaculate Conception, Washington, DC, 208, *209*, *210*, 212
Venetian Art Mosaic, Forum of the Twelve Caesars, Rockefeller Center, New York, 110, *110*
Vermilya-Brown Company, 233
Verosko, Kenneth, *Finished dome*, World Financial Center, Manhattan, 163, *165*
Viemeister, Read, *Key, First Flight*, Dayton, OH, 171–72, *171*
Villard Houses, Manhattan, *112*, 113, 186–88, *186*
V.I.P. Facilities, Ras al Mishab, Saudi Arabia, 203
Virginia State Capitol, Richmond, VA, 157
Virginia Theatre, Charleston, WV, 127, *127*
Vittorio Foscato, 11
Voorhees, Gmelin and Walker, AT&T Building, New York World's Fair (1939), 141, 233

Wald, Everett, Metropolitan Life Insurance Company North Building, Manhattan, 45, *46*
Waldorf-Astoria Hotel, Manhattan, 101, 104–5, 175, 228; flatware for, 105, *106*; Jansen Suite, 105; *The New Waldorf-Astoria: Park Avenue entrance*, *100*, 101, 105, *105*
Walker, Ralph Thomas, 131
Wall-mounted lamp shield, 66, *66*
Walsh, William Campbell, 34; Forum of the Twelve Caesars, Rockefeller Center, Manhattan, 110, *110*
Waring & Gillow, 229
Warner (Strand) Theatre, Syracuse, NY, 232
Warner and Mitchell, 43
Warner Brothers, 73, 115, 145
Warren & Wetmore, Grand Central Terminal, Manhattan, *75*, *76*, *77*, 94, 169
Washington, George, 131
Watteau, Antoine, 110
Wayner, Albert, 239
Weber, John E., Switzerland Building, New York World's Fair (1939), 133, 234
Weber, William, 239
Wedding present, *44*, 45
Weiner, Albert, 239
Weiss, Charles, 239
Wells, Joseph Morrill, interior design of Villard Houses, Manhattan, *112*, 113, 186, *186*, 188
White, Peter, *77*, 239; ceiling lighting, lobby, Buchanan Center for the Performing Arts, University of Wyoming, Laramie, *81*; Downlite design, 73; Lighting for East Building: Atrium, National Gallery of Art, Washington, DC, 73, *73*; *Raintree Fountain*, Sterling Forest Gardens, Tuxedo, NY, 61, *61*; *Rendering of the seal of the United States*, 199, *199*
White, Stanford, 26
Willet, Henry Lee, 86
Willet, William, and Ann Lee Willet, chancel window, Cadet's Chapel, United States Military Academy, West Point, NY, 86
William Baumgarten & Co., 21, 221
William H. Jackson Company, 26, 45, *47*
William L. Crow Construction Co., 234
William Pahlmann & Associates, Forum of the Twelve Caesars, Rockefeller Center, Manhattan, 110, *110*
Williams, Percy, The Bronx Theatre, The Bronx, 115
Williamsburg Trust Company, Brooklyn, 163
Willow cafeteria, Manhattan, 106
Wilson, David, 239
Wilson, David, *Nave window*, Lovers Lane United Methodist Church, Dallas, TX, 94, *94*
Wilson, Richard Guy, 7
Wiseman, Harrison, G., Hollywood Theatre, Manhattan, 119, *120*, *121*
women: employed in the Rambusch shops, 11; in stained-glass studio, 87
wood carving, 26
Workman, James M., Carolina Theatre, Greensboro, NC, 129
World Financial Center, Manhattan, 163, *165*
World's Columbian Exposition (Chicago, 1893), 131
World's Fair (New York, 1939). *See* New York World's Fair (1939)
World War I, 12
World War II, 12–13, 52, 70, 144–55
Wraae, Gustave, 34; apsidal mural, Holy Name Church, Columbus, OH, 33, *33*; baldachino, Holy Trinity Church, Newark, NJ, 55–56, *56*
Wright, Frank Lloyd, 65
Wright, Wilbur and Orville, 171–72

Yamasaki, Minoru, 167
York and Sawyer, New York Academy of Medicine, Manhattan, 189–90, *189*
York Glaziers Trust, 87
Young, Cliff, 239

Zadora, Pia, 93, *93*
Zimbalist, Efrem, 191
Zimmerman, Julian: *Mural*, L'Enfant Plaza Hotel, Washington, DC, 110, *110*; *Rotunda: cross section*, Legislative Assembly of British Columbia, Parliament Buildings, Victoria, BC, *201*, 202
Zimmerman, Richard, 239
Zivotovsky, Martin, 239
Zubor, Marco, 88
Zucker, Howard, 189, 239
Zukor, Adolph, 62
Zumwalt, Thomas, 203

*Dedicated to the memory of the author, Catha Jackson Grace,
who passed away as this book was going to press.*